The Unification Process in Germany

Forthcoming titles in the same series:

The German Question after the Cold War
Günter Minnerup
0 86187 124 3

Social and Economic Modernisation from Honecker to Kohl
Mike Dennis
0 86187 166 9

Party Politics in the New Germany
Geoffrey Roberts
1 85567 029 1

German Foreign and Defence Policy
Lothar Gutjahr
1 85567 072 0

Revolution in Eastern Germany
Roger Woods
0 86187 054 9

THE UNIFICATION PROCESS IN GERMANY

From Dictatorship to Democracy

Gert-Joachim Glaessner

Translated from the German by Colin B. Grant

St. Martin's Press
New York

First published in the United States of America in 1992

Printed in Great Britain

ISBN 0-312-08570-2

Library of Congress Cataloging in Publication Data

Glaessner, Gert-Joachim, 1944–
    The unification process in Germany: from dictatorship to
democracy / Gert-Joachim Glaessner: translated from the German by
Colin B. Grant.
        p. cm.
    Includes bibliograpical references.
    ISBN 0-312-08570-2
    1. Germany – History – Unification, 1990. I. Title
DD290.25.G57 1992
943.087'9–dc20   92-16646
                                                                         CIP

Contents

Preface

The momentous historical events which, at the end of the eighties, led first to revolution in the GDR and then, with breathtaking speed, to the unification of Germany gave rise to a complex variety of often contradictory reactions both within and beyond the confines of Europe. A tangible sense of relief at the ending of the Cold War and the removal of the ugly divisions which had scarred Europe for over forty years sat uneasily with growing apprehension in some quarters at the thought that a bigger, more self-confident and economically powerful Germany, freed of the constraints imposed by the Cold War, might soon come to represent – again – a threat to the stability of Europe and the world. Some commentators had doubts about the new Germany's ability to prove a reliable and predictable partner in European affairs. They were opposed by others who pointed to the signal success with which the old Federal Republic had established a widely admired democratic system and had played its full part in building up an ever more unified and harmonious western Europe after World War II. On this basis it is often argued that the Europeanisation of Germany represents the best guarantee of a stable future for a world in which a united Germany's economic muscle will almost inevitably be translated into increased political strength. For their part, Germany's leading politicians have shown themselves to be sensitive to the worries of the international community, repeatedly stating that Germany sees its future as a force for peace and as a committed member of the European Community.

It is against this background of uncertainty but also of opportunity that the series THE NEW GERMANY explores the factors which have shaped Germany's recent history and those which will exercise a major influence on its own future development and, by extension, that of the international community. Aimed at a wide readership, the series seeks both to inform and to stimulate discussion by focusing on issues which are at the heart of the contemporary debate about Germany's role in the post-Cold War and post-Wall world. Each volume contains a comprehensive selection (in English) of key documents, all of which are vital to an understanding of that debate. The combination of expert analysis and relevant documentation offers the reader an opportunity to engage with many of the most important issues and problems which will help to determine the future of the most powerful nation in Europe.

Having finally achieved unification after years of division, Germany now faces new challenges at a time of potentially dangerous change within the political and economic world-order. It is essential that these challenges and the nature of Germany's response to them should be as widely understood as possible.

Ian Wallace
Series editor

Introduction

'We are the people' rang the call of the hundreds of thousands who took to the streets of East German cities in Autumn 1989. It was these demonstrators who brought about the downfall of the regime of the Socialist Unity Party (SED).

In early 1990, however, the call had become 'we are one people': the demonstrators now demanding the rapid reunification of the two German states were no longer those of the previous Autumn. The 'people of the GDR' came into being only briefly when they swept away the old political order, after which this unified body politic disintegrated. Ralf Dahrendorf has observed that the rallying cry 'we are the people' as a maxim of the democratic state and its constitution was in fact only the 'mirror image of the total state which had just been dislodged'.[1]

As in other post-communist countries, the German Democratic Republic (GDR) had to endure the birth pangs of creating a society which had hitherto been unified in accordance with the ideological views of the 'party of the working class'. Any attempt at the articulation, association and organisation of interests outside those laid down by the party was prohibited. In the Autumn of 1989 'the people' were united in their rejection of the old order.

Unlike Czechoslovakia, Poland and Hungary the process of self-discovery by GDR society never really started; it was overshadowed by demands for reunification only weeks after the collapse of SED rule. In the eight months which separated the announcement made by the then Prime Minister of the GDR, Hans Modrow, on his return from Moscow (that the Soviet Union would have no objections to a reunification of the two German states) and German Unity Day on 3 October 1990, political events in the GDR were subject to three conflicting trends: *first*, the process of political organisation and differentiation led to the creation of a range of different parties, interest groups and associations which sought to respond to the many new problems confronting the people of the GDR during the transition process. This typically follows in the wake of an ousted dictatorship.[2] *Second*, the transitory nature of this process was increasingly overshadowed by a tendency to seek to create the preconditions for reunification as quickly as possible. In these months all the political groups and the *Volkskammer* of the GDR freely elected on 18 March 1990 tried to chart a course between the twin perils of outright annexation (*Anschluss*) by the Federal Republic on the one hand and retention of structures broadly unchanged from the past on the other. The principal advocate of the first course was the conservative DSU (Deutsche Soziale Union) whereas the successor party of the SED, the PDS (Partei des demokratischen Sozialismus), favoured the latter. *Third*, the political forces of government and opposition in the GDR found their room for manoeuvre increasingly constrained: their actions were determined by what amounted to a permanent election campaign and by their dominant sister parties in the West which dictated tactics and set the political agenda.

Against this background the two German states reunified in a way unforeseen by the architects of the Constitution of the Federal Republic. When founded in 1949 the Federal Republic was conceived of as a provisional order. No one could possibly have imagined that it would become a lasting state structure. The preamble of the 1949 Constitution (Basic Law) reads: 'All German people are called upon to achieve the unity and freedom of Germany in free self-determination.' Article 146 made the provision that 'this Basic Law shall cease to be valid on the day on which a constitution adopted by the free decision of the German people comes into force'.

However, the belief that the division of Germany could still be overcome in this century had evaporated over the years. The principles of the constitution did not seem to belong to the realms of *realpolitik* — at least until 1989. The situation was dramatically changed by the revolutionary upheaval in Central and Eastern Europe. Suddenly, German unity was placed on the international political agenda. Politicians in the East and West were at first hesitant and predictable in their responses: they counselled caution and circumspection. None the less, by early 1990 it was becoming clear that a measured, long-term *rapprochement* of the two states was rejected by the majority of East Germans — they wanted unity as quickly as possible, and in late January 1990 the Soviet Union opened the door for a future united Germany.

In the weeks following the first free elections in the GDR on 18 March 1990, the pace of the reunification process increased markedly. It was precipitated not only by the worsening economic plight and social crisis in the GDR but also be a reappraisal of the world political situation which seemed to favour rapid unification. It was felt that the window of opportunity opened by the Soviet Union and the revolution in Central and Eastern Europe should be used.

The first freely elected parliament and the first democratically legitimised government of the GDR needed to take three major decisions: *first*, how was German unity to be achieved? Was it to be brought about by the accession of the GDR to the Federal Republic or more slowly by means of a confederation; *second*, and intimately related to the above, should the GDR endow itself with a new constitution and build separate political structures for this transitional period? *Third*, after it had been decided that the GDR would accede to the Federal Republic, how could the interests of GDR citizens be secured?

A large number of people and politicians of the old Federal Republic in 1990 took the mistaken view that the accession of the GDR and hence the unity of the two German states would rapidly heal the economic, social and cultural division of their antagonistic social systems. Today it is clear that the reunification of the two German states on 3 October 1990 marked only the beginning of a long and arduous process through which they will grow together.

This book seeks to shed light on the causes and consequences of these developments in their various dimensions. It will explain the structural causes of the crisis, examine the motives of the actors involved, describe the process of transition from dictatorship to democracy and finally analyse the consequences of the transitional process for German political culture.

Notes

1 Ralf Dahrendorf, *Reflections on the Revolution in Europe*. London, Chatto and Windus, 1990, p. 98.
2 Cf. Juan Linz, 'Transitions to Democracy', in *The Washington Quarterly*, Summer, 1990, pp. 143–64; Guillermo O'Donell, Phillippe Schmitter, Laurence Whitehead (eds), *Transitions from Authoritarian Rule: Prospects for Democracy*, Baltimore, Johns Hopkins University Press, 1986.

1 *Deutschlandpolitik* and the aim of reunification

With the fall of the Berlin Wall on the night of 9 November 1989 a political objective had been reached which all the political forces in the Federal Republic had long considered a cornerstone of their agendas. However, until the Autumn of 1989 it had seemed idealistic to expect that this goal could be reached soon; German unity would at best come about in some distant future.

All the governments of the Federal Republic emphasised the aim of the Basic Law to seek the unity of Germany by peaceful means. This notwithstanding, they felt compelled by international political circumstances to pursue a pragmatic *realpolitik* with those who stood in the way of this aim: the Soviet Union and its 'proxies' in the GDR as they were known in the 1950s.

Although each year on 17 June sage speeches on the question of German unity were uttered in commemoration of the uprising in the GDR in 1953, a general consciousness evolved in the Federal Republic which saw no need to take any notice of the GDR. In conventional perceptions the Federal Republic was a synonym for Germany itself. The GDR was a broadly unknown and uninteresting country. Among young people in particular there was considerable indifference which the authorities tried by various means to counteract.

On closer inspection, however, matters were more complicated. Whereas the state and social system of the GDR met with suspicion, the people were not viewed this way. Reunification posed no problem for the vast majority of people; it was generally considered desirable but not something which had to be worked for. A representative survey conducted among young people in the early 1980s may illustrate the point[1] (see Table 1.1).

If the goal of German unity had not been enshrined in the Basic Law and been the will of all political parties, the people of the Federal Republic, unlike their compatriots in the GDR, would not have made it a demand. The longer the division of Germany into

Table 1.1 Young people in the Federal Republic between the ages of 14 and 21, 1981

When I think of the GDR	Interest in the GDR	No interest in the GDR
My thoughts, feelings tend to be . . .		
. . . that people have become indifferent to the GDR because the division of Germany has lasted so long	15%	46%
. . . that despite the division there is still a lot of common ground between West and East	64%	25%
Those who see German reunification as . . .		
desirable	79%	33%
realistic	4%	3%

Source: Infratest, May 1981

two states and social orders lasted the lower the likelihood that this aim would every be realised, particularly since this objective was never linked to the possibility of renouncing the Federal Republic's own normative conception of state and social order. The reunited Germany was to be a democratic Germany based on the model of the Federal Republic.

The 'magic formula' which succeeded in bridging this gap for over two decades, but which in recent years increasingly ran the risk of concealing it, was the keystone of the new *Ostpolitik* inaugurated by Willy Brandt in 1969:

Twenty years after the founding of the Federal Republic and the GDR we must prevent the German nation from drifting apart. That means we must live side by side in order to try then to live together . . . . In stating this aim we are not succumbing to any false hopes: interests, power relations and social differences cannot be dialectically resolved nor should they be obscured. But our negotiating partners should take heed that the right of self-determination enshrined in the Charter of the United Nations also applies to the German people. This right and the will to assert this right are not open to negotiation.[2]

The opportunities for overcoming the division of Germany had not improved after the first successes of Brandt's *Ostpolitik*, notably because the GDR, in agreement with its controlling power, rejected the notion of any future national unity.

Whereas up until the 1960s the GDR had — at least verbally — seen itself as the true keeper of a common German heritage, it now insisted that a distinct, socialist nation had evolved. According to Article 1 of the GDR constitution of 1949 Germany was an indivisible Democratic Republic, built on German *Länder*.

At that time the GDR, like the Federal Republic, still perceived itself as a provisional state which was part of a truncated nation. Despite the division of Germany there was until the early 1970s no doubt that this nation would continue to exist.

The revised 'socialist' constitution of 1968 stated that: 'The German Democratic Republic is a socialist state of the German nation. It is the political organisation of the working people in the cities and on the land who, united under the leadership of the working class and its Marxist–Leninist party, are building socialism.' This passage was revised in 1974 to read as follows: 'The German Democratic Republic is a socialist state of workers and peasants. It is the political organisation of the working people in the cities and on the land under the leadership of the working class and its Marxist–Leninist party.'

The changes quoted above signal a change in the way the GDR defined itself. They demonstrate the crucial problems of a state which came into being as a part of a divided nation in a politico–historical situation which foresaw no definitive solutions to the question of the German nation. Since the German question remained 'open' the social and political order which predated the creation of the GDR remained at least potentially an option.

By contrast, the constitution of 1968 and the revised version of 1974 defined the socialist GDR in accordance with the Soviet model, namely, the leading role of the working class and its Marxist–Leninist party, the basic forms of the organisations of the working people and the political foundations of the socialist order of state and society, the unity of powers, the alliance of all political forces, the structure and function of the political system and the claim that antagonistic interests had ceased to exist.

The changes to the constitution in 1974 eliminated the notion of the German nation and thereby indicated a break with the inherited *raison d'être* of the GDR which had hitherto stressed its role as the vanguard of a socialist future for the whole of Germany. Until this point the GDR had sought its legitimation in the fact that it had overcome the old class-based society and had therefore become the model for a future Germany.

The rupture of 1974 represented a reaction to the successes of the Federal government's *Ostpolitik* and the accession of both German states to the United Nations. At the same time it was an attempt to pre-empt the desired results of the CSCE Conference in Helsinki in 1975, namely that the existence of the GDR should not be put into question by the policy of *détente*. This in fact had been what the GDR had long demanded. It was also clear to all observers that this new self-definition could not have been made without the imprimatur of the Soviet Union.

Both *Ostpolitik* and the Helsinki Final Act were founded on mutual consensus by the two power blocs that a change to the status quo could only be achieved with force and was therefore impossible. At the same time they offered new opportunities for cooperation. These were the parameters in which the two German states tried to regulate their relations.

The GDR availed itself of every opportunity to prove its sovereignty. It insisted on the principles of territorial integrity and the maintenance of the status quo laid down in Helsinki. The Federal Republic appealed for the respect for human rights to which the signatories had committed themselves. All the political forces in the Federal Republic invested their energies in securing the most favourable conditions which would make the division of Germany as tolerable as possible while undertaking to improve the lot of the people in the GDR. Both the SPD–FDP coalition and its CDU–FDP successors failed however to resolve the ambiguities inherent in such a policy. The adherence to legal positions and the respective social and political orders on the one hand and the goal of unification on the other were mutually exclusive in the context of an *Ostpolitik* which did not really constitute an end to the Cold War.

This policy was based on a shared analysis of world political circumstances which foresaw the end of the division into opposing blocs as at best a remote objective — until 1989.

1.1 The aims of *Deutschlandpolitik*

The thirty years of *Deutschlandpolitik* pursued by the Federal Republic adhered to the following criteria:

1. The primary objective was not reunification but the right of self-determination for all Germans. Observers never seriously doubted that the people of the GDR would, if offered, opt for the Western system.
2. *Deutschlandpolitik* was subordinate to *Ostpolitik*. The primary objective lay in establishing a *modus vivendi* and a reconciliation with the neighbouring countries of Eastern Europe. Only lasting success in this area could offer any opportunity for a general improvement of the situation in Germany.
3. *Deutschlandpolitik* was subordinate to the policy of the Western alliance. The resolution of the division of Germany was

conceivable only in a European peace order (ill-defined to this day). An independent German line was seen as neither propitious nor desirable. The Federal Republic never seriously challenged its position in the West.

4. The combination of *Ostpolitik* and *Deutschlandpolitik* was possible only if the political situation in the socialist states was accepted in its existing form. The Helsinki Conference, which vouchsafed to the opposition in Central and Eastern Europe the right to dissent (consider Charter 77 in Czechoslovakia), produced a conflict of objectives in this policy since the new opposition groups subscribed to the very democratic order which *Ostpolitik* set out to achieve. Dissidents in these countries were not unjustified in accusing politicians and intellectuals in the West of bias toward the ruling political class. Circumstances in the GDR were different since it was only in 1989 that an identifiable structured political opposition had emerged.

5. The *Deutschlandpolitik* of the Federal government and the opposition failed to foresee the gravity of developments after Gorbachev assumed power. Observers only recognised the ramifications that the concept of a 'European Home' would have for a divided nation as late as 1989.

Despite the hopes of a new political order in Europe kindled by Soviet policy after 1985, there remained no signs of change in the objectives of *Deutschlandpolitik* until mid-1989. Thinking was still very much long term.

In what was received as a keynote declaration of *Deutschlandpolitik* the then Federal Minister for inter-German relations, Dorothee Wilms, said in a speech in 1988:

We are aware that the division of Germany will not be overcome in the near future because Europe itself remains divided .... The preconditions for unification simply do not exist — either in terms of internal German relations or in the relations between the four victorious allies of the Second World War.[3]

This was by no means the only statement of its kind.

The former Federal Chancellor Helmut Schmidt expressed a view not only widely held in the SPD when he wrote in September 1989: 'An eruption in the GDR would jeopardise the reform process in Eastern Europe.'[4] Helmut Schmidt felt that there was no prospect of a panacea for the German question. He reminded the German people of Poland which had been divided for over a century, again truncated in the twentieth century but which nevertheless had emerged a nation-state. 'I am confident that in the course of the next century the German nation will have a common roof under which freedom can shelter.'[5]

In October 1989, in a commentary entitled 'German unity and NATO membership are incompatible' the architect of Willy Brandt's new *Ostpolitik*, Egon Bahr, answered the question as to whether the unity of Germany as a state was now close to realisation: 'All identifiable indicators in East and West continue to point to the opposite. The major challenge until the year 2000 of banishing war by means of common security and non-aggression presupposes the stability of both blocs and their respective German states.'[6] Exactly one year later both German states were united and a member of NATO.

As late as 8 November, the day before the opening of the Berlin Wall, the Federal Chancellor Helmut Kohl stated in his report on the state of the nation before the *Bundestag*: 'Let us maintain — no matter how difficult this may be for us and especially our compatriots in the GDR — our *patient resolve* to tread the path of *evolutionary change* (my emphasis — G.–J.G.) which will lead us to the full respect for human rights and the free self-determination of all the German people.'[7] It was also emphasised that the Federal government remained committed to its policy of cooperation with the GDR in matters of the economy, environmental protection, science and culture but that the GDR would have to introduce reforms which would create the conditions in which 'this cooperation can really come to fruition'.[8]

A broad consensus existed in the Federal Republic that it would be a long time before (re-)unification would be achieved. This was the background to Willy Brandt's view that in its quest for reunification the Federal Republic was living a lie.[9] This view in turn prompted a reply from the Editor-in-Chief of the weekly *Die Zeit*, Theo Sommer, in Summer 1989 in which he said that the idea of German unity should be abandoned in favour of the freedom of the Germans in the GDR.[10] Helmut Schmidt protested vehemently against this view stating that no European neighbour would deny this goal to a German people which saw 'its own national unity and self-determination as nothing less than natural'.[11]

Sommer and Schmidt did not differ too greatly in their analysis of the situation. Both saw the unification of Germany as a nation-state as only a distant prospect.

Such opinions were also represented in the heart of conservative thinking as the following statement by the late Chairman of the rightwing-conservative CSU, Franz Josef Strauss, illustrates: 'Are we truly impelled, tortured, burdened and driven by reunification? It is not so much reunification in the sense of a recovery of the state unity of Germany as the longing for the restoration of democracy and conditions under which people can live in dignity in that part of Germany.'[12]

1.2 Contradictions between the theory and practice

The *Deutschlandpolitik* of the liberal–conservative coalition government has long been characterised by a growing contradiction between declarations of intent and practical policy-making. The prospects for a policy based on conciliation and cooperation in practical matters in Germany were anything other than favourable at the beginning of the 1980s. The great expectations for the implementation of the Helsinki Final Act of 1975 had been disappointed. If one considers relations among the European states, in particular between the two German states after the CSCE Final Conference, difficulties are uppermost in the memory: the expulsion of writers from the GDR and the hardening of the cultural policy line, obstacles put in the way of West Germans trying to visit the East, the crisis in Poland which precipitated the imposition of martial law in December 1981 and the long shadow it cast over Helmut Schmidt's meeting with Erich Honecker on the Werbellinsee near Berlin in 1981.[13]

The Soviet troops invasion of Afghanistan in December 1979 and in the same month NATO'S 'Twin-Track Decision' to deploy new middle-range nuclear missiles combined with new proposals for negotiations on disarmament, led to an acute deterioration in East–West relations.

Deutschlandpolitik also faced new difficulties. On 13 October 1980 the Chairman of the State Council, Erich Honecker, made demands in a speech delivered in Gera which amounted to a hardening of the policies of the SED leadership towards the Federal Republic. Honecker made further improvements in inner-German relations conditional in particular upon the recognition of GDR citizenship and the granting of embassy status to the Permanent Representatives of the Federal Republic in East Berlin and the GDR in Bonn.

The GDR leadership did none the less display a willingness to negotiate. Despite the strains in external policy imposed by a worsening in East–West relations, the following years clearly illustrated that the SED, although it insisted on West German acceptance of its far-reaching demands (indeed as it continued to do until the end of its rule in 1989), had no interest in witnessing a deterioration in its relations with the Federal Republic.

This development remained broadly unaffected by the change in government in Bonn in October 1982. In fact the GDR emphasised the responsibility incumbent on both German states for securing peace. Admittedly this stance was undoubtedly dictated by the desire to prevent the implementation of NATO's 'Twin-Track Decision' and the deployment of new medium-range nuclear missiles in the Federal Republic. However, it became increasingly obvious that in the following years the GDR leadership wished to acquire a degree of political independence for both German states in view of the dangerous escalation of tension between the United States and the Soviet Union. The governments of the Federal Republic and the GDR aimed not to heighten tensions but rather to contribute to *détente* by further developing treaty relations between two states on the faultline of the two world systems.

The SED had quickly signalled its interest in pursuing inter-German talks and negotiations with the new government. After 1982 intergovernmental contacts intensified and inter-German relations were extended. The mutual interest in good relations was so deeply felt that even serious strains such as the death of a transit passenger under questioning by East German border guards in 1983 or the occupation of the West German Permanent Representation by people who wanted to leave the GDR and the settling of about 24,000 GDR citizens in the Federal Republic in 1984 could be resolved.

A milestone in treaty relations between the two German states was reached with the conclusion of the Cultural Accord in 1986. It offered the prospect of closer cooperation in culture, the arts, education and science. Cultural and scientific meetings were to be encouraged and the exchange of publications, information and cultural and artistic events made possible.[14]

Erich Honecker's visit to the Federal Republic from 7–11 September 1987 was without doubt another important watershed in German–German relations since it meant *de facto* international recognition of the GDR.[15] His visit was foreshadowed by protests from the parliamentary CDU/CSU about the protocol of the visit — an honorary *Bundeswehr* guard, the playing of the two national anthems and the rising of the GDR flag which had always been derided as the 'flag of division'. The Federal Chancellor, Helmut Kohl, was forced to warn several times against unrealisable demands which could jeopardise the visit.

His predecessor Helmut Schmidt joined the debate about the Honecker visit in July. With the lyrical title 'One of Our Brothers' he wrote an article in which he warned the West German press against losing all sense of proportion and dignity. The visit he felt was a 'further step on a long and difficult road which is to lead to normalisation in the heart of Central Europe'. Schmidt personally credited Honecker with being a realist of long standing who had now become an old and wise man. 'I sense in him a German identity which goes beyond the sense of homesickness he feels for Wiebelskirchen and the Saar', where he was born. Schmidt concluded his article with a ringing appeal: 'For years we have spoken of the Germans in the GDR as our brothers and sisters. Let us now translate our words into action: even if we cannot ever become political friends with Erich Honecker let us at least extend a dignified welcome to him — receive him as our brother!'[16] These were without doubt the words of Schmidt the Christian, not Schmidt the politician.

Public opinion was ambivalent about the visit. On several occasions the Federal Chancellor underlined the basic position of the government in its adherence to the unity of the German nation as laid down in the Basic Treaty with the GDR. The government emphasised its commitment to the renunciation of the use of force as a central element in the policies of the Federal Republic as well as its recognition of existing borders. The division of Germany was only to be assured by peaceful means and by a process of mutual understanding.[17]

Kohl noted at a banquet held in Honecker's honour:

The sense of united nationhood is alive as it has always been and we remain resolute in our will to preserve it. This unity lives in a common language, in a shared cultural heritage and in a long and continuing shared history. Some have difficulty in imagining how this meeting can be reconciled with the continuity of German history. Our meeting is neither a beginning nor an end; it is a step in a continued process manifest in the quest for good neighbourly relations. This visit cannot and will not change anything in the differing views of both states on fundamental questions including the question of the division of Germany . . . . The preamble of the Basic Law is not negotiable because it expresses our belief. It seeks a united Europe and appeals to all the German people to accomplish the unity and freedom of Germany by free self-determination.[18]

1.3 The contradictions and limitations of *Deutschlandpolitik*

Only in retrospect does the Honecker visit emerge clearly as a watershed in relations between the two German states. The international prestige gained and later further confirmed by a state visit to France were undoubtedly factors which led to the failure of the political leadership in the GDR to recognise obvious symptoms of impending social crisis and to resist reform.

In December 1987 the GDR government officially protested at the 'interference' of Western politicians in the 'internal affairs' of the GDR after they had criticised it for refusing to admit SPD and Green politicians and for searching the premises of the *Umweltbibliothek* in the Zionist Church in East Berlin.[19] Relations were further strained by the mass arrests and expulsions of prominent opposition figures after the demonstrations in January 1988 commemorating the deaths of Rosa Luxemburg and Karl Liebknecht. In a *Bundestag* debate the leading Green deputy Petra Kelly called for people to have the 'courage to interfere' and to realise that 'internal and external peace are to be understood as an indivisible whole'.[20]

Despite the generally positive results of *Deutschlandpolitik* it became clear after Erich Honecker's visit to Bonn and the subsequent hardening in the position of the SED leadership that the Federal government, like the opposition SPD, was bereft of any political vision of the future. This can be explained in part by the fact that the pursuit of continuity in *Deutschlandpolitik* had encountered opposition in the ranks of the CDU/CSU themselves — hardly surprising in view of the negative stance of the parliamentary CDU/CSU towards the treaties with Eastern Europe ten years earlier. However, this position had never officially been revised. This made the political rhetoric of the various wings of the CDU/CSU so difficult to comprehend. Pragmatism, revisionism, rigid adherence to legal positions and the paucity of ideas for Germany's political future represented an odd and sometimes incompatible combination. Most of the hidden contradictions of *Deutschlandpolitik* became obvious when the general climate of international and German politics began to change with increasing speed. Like the Social Democrats but for different reasons, the Federal government ran into difficulties with policies which focused strongly on resolving human problems because the structure of society across the socialist countries was beginning to change. Neither government nor opposition had a strategy for dealing with the process of emancipation of GDR society from the party-state which would not presuppose an end to the *modus vivendi* with the authorities.

The parties of the government and the SPD opposition failed to grasp that a curious contradiction ran through their policies which would become even more acute in the years to come. The search for a consensus of interests with the East was still bringing improvements for the people while inadvertantly further consolidating orthodox régimes in Central and Eastern Europe.

Even after Helsinki both *Ostpolitik* and *Deutschlandpolitik* remained the exclusive preserve of government policy. The human-rights principles contained in 'Basket 3' of the Helsinki Final Act of the CSCE Conference were continually invoked but this stopped short of demonstrating solidarity with those in the GDR who fought for civil rights as prescribed in the Helsinki charter. (The situation was different in the East-Central European countries.) The reason for this was that the opposition in the GDR was extremely small and marginal and raised issues which were discomfiting for politicians in Western societies, namely radical disarmament, environmental protection, grassroots democracy, solidarity with the 'Third World'. The Honecker government shrewdly played on this contradiction.

However, the contradiction only became clear when the Soviet Union under Gorbachev changed its political course and the SED leadership started to shield itself from *glasnost* and *perestroika* by deploying more repressive measures. The changes in the Soviet Union not only upset the old political structures and those of the socialist alliance; they also had a far-reaching impact on the sensitivities of 'real socialist' societies. Hitherto marginalised dissident and opposition groups gained influence deep in the ranks of the governing communist parties and paved the way for new thinking, for new forms for the representation of political and social interests and growing national independence. All this posed a grave threat to the monopoly of power of the party leadership.

Even if no one in 1987–8 could have predicted the collapse of these systems, the scope of *Ostpolitik* and *Deutschlandpolitik* had undergone dramatic change. There were, however, no concrete efforts (such as the quest for new ideas in the early 1960s) which could have met this challenge.

The upheavals in the GDR elicited only predictable responses from the West German government and opposition: they appealed for greater freedoms but were prepared to sit down with the various party and state leaderships 'in the interest of the people'. For example, in November 1989 the Federal government welcomed the announcement of new travel arrangements made by the new SED leadership under Egon Krenz. It was this arrangement which would become the direct catalyst for the implosion of the political system. In the spring and summer of 1989 this proposal would have met with widespread support, but in November it succeeded only in bringing discontent to boiling point and therefore leaving the party leadership, as it judged the situation, with only one set of alternatives: either capitulation or the opening of the Wall.

The initial response to this historical event in conservative circles was ambivalent. Mounting doubts in the West about German loyalty to the Western Alliance had to be allayed. Reactions to West German efforts to secure greater independence in the deployment of new short-range nuclear missiles but, even more, to the response of the Federal government to the collapse of SED rule at the end of 1989 indicated that, despite the conformism and often hasty obedience of the previous decades, such doubts persisted.

The hastening pace of the process of German unification brought in its wake a growing number of critical commentaries from Germany's eastern and western neighbours who feared domination under a future united Germany. Chancellor Kohl's initial isolated stance and his hesitancy in giving unequivocal recognition to the permanence of the Polish Western frontier assisted only in rekindling deep-seated fears of a new *furor teutonicus* once thought banished forever.

The biggest opposition party, the SPD, was similarly unequal to the enormity of such change. Only the grand old man of the party, Willy Brandt, once reviled and slandered for his emigration from Nazi Germany, expressed his support for the goal of German unity. Here too, thinking was predominantly about the status quo, thus preventing the formulation of new ideas capable of mapping out a future course for *Deutschlandpolitik*.

None of the political forces in the Federal Republic was prepared to seize the opportunity to implement the objective of the preamble to the Basic Law — to 'accomplish the unity and freedom of Germany by means of free self-determination' — in less than one year. It was beyond the realms of their political imagination.

It would nevertheless be a mistake to believe that state unification signalled the end of *Deutschlandpolitik*. The 3rd October 1990 was just the beginning of a long process in the convergence of two systems which in forty-five years had evolved under completely different economic, political, social and psychological conditions. In this sense there will continue to be a *Deutschlandpolitik*. It will be a part of a domestic policy which has to ensure that, after political division, social division too is healed.

1.4 German unity as an objective of the Basic Law

Until 1989 it was agreed by all constitutional lawyers and politicians that any further German unity could only be achieved by means of Article 146 of the West German 'Basic Law' (constitution) which was expressly provided for this goal. It was beyond discussion that with reunification the German people would adopt a new constitution.[21] This was also in keeping with the intention of the architect of the constitution who had regarded the Basic Law as something provisional — in the words used by Carlo Schmid in 1949, as the foundation stone of a 'temporary dwelling' which should not receive the blessing which 'befits a permanent home'.[22] Since the Saar region had been placed under French administration after the war (where it was to remain until 1955), the Basic Law had made provision for a special Article (23) which was to enable the future accession of the Saar area. This 'Saar Article', unknown to most politicians, offered a useful mechanism in the extraordinary historic situation of 1989. The question remains, however, as to whether the experiences of over forty years' democracy in the Federal Republic and of the democratic transformation in the GDR do not require a common understanding among the German people about the basis of their future body politic.

The unification process was accompanied by a passionate and at times ideologically bitter debate about whether Article 23 or Article 146 represented the 'royal way' to German unity.[23] In fact, there was no 'royal way'.[24] The majority of the people of the GDR opted for a quick route toward unification and there were good reasons for having done so.

The advocates of Article 23 explained that this made it possible to give the process a political direction which was based on a proven constitutional order.[25] The Basic Law and finding of the Federal Constitutional Court ensured a 'high degree of rational constitutional law' which Article 23 upheld. They believed that the adaptability of the system and the stability of the Federal Republic had justifiably been identified with the Basic Law. Its retention would also be supported by the fact that it offered a working federal order and that the 'enormous pressures arising from the restoration of state unity for economic and finance policy, in addition to legislation, would be better absorbed on the basis of a stable and trusted constitution than in a new legal order'.[26]

Advocates of German unification under Article 146 of the Basic Law contended that only their path would guarantee the interests of the East German people since it presupposed a constitutional assembly.[27] Central to their argument was whether the new nation state would rest 'on national unity to which the constitution is subordinate' or 'stem from the democratic self-constitution of a political society on its current territory'.[28] Owing to its provisional character the Basic Law did not have to address 'the question of a reconciliation of constitution and nation' unresolved in modern German history. This reconciliation was now a real prospect. All supporters of Article 146 shared the view that it alone could enable East Germans to participate in the formation of a future state order.

It was justifiably pointed out that the appearances given by political debate deceived. Neither option necessarily precluded the other. Indeed, the advantages of each could have been pooled: 'An important argument in favour of the accession of the former GDR under Article 23, Section 2 of the Basic Law lies in the opportunity for addressing domestic and social policy issues of the constitution at a later stage after the ratification of unification.'[29] This task would then fall to the legal authorities in a reunited Germany.

This approach expressly admits of a unification treaty between the Federal Republic and the GDR. It represents a compromise in reformulating Article 146 to the extent that the Basic Law 'which holds for the whole German people after German unity and freedom have been achieved' will cease to operate on the day 'when a new constitution which has been endorsed by the free will of the German people' comes into force. Whether this is to happen remains a moot point.[30]

1.5 The European dimension of German unity

The GDR was never able to deny its provenance as the product of the strategic and ideological intentions of the victorious Soviet Union. Throughout its forty-year existence it suffered from a lack of legitimacy.[31] Provided that the political leadership could count on enforced mass loyalty it was never in serious danger as in the uprising of 1953, albeit since the SED had successfully secured the support of the people as the provider of an authoritarian welfare state by foul means rather than by fair. When, however, the welfare foundation began to subside under a moribund economy and its lease was effectively terminated, the whole building crumbled.

Within one year following the open outbreak of mass popular dissent the GDR became part of the Federal Republic — a state which had adopted an unequivocal Western orientation since its foundation. There was and still is basic agreement about this fact in (West) German society despite the unmistakable reservations among the political Left about the superpower role of the United States in the West. For this very reason then the fears of a new Rapallo Treaty proved groundless: Germany was no longer the pariah in the European community of nations as it had been in 1922 when it needed to ally itself with an outside power such as the Soviet Union.

The crux of European politics is not the likelihood that Germany will spawn a new nationalism and chauvinism but that Germany has, against its will, been forced into the role of a European superpower without any psychological preparation. This in turn fuels anxieties which perturb other European neighbours more than the fact that eighty million Germans could return to their old ways. Meanwhile, in Western European countries there is a remarkable discrepancy between official statements on the 'German question' and important sections of public opinion.

Some years ago the Italian Foreign Minister Giulio Andreotti made a statement which caused uproar and was seen by many as a reflection of popular belief. Andreotti said: 'We all agree that there must be good relations between the two Germanies . . . but we should not go too far . . . Pangermanism must be laid to rest. There are two German states and there should remain two German states.'[32] The former Federal Chancellor of Austria Bruno Kreisky remarked sarcastically that Andreotti had only said openly what everyone was secretly thinking. Was Germany's dream a nightmare for her neighbours? Or is not the situation less clear-cut?

In an article on the end of the Cold War, Nigel Hawkes, diplomatic editor of the *Observer* named what many in Britain considered to be the decisive aspect of all the discussions about the dissolution of political blocs and the democratisation process in Eastern Europe: fear of a Europe under German domination and the threat of conflict and instability this had produced in the past.[33] Discussions about Germany's role in Europe should be seen against this background. The geo-political position of Germany represents a problem for all her neighbours. As long as the Cold War determined the climate in Europe the Germans would remain firmly anchored in the Western Alliance. When internal and external political changes in Soviet hegemony in Eastern Europe precipitated a far-reaching transformation of the European political order, some uncertainty resulted as to the future direction Germany would take. Even before November 1989 there had been signs of uncertainty in Western public life. This resulted from the fact that old certainties were crumbling, the perception of the Soviet Union as the old adversary had to be revised and new political strategies devised. A fresh assessment was required of the new constellation of political power in Europe, the new role of the Soviet Union and of Germany's place in the 'European Home'.

Unease, not to say fear that Germany might express new geo-political pretensions, became widespread in the period immediately prior to the German unification process. In the Federal Republic a growing number of voices were raised in favour of what amounted to a rehash of the old ideas of neutrality. This fuelled fears in the West that Germany might choose to take an independent course. The breadth of these fears can be clearly seen from a range of press commentaries in 1989–90. For example, Peter Kellner writing in the *Independent* in summer 1989 remarked in an article tellingly entitled 'Keeping the Germans on a Leash': 'If West Germany is not tethered effectively to the wider international community, the long-term pressures inside the country towards *Alleingang* — going it alone and dragging Austria and East Germany into its orbit — could prove hard to resist.' These tendencies could turn into a dangerous and irresistible force in the politics of the Federal Republic: 'A new leash is needed.'[34] This is further underlined by the fact that the unification of the two German states introduces a new factor into European politics:

Germany will seek to regain the power to determine the fate of Europe. The only way to reduce the risk inherent in that prospect is to wrap the Bonn government even tighter into the community of free nations. As economic bonds replace military alliances that means that the European Community will become more important than NATO.[35]

Peter Torner, President of the Council on Foreign Relations even noted a 'bizarre nostalgia' for the Cold War.[36] Henry Kissinger spoke of 'a sudden nostalgia [that] has developed for the status quo'.[37] Lawrence Eagleburger was quoted as saying that the Cold War had produced a remarkable set of stable and predictable relationships between the great powers. Uncertainty about Gorbachev's prospects of success also contributed towards consolidating old positions.[38] Even the provincial press was alarmed. There was talk of the 'good old days' when the division of Germany into East and West was still clear.[39] The changes in Europe prefigure a leading role for Germany — of that there was and is no doubt — or as George F. Will put it in a commentary: 'Germany will be the head of the European House'.[40] The questions remain: what role will the enlarged Federal Republic play in the Western Alliance and in the European Community? How will the relationship of the Federal Republic with the former countries of the Soviet Union develop with a unified Germany remaining a member of the Western community? The position of both the government and the largest opposition party on this complex of issues is quite clear.

One of the questions raised in 1989 was: who are these Germans and can they be trusted?

Who are these people we see on our television [asked Mary McGrory in the *Washington Post* on 15 October 1989] these people who sing 'We shall overcome', carry candles and sass their police? They are East Germans, we are told. But they are not the Germans we remember from a generation past. They are not the goose-stepping, Heil-Hitlering, authority-loving people who followed a mad leader to war that devoured the world and decimated a generation, who acquiesced in — or at least made sure they didn't know much about — the extermination of 6 million Jews.[41]

The autumn of 1989 changed the image of 'the Germans'. For the first time in their history they risked an uprising against a dictatorship and fought for democracy and human rights. The question remains as to whether these events will leave a lasting imprint on the future image of the German people.

'Don't Trust the Germans' ran the title given by Roger Scruton, a leading conservative thinker in Great Britain, to an article he published in the *Sunday Telegraph* in June 1989 on the eve of a NATO summit and at the height of a debate on the development of new short-range nuclear missiles in Europe. The West Germans, he maintained, were no longer prepared to support the policies of the West. They were courting the idea of neutrality and unilateral disarmament. This endangered the Western Alliance and supported the long-term goal of Soviet policy to drive the Americans out of Europe. The result of this process would not be peace and lasting *détente* or a common European Home: 'The Iron Curtain will be raised, but only to fall again in the Atlantic. West Germany has now taken a decisive turn away from the Western Alliance.'[42] Scruton offers his readers a bitter reminder of a historical tendency in German politics to see Germany's central location in Europe as a justification for her claim to leadership. None the less, as a leading article in the *Independent* put it, 'very few people, least of all most West Germans, want a restoration of German hegemony in Europe'.[43]

It was the Federal Republic which had first decided to adopt the political ideals of Western democracies. However, many critical intellectuals question whether and to what extent this decision will last and whether it was not taken primarily for ideological reasons, that is to establish a clear demarcation (*Abgrenzung*) vis-a-vis communism and to set up a Western-style liberal democracy as a counter-model to the dictatorship in the GDR. In the history of the Federal Republic the perception of communism as arch-adversary served the needs both of foreign

policy and of German–German policy. It ensured the 'preservation of a power structure which cannot do without deterrence'
and made criticism of that power structure taboo.[44] Whether the
Western outlook of the Federal Republic was in fact no more than
a signpost in the East–West conflict was to become evident in the
process of radical upheaval in Europe.

As a country the Federal Republic was vague and ill-defined.
The population of a country which was only forty years old had
not developed a sense of national identity. German history was
broader and darker than that of the geographically and culturally
more limited Federal Republic.

The West Germans sought redemption first in hard work and then in
being good Europeans, thus making a crucial contribution both to
Europe's economic revival and to the creation of the European Economic
Community. Material success inevitably failed to satisfy the spiritual
needs of a people long inclined to abstract yearnings; and the West
Europeanism was soon complemented by Willy Brandt's *Ostpolitik*. The
federal system and the absence of a true capital favoured strong regional
development and cultural decentralisation, but did nothing to foster a
sense of identity.[45]

It was generally recognised, however, that in its Western part
Germany had developed into a stable democracy.

Its emergence as much the most prosperous, democratic and civilised
state to have flourished on German soil is a tribute to the hard work and
good sense of a people chastened by the horrors of war; and also to the
wisdom of the Western allies who shaped the Basic Law, or constitution,
on which it was founded.[46]

Can the Germans be trusted? Many commentators in recent
years have expressed their reservations on this issue. There does
seem to be a remarkable discrepancy between the opinion of
leading intellectuals in Western countries and ordinary citizens —
a contradiction which also runs through German society. While
well-known intellectuals such as Günter Grass and Jürgen
Habermas spoke of a 'bargain called Germany' (a reference to the
absorption of East by West Germany at what seemed little cost)
and 'Deutschmark nationalism', the overwhelming majority of
citizens welcomed German unity. Admittedly, they also stated in
all the opinion polls that the unification process was taking place
too hastily. Opinion polls in neighbouring European countries
present a variegated picture. In February 1990 the prestigious
French opinion research institute, Sofres, produced results showing that 58 per cent of French people reacted positively when
they were asked if they were in favour of German reunification;

Table 1.2   Do you favour or oppose the reunification of Germany?
(figures in %)

	Britain	France	Poland	USA
Favour	45	61	41	61
Oppose	30	15	44	13
Neither	19	19	14	9
Don't know	6	5	1	17

Source: The Economist, 27 January 1990: 29–34

28 per cent favoured the retention of the existing German states; 43 per cent expressed the view that reunification would complicate the political integration of Germany and 37 per cent were afraid that the position of France would be weakened by German reunification.[47] At the end of 1990 a study by the same institute showed that 58 per cent took a positive view of German reunification, 9 per cent were against reunification and 28 per cent expressed indifference.[48] A year earlier, at the beginning of 1990, a poll by *The Economist* and the *Los Angeles Times* had been conducted in Britain, France, Poland and the United States (see Table 1.2).

A poll by the French institute CSA which was also carried out at the beginning of 1990 in the Federal Republic, Spain, France, Great Britain, Italy, Hungary, Poland and the former Soviet Union produced the following results shown in Table 1.3.

All the poll findings indicate that the unification of Germany provoked a variety of deep-seated feelings, expectations and fears, or, in the words of the former French Foreign Minister Claude Cheysson in a BBC interview on 28 May 1989: 'Before the Germans were tempted by the wind of the East, our Germans [i.e. the West Germans] were fully integrated' into the Western Alliance and European Community — and now it was important to ensure that the situation stayed that way.

Above all else the fear that Germany might become too powerful dominates public opinion in Poland — the country which suffered most under Germany during World War II — and to a lesser extent in France (despite thirty years' official partnership) and in Great Britain. As might be expected, the reasons for this are complex. Underlying them is the historical experience of these countries with 'the Germans' — an experience itself intimately related to the question of the German nation-state and its role in the centre of Europe. In addition, the old fear of German romanticism, irrationalism and nationalism plays a part. Western reaction to the events of 1989 and 1990 demonstrate that

Table 1.3 Do you personally take a positive or negative view of German reunification? (figures in %)

	FRG	Spain	France	UK	Italy	Hungary	Poland	USSR
Very positive	31	48	17	21	41	23	9	17
Rather positive	49	25	51	40	37	45	17	34
Rather negative	15	4	17	15	8	16	26	17
Very negative	2	2	6	12	5	6	38	13
Don't know	3	21	9	12	9	10	10	19

Source: Frankfurter Rundschau, 19 February 1990: 16

despite the official pronouncements, attitudes towards the German people remain reserved, cautious and sometimes coloured by suspicion. Occasionally, sentiment verges on the bizarre as when, for example, Roger Scruton describes Germany as a vacuum in the heart of Europe, as

a tomb in which the remnants of Prussia once were buried and in which the ghost of a stricken people constantly reappears, calling for vengeance and redemption . . . . The Germans now wish to throw their arms away; their longing is based on guilt . . . . We should recognise in these things something of the exorbitant spirit which spoke through Hitler: the desire to transcend the patient work of politics, into a state of unity and grace.[49]

Heleno Saña expresses similar ideas derived from memories of German history. In his book *The Fourth Reich: Germany's Late Victory* he sees the German people as having two political choices:

Some want to dominate Europe from the outside, the rest from within. The first option is the more primitive, the second the more subtle, both hold out the promise of nothing good. For neither the one nor the other would bring about the de-Germanicisation which the world and not the least the Germans themselves need in order to free themselves of their megalomaniac obsessions.[50]

George Valance, editor-in-chief of *L'Express* echoes Zbigniev Brzezinski's view, expressed in an interview with *Le Figaro* (18 July 1990), that 'the end of the Cold War would leave two victors: the United States and Germany. And two losers: the USSR and France'. Valance, too, sees France losing out after German reunification:

German reunification constitutes a tremendous challenge to France. Since the war France has been lucky, very lucky . . . . The German economic giant is being transformed before our eyes into a political giant. The centre of Europe is moving towards Berlin as Paris takes on the aspect of a southern city. The future of the Continent is dealt with in Bonn, Moscow or Washington. Paris is just kept informed.[51]

Despite the positive attitude which Germany's neighbours in East and West have taken towards her wish to be reunited, doubts remain about the resolve and political reliability of the German people. A reunified Germany has still to prove that it is in a position to preserve the Federal Republic's forty-year-old democratic tradition despite its increased size and the threat of social and political conflict.

In 1949, at a celebration to mark the 200th anniversary of the birth of Goethe, Thomas Mann expressed his regrets that the ideals of European democracy had never enjoyed prestige or political power in Germany. Politicians in the Federal Republic subsequently embraced his hopes that a European Germany would grow to be a good home — one to which the world could respond positively rather than with fear 'because it has a place in the democratic religion of mankind'.[52]

In the process of German unification Thomas Mann's vision of a European Germany has been frequently invoked in an attempt to allay fears abroad. This kind of appeasement strategy is as antiquated as the fears it addresses. The problem does not lie in a German Europe of disreputable intentions but in the political geography of Europe in which Germany will take her place.

The basic decision in favour of adherence to a Western-liberal political and social order was taken on 3 October 1990. The decision to adopt a political order which the old socialist system had consigned to the dustbin of history appears to be a common feature of all the transformations in Eastern Europe. For this reason they may be termed 'constitutional revolutions'.[53] The peculiarity of the German revolution derives from the fact that the GDR was able to become part of a political order of some forty years' stability — in marked contrast to the painful transition anticipated in Poland, Czechoslovakia and Hungary, not to mention the Soviet Union. The problem is that the merging in the heart of Europe of two states which had hitherto belonged to two ideological systems and opposing alliances has, apart from internal difficulties, shifted the balance in Europe.

The accomplishment of German unity, the reunited Germany's membership of NATO and the European Community and the collapse of the Warsaw Pact and Comecon require the creation of a new European equilibrium covering the political, economic, military and cultural spheres. This also presupposes an analysis of the consequences of an eastward shift in Europe's centre of gravity. The Poles, Czechs, Slovaks and Hungarians have left the periphery of the Soviet empire and rejoined the centre of Europe.

The Germans in East and West had been the respective outposts of two opposing systems. Now suddenly they find themselves as an economic superpower in a radically altered political constellation in the heart of Europe. It is not necessary to be a devotee of the romantic ideal of some Central Europe *Mitteleuropa*)[54] to understand that the geopolitical coordinates have shifted eastward. Europe is coming together and Germany has still to find her role. As August Pradetto writes:

Until now Europe has been led by France and the Federal Republic of Germany. Economically speaking in the 1980s Germany was stronger but France was more dynamic. Germany is now set to become not only bigger than any other western European country; it is likely to register a much higher growth rate . . . . In future Germany will be the locomotive of the European train with the others having to follow suit. This will create economic and political tensions not only among the European states but also within their own borders.[55]

The revolutions in East-Central Europe have brought in their wake two irreconcilable tendencies: whereas Western Europe, despite its difficulties, tends towards integration and the dilution of the nation-state, the liberation of Eastern Europe from the clutches of Soviet socialism is inextricably linked to a new nationalism. After years of artificial uniformity in these societies, enforced by means of an ideologically determined policy, people are again becoming aware of their differences. A solution to the old and new ethnic, social and cultural 'cleavages' by rational and democratic means has, however, still to be found. This contradiction runs through the heart of Europe and Germany.

The people of the GDR owe their freedom in large part to the national movements in Eastern Europe. Without the radical change in Poland and Hungary and without Soviet acceptance that such change could not be arrested by force, there would have been no revolution. By extension, without Western Europe and the integration of the Federal Republic in the Western Alliance and the European Community, the Allies would not have sanctioned state reunification. However divergent the initial stances of the Soviet Union and the United States may have been at the outset of the reunification process, they shared the belief that a reunited Germany was not to become some sort of disruptive factor in the European political order. Disagreement arose over the means by which this was to be achieved. The anchoring of the Federal Republic in the Western community, accepted in the end by the Soviet Union, offers a safeguard against fears that Germany might again abandon liberal-Western ideas and play the unfortunate role of a medium-sized power with an authoritarian order at home and with chauvinistic ambitions abroad.

Ralf Dahrendorf is right to note that there are no signs that the process of European unification renders the nation-state obsolete in its critical tasks. Dahrendorf believes first and foremost that the nation-state in practical terms remains the realm in which basic civil rights are guaranteed.[56] The constitutional order of the Federal Republic fulfils such criteria.

Notes

1 Anne Köhler and Rudolf Eppinger, 'Einstellungen von Jugendlichen zur DDR und zur Deutschlandpolitik', *Schriften und Materialien zur Deutschlandpolitik und Europapolitik*, No. 3/1984, Munich: Studienstätte für Politik und Zeitgeschehen, p. 21.

2 Bundeskanzler Brandt, 'Regierungserklärung vor dem Deutschen Bundestag am 28 October 1969', *Bulletin* Presse- und Informationsamt der Bundesregierung, No. 132/1969, Sonderdruck, pp. 33–4.

3 Dorothee Wilms, 'Deutschlandpolitik im Rahmen der europäischen Einigung' (Rede vor dem Institut Francais des Rélations Internationales 25 January 1988 in Paris) *Texte zur Deutschlandpolitik*, Bundesministerium für innerdeutsche Beziehungen (ed.), Reihe III/vol. 6 — 1988, Bonn, p. 34.

4 Helmut Schmidt, *Die Zeit*, 22 September 1989.

5 Helmut Schmidt, 'Was ist der Deutschen Vaterland? Ein endgültiger Verzicht auf die Einheit würde nur das Misstrauen unserer Nachbarn in Ost und West verstärken, *Die Zeit*, No. 29, 14 July 1989, p. 4.

6 Egon Bahr, 'Einheit und NATO sind unvereinbar', *Vorwärts*, No. 10, 1990.

7 'Bericht der Bundesregierung zur Lage der Nation im geteilten Deutschland', *Bulletin* Presse- und Informationsamt der Bundesregierung, No. 123, 9 November 1989, p. 1059.

8 'Bericht der Bundesregierung', op. cit., p. 1058.

9 Willy Brandt, 'Deutsche Wegmarken', *Der Tagesspiegel*, 13 September 1988, p. 9.

10 Theo Sommer, 'Quo vadis Germania? Eine Standortbestimmung der Bundesrepublik nach den Besuchen von Bush und Gorbatschow', *Die Zeit*, No. 26, 23 June 1989, p. 3.

11 Helmut Schmidt, 'Was ist der Deutschen Vaterland?', loc. cit.

12 Franz Josef Strauss, 'Die moralische Substanz der Nation bleibt erhalten. Beitrag von Franz Josef Strauss beim Münchner Podium 84 ''Reden über das eigene Land: Deutschland''', *Frankfurter Rundschau* (Dokumentation), 2 January 1985, p. 16.

13 Cf. 'Das deutsch – deutsche Treffen am Werbellinsee. Dokumentation zum Treffen des Bundeskanzlers der Bundesrepublik Deutschland, Helmut Schmidt, mit dem Generalsekretär des ZK der SED und Vorsitzenden des Staatsrates der DDR, Erich Honecker', 11--13 December 1981, Bundesministerium für innerdeutsche Beziehungen (ed.), Bonn, 1982.

14 Cf. *Beziehungen der Deutschen Demokratischen Republik zur Bundesrepublik Deutschland*. Dokumente 1971–1988, Berlin (DDR), Staatsverlag, 1990, S. 134.

15 Cf. *Der Besuch von Generalsekretär Honecker in der Bundesrepublik Deutschland. Dokumentation zum Arbeitsbesuch des Generalsekretärs der SED und Staatsratsvorsitzenden der DDR, Erich Honecker, in der Bundesrepublik Deutschland im September 1987*, Bonn, Bundesministerium für inner deutsche Beziehungen (ed.), 1988; *Ein Erfolg der Politik der Vernunft und des Realismus. Offizieller Besuch des*

Generalsekretärs des Zentralkomitees der Sozialistischen Einheitspartei Deutschlands und Vorsitzenden des Staatsrates der Deutschen Demokratischen Republik, Erich Honecker, in der Bundesrepublik Deutschland vom 7-11 September 1987, Berlin (DDR), 1987.

16 Helmut Schmidt, Einer unserer Brüder. Zum Besuch Erich Honeckers, *Die Zeit*, No. 31, 24 July 1987, p. 3.

17 Cf. Der Besuch, op. cit., p. 17.

18 Ibid., pp. 26–7.

19 *Texte zur Deutschlandpolitik*, Bundesministerium für innerdeutsche Beziehungen, (ed.), Reihe III, Vol. 5, 1987, p. 361.

20 *Texte zur Deutschlandpolitik*, Bundesministerium für innerdeutsche Beziehungen (ed.), Reihe III, Vol. 6, 1988, p. 43.

21 Cf. Helmut Simon, '''Vom deutschen Volk in freier Selbstbestimmung . . .'' Die geeinte Nation braucht ihre Verfassung', *Die Zeit*, No. 29, 13 July 1990, p. 9.

22 Cf. Ernst Benda, 'Das letzte Wort dem Volke. Auch die ostdeutschen Bürger müssen sich unsere Verfassung zu eigen machen', *Die Zeit*, No. 38, 14 September 1990, p. 13.

23 Cf. Robert Leicht, 'Königsweg zur Einheit. Das Saarland als Beispiel: Wie ein abgestufter Beitritt zur Bundesrepublik gelang', *Die Zeit*, No. 10, 2 March 1990, p. 7; Ernst Benda, '''Königsweg'' oder ''Holzweg''. Professor Ernst Benda über verfassungsrechtliche Fragen der deutschen Vereinigung', *Der Spiegel*, No. 18, 30 April 1990, pp. 75–80.

24 Jürgen Seifert, 'Ein bloßer Beitritt wird der DDR nicht gerecht. Verfassungsfragen der deutschen Einigung', *Frankfurter Rundschau*, No. 67, 20 March 1990, p. 16; Hans-Joachim Mengel, 'Keine Zeit für eine neue Verfassung? Der Einigungsprozeß mit der DDR erschöpft sich im Transfer eines wirtschaftlichen Systems', *Frankfurter Rundschau*, No. 155, 7 July 1990, p. 3; Ulrich K. Preuss, 'Auf der Suche nach der Zivilgesellschaft. Der Verfassungsentwurf des Runden Tisches', *Frankfurter Allgemeine Zeitung*, No. 99, 28 April 1990; Ulrich K. Preuss, 'Grundgesetz-Chauvinismus oder . . .', *Die Tageszeitung*, 3 March 1990, p. 2; Christian Starck, Das Grundgesetz für Deutschland — Schritt für Schritt. Beitritt der DDR oder ihrer Länder — die schonende Lösung der deutschen Frage', *Thüringer Tageblatt*, No. 102, 3 May 1990, p. 4.

25 Leicht, Königsweg, op. cit.

26 Starck, op. cit.

27 Seifert, op. cit.

28 Preuss, 'Grundgesetz-Chauvinismus', op. cit.

29 Herwig Roggemann, 'Zur Reformverfassung einer gesamtdeutschen Bundesrepublik — Ein verfassungspolitischer Diskussionsbeitrag', *Neue Justiz*, No. 5, 1990, p. 183; Herwig Roggemann, 'Die Verfassungsentwicklung der deutschen Staaten auf dem Wege in die gesamtdeutsche Föderation, *Juristische Rundschau*, No. 7, 1990, pp. 265–72.

30 Cf. Article 4,6 of the Unification Treaty between the Federal Republic of Germany and the German Democratic Republic.

31 Cf. in detail: Sigrid Meuschel, *Legitimation und Parteiherrschaft. Zum*

Paradox von Stabilität und Revolution in der DDR 1945–1989, Frankfurt/Main, Suhrkamp, 1991.

32 Quoted in Theo Sommer, 'Lieber zweimal Deutschland als einmal', *Die Zeit*, No. 39, 21 September 1984, p. 1.

33 Nigel Hawkes, 'Fatherland in display of maternal instinct', The *Observer*, 18 June 1989.

34 Peter Kellner, 'Keeping the Germans on a leash', The *Independent*, 12 June 1989.

35 David S. Broder, 'Start Planning for a new era and a new Germany', *International Herald Tribune*, 15 November 1989.

36 Peter Tarnoff, 'A Bizarre Nostalgia for the Cold War', The *New York Times*, 19 September 1989.

37 Henry Kissinger, 'Living with the inevitable', *Newsweek*, 4 December 1989, pp. 22–5.

38 Elmo Zumwalt and Worth Bagley, 'When will Mikhail run out of steam?', The *Washington Times*, 11 October 1989; Richard Pipes, 'The Russian's are Still Coming', The *New York Times*, 6 October 1989.

39 'Good riddance to the Cold War', The *Hartford Courant*, 24 September 1989.

40 *International Herald Tribune*, 1 December 1989.

41 Mary McGrory, 'Have the Germans really changed?', *Washington Post*, 15 October 1989, pp. B1–B5.

42 Roger Scruton, 'Don't trust the Germans. Far from offering the greatest hope for the future of Europe, West Germany's eagerness for detente with the Soviet Union poses a serious threat to our security', *Sunday Telegraph*, 21 June 1989.

43 'The best Germany we have had', The *Independent*, 25 May 1989, p. 24.

44 Max Frisch, 'Wir hoffen', Frank Grube and Gerhard Richter (eds.), *Der SED—Staat*, Munich, Piper, 1977, p. 16.

45 'The best Germany we have had', op. cit.

46 Ibid.

47 Alfred Grosser, 'Es könnte doch viel schlimmer werden . . . Eine Kritische Betrachtung aus Paris', in Ulrich Wickert (ed.), *Angst vor Deutschland*, Hamburg, Hoffmann & Campe, 1990, p. 148.

48 'Das Profil der Deutschen. Was sie vereint, was sie trennt', *Spiegel Special*, 1, 1991, p. 27.

49 Scruton, 'Don't trust the Germans . . .', op. cit.

50 Heleno Saña, *Das vierte Reich. Deutschlands später Sieg*, Hamburg, Rasch und Röhring, 1990, p. 267.

51 Georges Valance, *France Allemagne: Le retour des Bismarck*, Paris, Flammarion, 1990, p. 9.

52 Thomas Mann, 'Goethe und die Demokratie', in *Politische Schriften und Reden*, vol. 3, Frankfurt-on-Main, Fischer, 1968, p. 214.

53 Cf. Ulrich K. Preuss, *Revolution, Fortschritt und Verfassung. Zu einem neuen Verfassungsverständnis*, Berlin, Wagenbach, 1990.

54 Hans-Peter Burmeister, Frank Boldt, György Mészáros (eds.), *Mitteleuropa — Traum oder Trauma? Überlegungen zum Selbstbild einer Region*, Bremen, Edition Temmen, 1988.

55 August Pradetto, 'Zusammenbruch des "Realsozialismus", deutsche Einheit und europäische Integration', *Europäische Rundschau*, **13**, 1990, No. 4, p. 50.

56 Ralf Dahrendorf, *Reflections on the Revolution in Europe* (in a letter intended to have been sent to a man in Warsaw), London, Chatto and Windus, 1990, p. 124; here, Dahrendorf is arguing against Peter Glotz, 'Renaissance des Vorkriegsnationalismus?', *Die neue Gesellschaft/Frankfurter Hefte*, **37**, 1990, No. 1.

2 Structural defects of 'real socialism': causes and antecedents of the crisis

The German Democratic Republic (GDR) was an 'occupation régime' (Samuel Huntington), that is a political system which came under Soviet occupation in the aftermath of World War II and the unconditional surrender of the National Socialist régime as a piece of 'wreckage' of German history. Like the Federal Republic of Germany the GDR was the product of the Cold War, the disintegration of the anti-Hitler coalition and of the changed geopolitical interests of the superpowers. It was only in the process of becoming a state that the Soviet zone of occupation, the later GDR, explicitly accepted the fundamental principles of the Stalinist notion of transformation: a revolution from above.[1]

In 1948 in the wake of the controversies about 'Titoism', the SED openly endorsed these Stalinist principles. It proclaimed itself a 'party of a new type' thereby accepting the reduction of the idea of the Leninist vanguard to the ideological and politico-strategic leading role of the party; here, the historical role of the proletariat is confined to the fulfillment of tasks set by the party. The SED could not rely on the broad consensus or active support of the people in the execution of these tasks. East German communists never succeeded in gaining popular legitimacy.

The SED failed to gain legitimacy because it was not prepared to undertake a basic and thoroughgoing change in its understanding of the structure and functioning of a socialist society developed in the time of Stalinism. This understanding can be summarised briefly as follows: the SED, like every other communist party, defined itself as a vanguard party with the historical mission of building socialism and communism. This in turn presupposed a total concentration of power in its hands; there was no question of any power sharing. For the SED the realisation of its objectives necessitated centralised policy based on uniform principles. Only on the basis of the unity of party, state and society could there be any question of a functional division of powers among the party, executive, legislature and judiciary and among the institutions of the state and the 'social organisations' they controlled. Any attempt to separate the various components of the political system — the Marxist–Leninist Party, the state, the legal system, mass organisations and the allied parties — was considered to be a general attack on the very foundations of the state and social order.[2]

The key mechanism in the functioning of the state was 'Democratic Centralism'. It secured the supremacy of the communist party in all areas of society. Its removal would have meant the end of SED influence over the recruitment of personnel, over vetting mechanisms and the parallel structure of the party apparatus and state administration.[3]

Within this normative framework the communist party employed the state as the primary means by which to secure its political goals. It dictated the political direction of the state institutions and intervened whenever it was considered expedient in the day-to-day workings of the state apparatus. The party monitored the execution of its directives through the state apparatus and ensured the selection, training and political education of all employees who worked in state institutions (cadres). With its direction and control of all institutions in the field of economic planning the ruling communist parties heavily influenced the economic and social development of the social system as a whole.

Since the beginning of their rule communist parties have used the state in order to achieve their political and social objectives. The politics of the party were synonymous with the politics of the state. This was not without its contradictions: while the party espoused a theory of revolution and of the creation of a socialist state which professed its indebtedness to Marx and Engels and wanted to abolish the state as an instrument of repression, the 'dictatorship of the proletariat' which was established in the Soviet Union as the dictatorship of the party (and which widened further still after the Second World War) were anything other than a step toward the abolition of the state. On the contrary, the communist parties constructed a powerful, centralised state in which all the means of power were concentrated and which translated its socialist objectives into practice.

The SED created organisations and institutions inspired by the Soviet model which were to guarantee a 'bond with the working people'. They consisted primarily of the parliaments, local people's assemblies and the 'National Front' of allied parties and mass organisations. The people's assemblies (*Volkskammer*, regional, local and district diets, municipal and regional councils) were all conceived as the alliance of the working class and other classes and social strata (cooperative farmers, the intelligentsia and other working people) at the state level. The notion of such an alliance can also be seen in the constituency of the 'Block Parties' in the 'National Front' such as the Christian Democratic Union (CDU), the Liberal-Democratic Party of Germany (LDPD), the Democratic Farmers Party of Germany (DBD) and the National Democratic Party (NDPD). Until new elections were held in May 1990 the SED and the above parties were joined by some mass organisations in the people's assemblies: the Free German Trade Union Confederation (FDGB), the Democratic Women's League of Germany (DFD), the Free German Youth (FDJ) and the *Kulturbund* (KB). The Association for Mutual Farmers Assistance (VdgB) gained representation after 1986. Until late 1989 these parties and organisations unquestioningly recognised the SED as the leading political force and the need for their unconditional subordination to its leading role. Ostensibly, this alliance reflected the close 'cohesion of allied classes and social strata in the GDR'.[4]

In accordance with Leninist tradition the mass organisations were seen by the SED as 'transmitters' — as organisations which were to operate like transmission belts in translating the will of the SED into social practice (most notably the trade unions and the party's youth organisation, the Free German Youth). In addition, the mass organisations were conceived as 'schools of socialism'; they were to bring non-party members and young people into the fold, organise and mobilise them and provide the SED with new members. However, these organisations differed somewhat from the Stalinist period in so far as they enacted in part the role of representing their members' interests *vis-à-vis* the party or the state apparatus, although this role in turn dictated that such representation remained within the confines set by the party. They were little more than bureaucratic-interest organisations in a centralised party system and not pressure groups in the democratic sense.

Finally, the party organised and vetted all the means of political and ideological influence, agitation and propaganda. The means of mass communication, agitation and propaganda and mass schooling were intended to foster or consolidate a 'socialist consciousness' among the population. The press, radio, television and almost all the publishing houses and many educational institutions were either owned by the SED or subject to its control.

Cooperation between the SED and the other parties and mass organisations was, in the words of involved parties before October 1989, 'characterised by shared socialist ideals; by the principles of comradely cooperation and the shared determination to reach the goals of society for the benefit of the people'.[5]

This basic understanding of the structure and functioning of the political system was common to the SED and all other ruling communist parties. To this extent the social and political crisis of the GDR can also be seen as part of a more general crisis of post-Stalinist socialism in countries where the socio-economic and political system of the Soviet Union has been imposed. A search for the determinants of the crisis in the system reveals an inter-related complex of economic, political, social and cultural causes. Aside from poor economic performance and the growing technology gap between the GDR and other countries, by far the most crucial phenomenon in recent years was the increasingly manifest emancipation of society from the self-arrogated leading role of the communist party. The parties wished to create uniform societies and to fashion a new 'socialist man' in their image. In reality, however, in the GDR as in other socialist countries a cultural and social change had taken place. Over a period of years clear trends had evolved which were not unlike those in Western industrialised countries: the structure of society was becoming more differentiated; new attitudes and value orientations were emerging and the influences of international culture and civilisation could no longer be artificially suppressed as they had been as recently as the early 1960s when the party leadership attempted to ban the viewing of Western television broadcasts. None the less, the active participation of the population in this process of change was blocked by the Wall and closed borders. The sense of imprisonment and attendant dissatisfaction grew without eliciting any response from the SED.

Since 1985 another factor which posed a grave danger to the forces of orthodoxy entered the frame: *Glasnost* and *Perestroika* in the Soviet Union. The process of a transition from a dictatorship which claimed absolute hegemony to an enlightened authoritarianism and possibly to a democracy which, until now without recourse to war, is unique in terms of world history and could not avoid affecting the countries which had once constituted the socialist bloc. The rapid and at times abrupt ideological and social changes emanating from the Soviet Union which touched other socialist countries in recent years at once shook the foundations of the internal order of these states and the alliance itself. The dissolution of the erstwhile socialist bloc into several individual, national and as yet barely comparable variants has now reached an advanced stage and has brought a fundamental change to the political face of Europe.

One of the most basic causes of the crisis of Soviet-type socialism lies in the fact that the inherited authoritarian and centralised structures of the political and economic system impeded the process of modernisation. The political system was unable to meet the scientific-technological, economic, social and cultural challenges which had faced the socialist countries for two decades or more. The impending economic disaster which confronted the GDR in 1990, on a scale which not even those who had remained deeply sceptical of GDR statistics could foretell, illustrates that the current plight has not been produced by specific or accumulated errors but by structural defects inherent in the system — in sum, the belief that a modern, industrial society could be planned and regulated from the centre. This belief could not be fulfilled in the economy or in the social or cultural spheres. Attempts in this direction succeeded only in producing authoritarian political and social systems which were inflexible, unadaptable and which, when faced with the need for modernisation, offered only a belated or half-hearted response.

For a short period in the 1960s, however, it did still appear that Soviet-type socialism was capable and desirous of reform. This hope was dashed on 21 August 1968 in Prague. Since the early 1960s there had been several attempts to cast off the fetters of the old Stalinist system and to emphasise the ideological and political independence of the other German state. The 'New Economic System of Planning and Management' (NÖS) inaugurated in 1963 acted as a pilot project for other socialist countries. The terminological proximity to Lenin's 'New Economic Policy' (NEP) was no coincidence. However, this experiment had to be modified after the fall of Khruschchev in 1964 and then abandoned altogether in 1968–9.

The latitude for reform permitted by the Soviet Union had become severely limited. In different political circumstances the NÖS could indeed have become a model for system reform — albeit of a technocratic character — for the other socialist countries. In the mid-1960s the party leadership under Walter Ulbricht formulated new ideas in various political areas which were independent of the Soviet position. The SED abandoned the claims that communist society could be attained in the foreseeable future. In the place of utopian visions of the future emerged the notion of a 'socialist community of people' — a socialist society free of conflict but which in fact merely concealed the real conflicts. The SED was convinced that with the help of scientific methods derived from systems theory and cybernetics it could engineer the building of a modern form of socialism. It adopted an independent, obstinate stance in questions of East–West relations and in the German question but could not sustain this for long.

The definitive end of all attempts at reform in the Soviet Union came together with a recentralisation of the planning and management mechanisms. The supression of the Prague Spring of 1968 brought to an end all efforts to introduce structural reforms and produced a return to the old, politically controlled centralism which lasted a further two decades.[6]

The replacement of the long-standing party chief Walter Ulbricht and the assumption of the chairmanship by Erich Honecker in 1971 not only paved the way for a more realistic international policy for the SED but also represented the prerequisite for economic and social policies which also clearly bore the hallmarks of an independent stance. The fact that during the Brezhnev years the SED leadership took a remarkably independent line is often forgotten today.

In the first half of the 1970s the SED set new priorities in economic and social policy and improved its popular standing by means of a paternalistic social policy. The world economic crisis of the mid-1970s intervened to wreck the wide-ranging plan for the 'unity of economic and social policy'. The relative stability and economic strength of the GDR enabled certain new priorities to be set in foreign policy and security matters while the policies pursued by the Honecker leadership during the new Cold War of the early 1980s also helped to ensure that relations between the two German states survived all the dangers more or less intact.

A further area in which the SED sought to secure legitimation — cultural policy — alternated between liberalisation and repression. But in general terms, compared to the 1950s and 1960s there was a marked improvement in the cultural climate in the GDR.

The new social developments such as changes in the values held in particular by the younger generation and the advent of new issues, for example the environment, peace, individual self-determination left the SED leadership bereft of understanding or any demonstrable political vision. There had long been a clear need for reform here. In the last years a large number of informal groups and associations had defied the obstacles put in their way and had formed for the most part under the auspices of the Evangelical Church. References made to the events of 1989 as a 'protestant revolution' are not mere coincidence.[7] The churches protected the various opposition groups and deeply informed their ideology, values, political beliefs and forms of action. In the Ulbricht years such attempts would have been nipped in the bud.

However, in a thoroughgoing liberalisation of the political system, the SED could not take this step. Instead, as the calls for internal reform became more vocal it retreated into orthodox positions. In so doing the SED squandered the credit it had so painstakingly built up in the 1970s and early 1980s. What would have been regarded five years earlier as a liberal attitude seemed, in the light of the dynamic process of change in the Soviet Union and in other socialist countries, to be a dogged adherence to repression and moribund ideas.

Notes

1 Cf. Gert-Joachim Glaessner, *Herrschaft durch Kader. Leitung der Gesellschaft und Kaderpolitik in der DDR am Beispiel des Staatsapparates*, Opladen, Westdeutscher Verlag, 1977.
2 *Einführung in die marxistisch–leninistische Staats- und Rechtslehre*, Berlin (DDR), Staatsverlag, 1986, p. 59.
3 Cf. in detail Gert-Joachim Glaessner, *Die andere deutsche Republik. Gesellschaft und Politik in der DDR*, Opladen, Westdeutscher Verlag, 1989, pp. 90–150; *DDR. Gesellschaft Staat Bürger*, Berlin, (DDR), Staatsverlag, 1978.
4 *Handbuch Deutsche Demokratische Republik*, Leipzig, VEB Bibliographisches Institut, 1979, p. 234.
5 *Marxistisch-leninistische Partei und sozialistischer Staat*, Berlin (DDR), Staatsverlag, p. 115.
6 Andrzej Korbonski, 'The Politics of Economic Reforms in Eastern Europe: the Last Thirty Years', *Soviet Studies*, 1989, No. 1, pp. 1–19, p. 11.
7 Cf. Ehrhart Neubert, *Eine protestantische Revolution*, Osnabrück, Kontext Verlag, 1990.

3 The collapse of the old system

3.1 Prelude to the crisis

A session of the Central Committee of the SED in December 1988 was the scene of an unprecedented statement by the General Secretary of the Party, Erich Honecker. He said that there was 'no model which held for all the socialist countries'. Instead, Honecker referred to a socialism 'in the colours of the GDR'.[1] These statements were reminiscent of the famous essay from the early days of the SED in 1946 in which reference was made to a 'particular German road to socialism'.[2]

On closer inspection, however, it becomes clear that talk of circumstances specific to the GDR served only to distance the party from the reform of Soviet communists under Mikhail Gorbachev. The Western media had always accused SED policy of being too Russian and, it was alleged, now exhorted the party to 'march into anarchy' since in the eyes of Honecker and the party leadership this would be the expected result of *Glasnost* and *Perestroika*. The SED would not however heed these 'new "friends" of the Soviet Union'.[3]

Honecker's speech was quite rightly perceived in large sections of the party and in the GDR generally as a rejection of any reform. The party leadership under Honecker was to remain loyal to this policy until the end.

Honecker did seem to have some valid arguments in his favour. Was not the GDR the most industrially developed country in Eastern Europe? Did it not register the highest standard of living in Comecon? Had not the policies of *Glasnost* and *Perestroika* already resulted in major economic and social problems? This notwithstanding, the leadership failed to cope with one key aspect: for the first time since the early 1960s and the suppression of the 'Prague Spring' the policies of *Glasnost* and *Perestroika* had cultivated the vague hope of a reform of administrative socialism. A large number of intellectuals and SED members now expected the party to embrace these initiatives. According to the former member of the politburo, Günter Schabowski, Glasnost had met with such enthusiasm because 'one of the key contradictions between the people and the leadership in the GDR lay precisely in the lack of openness'.[4] Honecker had, he believes, wholly underestimated the ideological sea-change which *Glasnost* had introduced.

This is undoubtedly true. None the less it must be remembered that this phenomenon was much more widespread than many who lived in the GDR are now prepared to concede. Social conflicts in the GDR pervaded the leading party with its two million members. This was the 'expression of a GDR phenomenon, and an SED phenomenon: the party included both those who banned films and those who had made them; it included the judges and prosecutors who pronounced hardline political sentences and defence lawyers who in the same trials called for acquittal'.[5]

Moreover, dozens of academic institutes provided 'analyses' which appeared to corroborate the optimistic world view of the party leadership. There was no critical social science and no clandestine or samizdat publications as in other socialist countries.

The published results were as far removed from reality as the image of the state of the GDR purveyed by the press.

Instead of advising on the solution of problems, general slogans were disseminated and stereotypically repeated in an effort to right something which is still wrong . . . . Instead of seeking the trust of our party comrades and all the people and winning them over for active cooperation in the resolution of problems, the press continually tried to suggest a picture of the GDR which deviated further and further from the everyday experiences of ordinary people. Conflicts were suppressed and important answers often replaced by bureaucracy and intimidation.[6]

These were the self-critical words of Honecker's successor, Egon Krenz, in the last session of the Central Committee of the SED in November 1989. This was indeed one of the reasons for which *Glasnost* had become a utopia in the GDR: the people were as oblivious as most party members to the fact that reality was far removed from its ideologically prefabricated portrayal in press, radio and television which were in turn subordinate to repressive regulations and 'language rules'. The editors-in-chief of all the media would be called to weekly briefings (*Argumentationen*) in the Central Committee building in order to ensure media uniformity.[7]

The above fact helps to explain a joke often heard in the

Autumn of 1989: a man goes to the police and applies, like tens of thousands at the time, for an exit visa. He is asked where he would like to go and replies: 'To the GDR.' When informed that he is already there he says: 'No, I mean the GDR I read about in the paper.'

This distortion of reality was not without its repercussions. Propaganda became a law unto itself and formed the world view of those who used it. (One of the most depressing experiences one can have in dealing with confidential documents and interviewing former leading politicians is to observe that they use the same wooden, stereotyped language to which they subjected the people.)

Some leading political figures only grasped that they themselves had seen reality through ideological lenses when it was already too late. At the tenth session of the Central Committee of the SED (8–11 November 1989) which decided to open the Wall, Egon Krenz conceded that the 'problems and questions discussed today in total openess . . . [had not] come about overnight or in the previous summer'. The SED had started from false economic premises, misinterpreted the international situation and indulged in utopian thinking.[8]

The further changes in the Soviet Union, Poland and Hungary progressed, the greater the uncertainty in the gerontocratic leadership of the SED. It cocooned itself in a web of self-delusion and saw every attempt at change as an attack by the class enemy. The mass exodus of predominantly young people was — as on 13 August 1961 when the Berlin Wall was built — attributed to the negative influence, propaganda campaigns and wartime reporting techniques of the Western media which gave the 'stage directions to encourage citizens to leave the GDR'.[9]

The central organ of the SED, *Neues Deutschland*, stated on 2 October 1989 that no tears should be shed for those who had left the GDR. This sentence, which provoked outrage in the GDR, was apparently penned by Erich Honecker himself and forwarded to the party newspaper through the Agitation and Propaganda Section of the Central Committee of the SED.[10]

3.2 The end of the Honecker era

The fortieth anniversary of the founding of the GDR on 7 October 1989 was intended by the SED to be an occasion when the historic achievements of the GDR could be displayed to the eyes of the world.

In an address, which carried the grandiloquent title: 'Through the people and for the people great things were achieved' Erich Honecker painted a veritably idyllic picture of the situation in the GDR. The GDR was crossing the threshold into the third millenium, secure in the knowledge that the future belonged to socialism even if 'influential forces in the FRG' were awaiting the chance to 'overturn the results of World War II and post-war history by a coup'. Instead of addressing the real problems facing the GDR, Honecker referred to a 'policy of continuity and renewal' which would ensure that in future 'socialism' would glow in the 'colours of the GDR'. While thousands were leaving the country or demonstrating on the streets, Honecker was speaking of a 'trusting debate in town and country' underway in preparation for the 12th Party Congress.[11] In the illusory world of a political leadership which saw its life's work threatened by external forces the party and the people remained united for the common cause. Honecker's successor, Egon Krenz, later said of a speech which described the situation in the GDR that it portrayed the country as an 'island of the blessed'. Günter Schabowski spoke of a 'problem-expurgated speech'.[12]

At the same time tens of thousands were demonstrating on the streets calling for a different kind of republic. Their talisman was Mikhail Gorbachev who had been invited to the celebration by the SED leadership and had politely digested the proceedings. Gregor Gysi, later to become the Chairman of the reformed PDS (Party of Democratic Socialism), described the situation on 7–8 October as 'ghost-like':

Tens of thousands of young people holding candles stood at the feet of Honecker and Gorbachev and shouted both the 'official slogan', 'the GDR is our Fatherland' and 'Gorby, Gorby!'. Only a few hundred metres or kilometres away there were thousands of 'illegal' demonstrators also calling 'Gorby, Gorby!' and singing The Internationale — the song which fights for human rights.[13]

The extent of insecurity in the population and in the ranks of the SED is illustrated by an analysis of the 'Central Assessment and Information Group' of the Ministry for State Security on 8 October 1989 which discusses reactions to the internal political situation in the GDR. Many 'progressive forces, in particular members of the SED' believed 'that the socialist state and social order in the GDR are in grave jeopardy'. The 'system of the direction and education of political, ideological and economic processes in the GDR' had stagnated, the 'palpable worsening of existing internal political problems and difficulties and the mass exodus indicated a general social crisis in the GDR' which the party could no longer contain. The GDR was already in a situation 'like that just before the counterrevolutionary events of 17 June 1953'.[14] This assessment was to prove correct; the party, however, clearly took no notice.[15]

The anniversary celebrations of the GDR degenerated into a fiasco. The bombast with which the Honecker leadership tried to laud the GDR merely served to precipitate the crisis and acted as a catalyst for the popular uprising. The celebrations became an embarrassing valedictory to a political and social system which had proved incapable of compromise or reform and of a political élite which mistook for reality its belief in its own proclamations of success. The failure of the leadership to introduce a reform of the political and economic system before it was too late at first pushed the GDR to the precipice of a civil war and proved to be the final nail in its coffin. Only fortuitous circumstances prevented the peaceful revolution of 9 October 1989 in Leipzig from being put down like the demonstrations in Tianamen Square.[16]

When only eleven days after the fortieth anniversary celebrations of the GDR, the SED General Secretary, Erich Honecker, was toppled, many long-time observers were reminded of spring 1971 when Honecker's predecessor, Walter Ulbricht, suffered the same fate.[17] Since the foundation of the GDR, power had been vested in two party chairmen. During the same period the Federal Republic of Germany had six chancellors: Konrad Adenauer, Ludwig Erhard, Kurt-Georg Kiesinger, Willy Brandt, Helmut Schmidt and Helmut Kohl. It was evident that the new leader of the SED, Egon Krenz, would be a transitional figure. However, no one at this time could have predicted that for a mere two months Krenz would be the last general secretary of an all-powerful state party and ultimately liquidator of a failed political and social experiment.

The road to the downfall of such an omnipotent general secretary was long and again testifies to the inability of the political system to reform itself from within. The staging posts will be briefly outlined below.

It was only on 11 October that the politburo of the SED issued a statement on the situation in the GDR which had been drafted under almost conspiratorial circumstances and carefully wrested from the incumbent general secretary. The statement had been preceded by a dramatic turn of events. In September thousands of GDR citizens had tried to leave the GDR by travelling through Hungary, Czechoslovakia and Poland. Hundreds camped down in the worst conditions imaginable in the grounds of the West German embassy in Prague. On 25 September the Czechoslovak party leadership had informed the SED leadership that it was no longer prepared to bear the consequences of an exodus now reaching panic proportions. It was afraid that the exodus from the GDR might jeopardise the internal political situation in Czechoslovakia. The question was whether the frontier between Czechoslovakia and the GDR was to be closed. This would have had unforeseeable consequences. The SED general secretary proposed an 'exceptional measure' to allow the people camped in embassy grounds to travel across GDR territory and settle in the Federal Republic.[18] On 4 October violent demonstrations took place in Dresden when people desperate to leave the GDR tried to storm the central railway station and climb aboard trains passing through *en route* for the Federal Republic. For the first time and much too late there were signs that the leadership was appreciating the true situation.

The people were offered a constructive and open dialogue. Regret was expressed at the exodus from the GDR:

Socialism needs every individual. There is room and a future for all. Socialism is the future of coming generations. For this reason we cannot be indifferent to the departure of people who worked and lived in the GDR . . . . The reasons for their leaving may be manifold. We must and will look for these reasons here — each one of us and together.[19]

The leadership emphasised the need for solidarity, proposed a 'democratic community' and called for 'active cooperation'. At the same time, however, accusations were made of far-reaching provocation by imperialist forces which had taken in many of the refugees. Most importantly, hopes of a decisive change to the structures of state and society were dampened: the GDR possessed 'all the necessary forms and forums of a socialist democracy'. They were to be made 'more comprehensive' — which, translated from SED language, means that they had hitherto not been used enough.[20] The concept of a 'forum' was an oblique reference to the opposition group 'New Forum' which at the time stood in the vanguard of the protest movement.

The issue of removing travel restrictions had become a key indicator of the willingness of the SED leadership to change course and initiate *in extremis* a far-reaching reform of the system. Even if the party had exhibited this will by October, it would have been too late. The people and broad sections of the SED membership were no longer prepared to give credence to the willingness to reform of the SED leadership under Erich Honecker. His removal was already seen as overdue.

Preparations for Honecker's removal from office had been underway since late summer 1989 in a tight circle of some Politburo members. The fortieth anniversary of the foundation of the

GDR acted as a magic catalyst. The last definite open sign of preparations came in a meeting of the Minister for State Security Erich Mielke, Egon Krenz, Günter Schabowski and the Central Committee Secretary for Security, Wolfgang Herger in the central building of the State Security Ministry. (The planned palace coup could not take place without the agreement or at least toleration of the Ministry for State Security.)[21] Clearly this meeting discussed the details of what Erich Honecker was later to call an 'internal party and state *putsch*'. The conspirators had obviously secured the support of Soviet advisers in the ministry and other organs of state security.[22] A comment made by the 'security chief' of the SED, Wolfgang Herger, reveals that for the all-important politburo session on 17 October the conspirators had even assumed that Honecker would leave the sitting and warn his security officials. But even here they had taken precautions: prior to the decisive politburo meeting a group of reliable members of the state body guard had been posted in a room adjoining the meeting room on the recommendation of Erich Mielke.[23]

Erich Honecker blamed his removal on the conspiracy of dark forces and traitors in the party's midst:

My fall as head of party and state was the result of a far-reaching plot by schemers who remain hidden. Those who are now boasting that they were responsible are small fry by comparison. What you have here is a major process which didn't just emerge overnight but is a long-term attempt to change the European, no, the world stage.[24]

Honecker is here alluding to a Soviet conspiracy which was designed, he believed, to prevent him from blocking a movement allegedly discernible since 1987 to overcome the division of Germany. This conspiracy theory is remarkably reminiscent of the circumstances of the fall of Walter Ulbricht in 1971. The conspirator then, either with the passive acceptance or active connivance of the Soviet Union, was Erich Honecker.[25]

The fall of Honecker and the dismissal of Joachim Herrmann, Politburo member for agitation and propaganda, and Günter Mittag, Politburo member responsible for the economy and secretary to the Central Committee, was intended to liberate the party. The election of the Politburo member and central committee secretary for security (he was therefore responsible for the brutal police intervention on 7–8 October), Egon Krenz as the general secretary of the SED and a few days later as chairman of the State Council and National Defence Council (with twenty-six against and twenty-six abstentions in the *Volkskammer* vote) left the impression that the SED leadership was content with cosmetic change only.

Protestations made by Egon Krenz and the Politburo that they wished to introduce new politics found little credence. Honecker's removal was too reminiscent of a palace coup. According to Günter Schabowski, Krenz was the 'lowest common denominator' for the Politburo members prepared to accept personnel changes in the Politburo.[26] To the majority of GDR people he was the loyal protegé of Erich Honecker and the man responsible for the ballot-rigging in the communal elections in spring 1989[27] which helped to strengthen open opposition.

The Central Committee elected Egon Krenz as the new general secretary and nominated him as Honecker's successor for the posts of chairman of the State Council and the National Defence Council for which he had already been deputy in his capacity as Central Committee secretary for security. A Central Committee statement described this decision as a turning point (*Wende*) which would enable the SED to 'regain the political and ideological offensive'.

There were then conflicting signals in a politically heated situation: promises of a new beginning and at the same time talk of political and ideological offensives and the old accretion of power to the general secretary of the party. The fact that Honecker's removal was declared not as dismissal but as retirement for health reasons leaves the credibility of the intended renewal or turning point open to doubt.

A number of decisions of the new party leadership would have been received a few weeks or months earlier as decisive steps forward: on the day of his election Krenz met a leading church figure — the first such communication after a long silence. He pursued open discussion with workers about the political situation. The banning in 1988 of the Soviet journal *Sputnik* which had provoked a public outcry even in the ranks of the SED was overturned. The State Council declared an amnesty for anyone convicted of 'crossing the border illegally' and political prisoners were also to be released.

In view of the gravity of the situation the new SED leadership tried to salvage what it could. On the day before the big Berlin demonstration on 4 November 1989, which would be a prelude to liberation from the constraints of the old system and briefly fuelled hopes of some kind of socialist alternative society, the Politburo of the SED had a meeting. In the *ad hoc* television address which followed Krenz gave a broad outline of the SED's action programme. It contained what in earlier days would have been seen as far-reaching political concessions. Now they were recognised as the half-hearted efforts of a party desperately clinging to power. Other pledges included: freedom of travel, extensive changes to penal law, a reform of the political system and means of economic management, the education system, media and, most significantly, a widening of the public realm.[28] The points made in this programme were taken up in the following weeks in several speeches and party programmes, modified and incorporated in the resolutions of the extraordinary Party Congress of the SED.[29]

Following the election of Egon Krenz, SED political strategy had also amounted to a damage limitation exercise. Initial hopes that concessions on points of detail would appease popular discontent soon proved ill-founded. The people of the GDR refused to believe that the SED leadership was able and willing to reform the political system and to overcome post-Stalinist socialism. The rebellion of the SED grassroots in the wake of new revelations of corruption, abuse of office and illegal deals, including officially tolerated arms trafficking, not only signalled the end of the Krenz 'era' after only forty-eight days; it also sealed the end of the SED.

3.3 The end of a state party

On 3 December 1989 the entire Politburo of the SED resigned in an act unprecedented in over seventy years of Communist Party history. The resignation was sparked by a revolt at the party grassroots which had been caught up in the popular mood for change and no longer trusted its new leadership to initiate root and branch reform.

The fall of the Central Committee and the SED Politburo and the involuntary resignation of Egon Krenz as chairman of the State Council and the National Defence Council on 6 December illustrated the complete collapse of a political strategy devoted solely to damage limitation. Yesterday's revolutionaries either would not or could not grasp that a revolution was underway and that they were its 'counter-revolutionaries'.

Despite a remarkable capacity of the 'renewed' SED leadership to adapt to changed circumstances, it was unable to regain the initiative. For weeks the leadership was left with no choice but to follow in the train of the opposition movement.

The fall of Honecker could not prevent the collapse of the old order. The mass exodus of predominantly young people continued. Opposition groups made further gains. The belief that only a radical and far-reaching reform could halt the disintegration reached into the deepest ranks of the SED.

There had long been attempts in the SED on the part of individuals and small groups to initiate extensive reforms.

However, for various reasons they had never gone beyond the state of discussions in small circles. Entrenched ideas of party discipline and the imperative never to endanger the 'unity and purity of the party' had ensured that problems had been addressed in the style of a family discussion. Any member who did not obey the rules of the game would in the past have been thrown into jail.[30] Since the 1970s, and more noticeably after 1985, an expulsion was enough to bring subversive party minds under control. Now long suppressed opinions and disappointment came to be openly expressed. A large number of SED intellectuals diagnosed a latent crisis in the SED which the political means traditionally employed by the party would be unable to resolve.

At the tenth session of the Central Committee from 8–10 November 1989 an 'SED Action Programme' was launched. It contained and elaborated on the major statements made by Egon Krenz in his speech. The programme stated that 'it was necessary to have peaceful mass protests, declarations of political organisations, the constructive contributions of church circles and mounting pressure from the grassroots of our own party and a learning process in the party leadership before rigid political structures could be broken and the first steps toward change could be taken'.[31]

Practical political reality offered a different picture. Large sections of the *Apparat* and the leadership of the SED continued until 3 December to defend resolutely their positions, conceal reality and manipulate events — especially preparations for the Party Congress.[32]

The SED leadership had initially hoped to maintain its position until the XII Party Congress which had been brought forward to spring 1990. However, after much hesitation it agreed to an extraordinary Party Congress to be convened in Berlin in December.[33] There were bitter behind-the-scenes struggles about the Congress programme and the election of party delegates. The party apparatus used all the means at its disposal to ensure that a majority in favour of the dissolution of the SED would not be delegated.

The bitterness with which the struggle was pursued can be seen in a public appeal issue by the SED district leadership at the Humboldt University in (East) Berlin. All SED members were called on

to elect only delegates to the extraordinary Party Congress who can prove through their self-criticism and honest attitudes and acts that they have learnt the lessons of the past and are resolute in their belief in a renewal of socialism. . . . Elect delegates who will safeguard the radical reformation of our party from the grassroots to the general secretary.[34]

The run-up to the Party Congress was marked by mounting grassroots' discontent with the vascillations of the party leadership which conceded concrete reforms only under duress. When it became clear that the Politburo under Egon Krenz would not abandon this stance the party grassroots swept away the leadership. The resignation of all the ruling bodies on 3 December delivered the last rites to the old guard. Earlier, the old Central Committee had expelled twelve members of the Politburo from the party including the former general secretary, Erich Honecker, the former minister for state security, Erich Mielke, the former president of the *Volkskammer*, Horst Sindermann, the long-serving minister president, Willi Stoph, and the chairman of the Free Trade Union Confederation (FDGB), Harry Tisch.[35]

A 'working committee' was set up to act as a transitional leadership. It included known reformers such as the Mayor of Dresden, Wolfgang Berghofer, and Gregor Gysi who was to become the chairman of the Party of Democratic Socialism (PDS) — the successor party to the SED. This working committee brought the Party Congress forward to 8 December and submitted a signed paper intended as the basis for 'a reformation of the SED as a modern socialist party'.[36]

The paper stated that only a radical break with 'Stalinist structures' could 'give a new political home' to SED members who 'subscribed to a society based on freedom, justice and solidarity'.[37] Stalinist socialism had been unable to respond to any of the compelling problems facing humanity in the economic, social, security, ecological and cultural spheres. It was, the paper went on, part of these problems. A 'third path' was needed — one which eschewed 'administrative socialism and the rule of transnational monopolies'.

The part of the paper devoted to concrete problems repeated all the demands — now also supported by the SED — for a fundamental reform of the political system and the economy. None the less, reformers quite clearly faced problems in dealing with an old apparatus which was still capable of a Bonapartist *putsch*. The greatest potential dangers for radical reform lay in the Ministry for State Security and the SED special units.[38]

The first sessions of the extraordinary Party Congress took place on the night of 7–8 December in (East) Berlin. Party membership had dwindled from 2.3 million to barely 1.8 million. On the same day news emerged that charges were to be brought by the state against Erich Honecker, Erich Mielke, Willi Stoph,

Günter Kleiber, Werner Krolikowski and Hermann Axen and that the accused — excluding Honecker who was in very poor health and Axen who was in Moscow for an operation — were already in custody.

It was against this background that the new prime minister, Hans Modrow, made an emotional address to the 2,750 delegates in which he warned of the dangers of a collapse and self-dissolution of the SED. The party had to be saved from destruction and disintegration. He went on: 'Let us make [this Party] clean and strong so that every comrade can look the people in the face! Let us make it strong so that it can serve social progress in our country; for me that means serving the people.'[39]

Any resolution of the crisis in the GDR was seen as requiring the whole of society. Modrow's appeal had been prefaced by the dramatic deterioration of the situation in the GDR in the days before. Further revelations about corruption and abuse of office, the imprisonment of almost the whole of the old leadership and attacks on state security buildings had heightened tensions. Modrow called for the respect of justice and the rule of law and pledged that the government would do its utmost to uncover illegal activities. However, he added the caveat that 'in uncovering abuses of office and corruption there can be no law-breaking'.[40]

The working committee's report delivered by Gregor Gysi also contained a key statement against the dissolution of the SED. Instead, there were demands for a complete 'break with bankrupt Stalinist, that is administrative centralised socialism in our country'. The document proposed a 'third path of a socialist nature' based on 'radical democracy and the rule of law, humanism, social justice, protection of the environment and genuine sexual equality for women'. In pursuing these aims the party would refer back to 'social-democratic, socialist, non-Stalinist-communist, anti-fascist and pacifist traditions'.[41]

The debate which followed revealed three irreconcilable positions of principle: one, the dissolution of the SED and formation of a new socialist party; two, reformation and renaming of the SED; three, retention of the name SED (here, the extent of renewal remained somewhat vague).

The statements by Modrow and Gysi provide three main arguments against the dissolution of the SED: the fear was that if the SED dissolved itself the position of the only remaining half-functioning state institution, the Modrow government, would become untenable. The result would have been a 'political vacuum which no one could have filled and which would have exacerbated the crisis bringing untold consequences'.[42] Gysi and

Modrow believed secondly that this would have implied the exclusion of SED influence from decisions of state and thirdly that if the SED dissolved itself, it would forfeit its enormous assets (property, publishing houses, scientific institutes etc.) and jeopardise the lives of employees there.[43] These fears soon became reality anyway, only to be compounded by the hesitancy of the SED. As a result, the party could reap no political dividends from its gradual retreat from positions of accumulated power nor deny its past.

The Congress decided, with 647 against and seven abstentions, to give the party a new name: the 'Socialist Unity Party of Germany — Party of Democratic Socialism' (SED–PDS).[44]

Even in the run-up to the Party Congress it had become clear that the old party structures would have to be abolished if the party was to stand any chance of survival: the Politburo, General Secretaryship, Central Committee and Central Party Control Commission were to be abolished and replaced by the chairman, deputies, presidium, party executive and arbitration commission customary in democratic parties.

In a secret ballot 95.32 per cent of delegates elected the Berlin lawyer Gregor Gysi to the position of chairman. His deputies were to be the head of government, Hans Modrow (99.4 per cent), the mayor of Dresden, Wolfgang Berghofer (who also became the director of the commission on the political system) and Wolfgang Pohl, first secretary of the Magdeburg regional executive (who also assumed the chair of the commission for organisation and party activities).

At the end of the first session the Party Congress submitted a discussion document in which it distanced itself from the policies of the SED.

The delegates . . . consider it their duty to apologise sincerely to the people in the name of the party for the grave crisis into which the old leadership of the SED has plunged our country. We are prepared to bear this guilt. We offer our sincere thanks to the responsible citizens of our country who forced radical change by their courageous and peaceful struggle and who in doing so offered us the opportunity for revolutionary renewal. The extraordinary Party Congress has completed the break with the subjugation of the people under party power and the dictatorship of the leadership over the party grassroots. It proposes party members . . . guidelines for a democratic socialism beyond Stalinist pseudo-socialism and the rule of profit.[45]

The difficulties of such a new beginning became clear a week later in the continuing sessions of the Party Congress. Debate was characterised by a general admonition of the old leadership on the one hand and vindication of the 'majority of honest comrades' on the other. A clear distance also emerged between the intellectual party reformers and the majority of 'ordinary' delegates. Many delegates were professional functionaries fearful of the unemployment and lower standards of living which a failure to save the party would produce. Many lauded the positive aspects of the past and spoke of the successes which had been achieved despite everything. They also warned of the dangers of the future such as rising unemployment, crime, nationalism and right-wing extremism.

The party leadership under Egon Krenz was accused of failing to have a political vision and making a radical break with the past. None the less, in spite of all the more critical statements made at the extraordinary Party Congress, this criticism can also be levelled at the new party leadership. The party leadership committed without doubt a fundamental, albeit in the circumstances understandable, error in resisting the totally new beginning which only dissolution could have provided. Only this step would have issued a clear public admission that the party was morally and politically bankrupt.

All the arguments advanced in favour of a retention of the SED proved untenable. Despite the popularity of Hans Modrow, the government failed to secure public confidence. The SED–PDS failed to lend credibility to the political transformation it had undergone. Even party assets could only partially be salvaged. Only SED influence on matters of state could still be maintained — at a price: even under its new reform-minded leadership the SED–PDS squandered much political capital by its inability, despite all efforts undertaken, to cast off the fetters of old thinking and the structures of the old apparatus. It remained largely powerless in the face of a rapidly changing political climate.

Notes

1 *Mit Blick auf den XII. Parteitag die Aufgaben der Gegenwart lösen. Aus dem Bericht des Politbüros an die 7. Tagung des Zentralkomitees der SED.* Berichterstatter, Genosse Erich Honecker, Berlin, Dietz, 1988, pp. 10, 91. This term was borrowed — unintentionally — from the vocabulary of French communism in its 'Eurocommunist' phase.
2 Cf. Anton Ackermann, 'Gibt es einen besonderen deutschen Weg zum Sozialismus?' *Einheit*, No. 1, 1946, pp. 22–32.
3 *7. Tagung des Zentralkomitees der SED*, loc. cit., p. 11.
4 Günter Schabowski, *Das Politbüro. Ende eines Mythos. Eine Befragung*, Reinbek, Rowohlt, 1990, p. 36.
5 Gregor Gysi and Thomas Falkner, *Sturm auf das grosse Haus: Der*

Untergang der SED, Berlin, Edition Fischerinsel, 1990, p. 16.

6 Egon Krenz, 'In der DDR — gesellschaftlicher Aufbruch zu einem erneuerten Sozialismus', *Neues Deutschland*, 9 November 1989, p. 3.

7 Cf. Ulrich Bürger, *Das sagen wir natürlich so nicht! Donnerstag — Argus bei Herrn Geggel*, Berlin, Dietz, 1990.

8 Egon Krenz, op. cit., p. 3.

9 'Kampagne gegen die DDR im Stile des kalten Krieges', *Neues Deutschland*, 25 August 1989, p. 2.

10 Egon Krenz, *Wenn Mauern fallen. Die friedliche Revolution, Vorgeschichte — Ablauf. — Auswirkungen*, Vienna, Paul Neff, 1990, p. 30; Interview with Wolfgang Herger (head of the party security apparatus of the SED).

11 Erich Honecker, 'Durch das Volk und für das Volk wurde Grosses vollbracht', *Neues Deutschland*, 9 October 1989, p. 3.

12 Krenz, *Wenn Mauern fallen*, op. cit., p. 88; Schabowski, *Das Politbüro*, op. cit., p. 75.

13 Gysi and Falkner, *Sturm auf das grosse Haus*, op. cit., p. 19.

14 *Hinweise auf Reaktionen progressiver Kräfte auf die gegenwärtige innenpolitische Lage in der DDR*, MfS, ZAIG, 0/227, 8 October 1989, in *Ich liebe euch doch alle! Befehle und Lageberichte des MfS Januar–November 1989*, Armin Mitter and Stefan Wolle (eds), Berlin, Basisdruck, 1990, p. 204.

15 This information was gained from interviews by the author with former members of the Politburo of the SED.

16 Cf. *Der Spiegel*, No. 48, 27 November 1989, p. 19; *Die Tageszeitung*, 24 November 1989, p. 5. There are conflicting reports about who was responsible for preventing the use of live ammunition against demonstrators. It can be safely assumed, however, that the version of events circulating in autumn 1989 that Egon Krenz personally intervened to prevent a bloodbath, is incorrect. Cf. Gysi and Falkner, op. cit., p. 19.

17 Cf. Peter Przybylski (ed.), *Tatort Politbüro. Die Akte Honecker*, Berlin, Rowohlt, 1991.

18 Schabowski, op. cit., p. 58; cf. also Cordt Schnibben, 'Wie Erich Honecker und sein Politbüro die Konterrevolution erlebten (II)', *Der Spiegel*, No. 17, 23 April 1990, p. 88.

19 'Erklärung des Politbüros des Zentralkomitees der Sozialistischen Einheitspartei Deutschlands', *Neues Deutschland*, 12 October 1989, p. 1.

20 op. cit.

21 Schabowski, op. cit., p. 80; Herger, interview, op. cit.; Markus Wolf, 'In eigenem Auftrag. Preprint "Der General und die Revolution"', *Stern*, No. 48, 1990, p. 110; interestingly, Egon Krenz omits to mention this meeting in his *mémoires*.

22 Reinhold Andert and Wolfgang Herzberg, *Der Sturz. Erich Honecker im Kreuzverhör*, Berlin, Aufbau, 1990, p. 375.

23 Herger, Interview, op. cit.

24 Andert and Herzberg, op. cit., p. 21.

25 Cf. Gerhard Naumann and Eckhard Trümpler, *Von Ulbricht zu*

Honecker. 1970 — ein Krisenjahr der DDR, Berlin, Dietz, 1990.
26 Schabowski, op. cit., p. 67.
27 Cf. the self-depiction of Krenz (*Wenn Mauern fallen*, op. cit., p. 126) who denies any knowledge of who manipulated the communal elections in May 1989.
28 'Fernseh- und Rundfunkansprache von Egon Krenz an die Bürger der DDR', *Neues Deutschland*, 4–5 November 1989, p. 1.
29 Cf. on this debate in detail Gert-Joachim Glaessner, 'Vom "realen Sozialismus" zur Selbstbestimmung'. Ursachen und Konsequenzen der Systemkrise in der DDR, *Aus Politik und Zeitgeschichte*, B 1–2/1990,5 January 1990, pp. 3–20.
30 This deterrent continued to operate. Only after the downfall of the SED did some older party members speak of their depressing experiences. Cf. Walter Janka, *Schwierigkeiten mit der Wahrheit*, Berlin, Aufbau, 1990; Gustav Just, *Zeuge in eigener Sache*, Berlin, Buchverlag Der Morgen, 1990.
31 'Schritte zur Erneuerung. Aktionsprogramm der SED', *Neues Deutschland*, 11–12 November 1989, p. 1; for an account of its development: cf. Gysi and Falkner, op. cit., p. 43.
32 Cf. 'Im Apparat wird noch manövriert' (reader's letter from Dieter Folde, lecturer in politics in the Central Committee of the SED), *Neues Deutschland*, 6 November 1989, p. 3.
33 'Politbüro der SED schlägt ausserordentlichen Parteitag vor', *Neues Deutschland* 13 November 1989, p. 1; 'Beschluss zur Vorbereitung und Durchführung eines ausserordentlichen Parteitages der SED', *Neues Deutschland*, 14 November 1989, p. 1.
34 'Delegierte zum Parteitag sorgfältig auswählen. Appell der Kreisleitung der Humboldt-Universität Berlin', *Neues Deutschland*, 20 November 1989, p. 3; according to Dieter Segert this appeal was only published in *Neues Deutschland* after several attempts and editorial alterations.
35 'ZK der SED trat zurück', *Neues Deutschland*, 4 December 1989, p. 1.
36 'Für einen alternativen demokratischen Sozialismus. Diskussionsstandpunkt des Arbeitsausschusses zu der von der Basis ausgehenden Neuformierung der SED als moderne sozialistische Partei', *Neues Deutschland*, 8 December 1989, p. 3.
37 Ibid.
38 Ibid.
39 'Souveräne DDR muss ein solider Baustein für europäisches Haus sein' (speech by Hans Modrow), *Neues Deutschland*, 9–10 December 1989, p. 1.
40 Ibid.
41 'Wenn wir alle für die neue Partei streiten, wird sie stark bleiben' (speech by Gregor Gysi), *Neues Deutschland*, 9–10 December 1989, p. 1.
42 Ibid.
43 Cf. *Wenn wir alle für die neue Partei streiten, wird sie stark bleiben* (speech by Gregor Gysi), Ausserordentlicher Parteitag der SED/PDS Partei des demokratischen Sozialismus, Berlin, Dietz, 1990, p. 25.

44 'Parteivorsitzender Gysi: Hart arbeiten für die Rettung des Landes und unserer Partei', *Neues Deutschland*, 11 December 1989, p. 1.
45 'Bruch mit der machtpolitischen Überhebung der Partei, mit der Diktatur der Führung vollzogen. Als Dokument beschlossen: Bericht zur Diskussion auf dem ersten Beratungstag des ausserordentlichen Parteitages', *Neues Deutschland*, 11 December 1989, p. 3.

4 Dual rule: the GDR before the elections

During the revolutionary changes in Eastern Europe, debate focused on two fundamental alternatives: reform or rupture. The transition from authoritarianism to democracy tends, as was the case in the GDR, to be initiated by factions in the old régime which consider the possibility of a reform leading to some form of political democracy. The opposition normally favours a fundamental break with the existing institutional order and political ideology. However, the strategy of a clean rupture is, as Juan Linz has pointed out, 'viable only in a revolutionary or potentially revolutionary situation . . . . Paradoxically, the transition is sometimes made possible by the simultaneous formulation of both positions as postures, for bargaining purposes rather than as final stands.'[1]

In such circumstances an 'élite settlement' was concluded between a reluctantly reformist government and new political groups which advocated a rapture with the past. The means of this agreement was the 'Round Table'. Modelled on Polish and Hungarian experience, the Round Table comprised representatives of opposition groups and the SED and some old parties and organisations — each with equal rights. It was an instrument of 'transition by transaction'. (Parallels with the Spanish *reforma-pactada-ruptura-pactada* model are manifest.) This path which led from authoritarianism to democracy 'tends to focus on élite-settlements, the roles of the leaders of the régime and the opposition, the ''bunker'', the democrats, and the revolutionaries, and inevitably reduces the role of the people.'[2]

The opposition sought to use the Round Table as a means by which to veto and control government actions. As events unfolded it turned into a form of parallel government which gave itself the right to advise the executive at any time.[3] The Round Table was accorded certain *de facto* legislative and executive functions. In return, it also conferred a certain legitimacy on the government. This 'dual rule' lasted until the elections of 18

March 1990. When the new political groups then called for a continuing role for the Round Table, they were reminded of the rules of parliamentary system.

4.1 The role of the *Volkskammer* and the Modrow government

At state level, attempts at cautious correction were rapidly overtaken by revolutionary events. Here, too, the pillars of state which underpinned the old system proved as resistant as the SED.

In the dramatic days of October and November 1989 the GDR parliament, the *Volkskammer*, appeared to have ceased functioning. In contravention of statute, the presidium of the *Volkskammer* defied the appeals of more than a third of all members to convene a sitting.[4] The only act of the *Volkskammer* after the *Wende* was the election of Egon Krenz as chairman of the State Council and chairman of the National Defence Council on 24 October. For the first time in an election of a chairman of the State Council of the GDR (the third) votes had been cast against (twenty-six) and there were abstentions (twenty-six) from the Democratic Bloc of allied parties. Erich Honecker had already been relieved of his functions *in absentia*. The president of the *Volkskammer*, Horst Sindermann, praised Honecker's achievements: 'We will not allow the human greatness and integrity of the revolutionary and comrade Erich Honecker to be attacked.'[5]

The *Volkskammer* then adjourned proceedings and sat again only on 13 November. The reason for this lay in the deliberate filibustering of the Presidium which clearly wanted to prevent what was to happen at the next sitting: hitherto the willing follower of all directives from above, the *Volkskammer* rebelled.

The 'supreme people's assembly' came together on 13 November for its eleventh sitting only after the resignation both of the Stoph government on 7 November and of the entire Politburo of the SED during the tenth session of the Central Committee on 8 November and the opening of the Berlin Wall on 9 November.[6] At this point the last remaining state leaders, the president and members of the Presidium, were replaced. The then regional boss of the SED in Dresden, Hans Modrow, was elected to the post of prime minister.

In the initial 'reform euphoria' of November–December 1989 it seemed that the old system could simply be cast aside to make way for a new democratic, socialist culture in the GDR. However, it soon became clear that the resistance of the post-Stalinist system of rule to extensive change was a factor not to be underestimated. The contradictions of the new government under Hans Modrow bear this out.

In his first government statement of 17 November 1989 Modrow had promised fundamental political change and requested the trusting faith of the people. He announced a far-reaching reform programme, the rule of law, an accountable judiciary, a new election law and free elections in 1990, an amended law governing the Ministerial Council, penal reform and the establishment of a constitutional court.[7]

Any economic reform would have to increase the independence of economic agents, reduce planning and direction from the centre and promote a meritocracy. Problems of the environment, urban development and education were given especial urgency, and state interference in cultural life was to be brought to an end. These were areas which, either by neglect or ideological saturation, had been formative in sowing unrest in the GDR.

In December the Modrow government was able to help defuse tensions. With their vested interest in ensuring stability in a changing GDR, Western powers and the Federal Republic helped the Modrow government to enhance greatly its popularity and stability up to the new year. Many of the objectives and pledges made at the time of the formation of the new government in November — that is *before* the resignation of the interim leadership of Egon Krenz on 3 December — had been overtaken by the sheer pace of events. This is particularly true of attitudes towards the unification of the two German states. Here, Modrow increasingly adopted an independent line at odds with his party, the PDS.

In his government declaration Modrow proposed to the Federal Republic a confederation which was to go much further than the treaties currently in force. The proposed forms of such German–German cooperation became clear when on 5 December and at New Year almost all restrictions on travel between the two states were abolished. This confederation assumed its first form with the visit of the federal chancellor to Dresden shortly before Christmas. Even sections of Helmut Kohl's 'ten-point plan', so controversial in the West, were positively received by the GDR government. Last, Modrow announced that the GDR would pursue an independent policy towards Europe.

After a visit to Moscow on 30 January 1990, and much to the open displeasure of his own party, the head of government proposed that Germany should once again be, in the original words of the East German national anthem, the 'united fatherland' of all the people belonging to the German nation. In so doing Modrow was taking up the demands which were growing in resonance at the weekly mass demonstrations. By contrast, the SED-PDS at this time had rejected the desire for German unity as an expression of nationalistic and chauvinistic tendencies.

Europe is entering a new stage in its development. The post-war chapter is being closed. The foundations necessary for the peaceful and neighbourly cooperation of all peoples are being laid. The unification of both German states is on the agenda . . . . A final resolution to the German question can only be assured in the free self-determination of all Germans in both states in cooperation with the Four Powers and in accordance with the interests of all the European states. This solution must support the process of European unity which should banish once and for all the military threat from our continent. The *rapprochement* of the two German states and subsequent unification should be seen by no one as a threat.[8]

With this declaration before his party Modrow bade farewell to the isolationism of the Honecker era which sought the creation of a socialist nation in the GDR. An off-the-record portrayal of Modrow's term of office reveals the following quotation: 'I'm tired of showing myself to be against the will of more and more Germans and running behind events. They could then at some stage become a law unto themselves and if the street takes control of the German question, then we can say goodbye to the demonstrations of October and November 1989 with the appeals for "no violence!".'[9] The results of the elections to the *Volkskammer* on 18 March proved that the question of German unification came to dominate the agenda which carried all political figures — with varying degrees of success — in its wake.

This relative openness towards new political circumstances contrasted with palpable intransigence when it came to the need for a fundamental change from within. When demonstrators' demands for a rupture with the old system grew increasingly vocal, it became clear that the government was faced with the same dilemma confronting most governments in periods of radical change: oscillating between reform and rupture and subject to the rapid acceleration of all political processes, the government proved unable to formulate any policies. With the opposition unable to take up the reigns of power the result was a diffuse mixture of change and entrenchment.

The government had a head start in the matter of filling the power vacuum inherited from the fall of the old guard. One of the principal reasons for this lay in the continuity of governing personnel and in particular in their dependence on the SED-dominated state apparatus. The decades of a power monopoly gave the 'old comrades' of the SED an advantage and made them indispensable.

4.2 The Round Table

The institution of a Round Table which would bring together all social groups for consultations on the crisis in the GDR was the most important demand of the opposition. By the time the Round Table had its first meeting on 7 December 1989, a dangerous power vacuum had come about. It could not be ruled out that various reactionary forces might seek to exploit this situation for the purpose of restoring the old order. While the demise of the SED threatened to deprive the government of its key support, the opposition did not have the vision, personnel or organisation to assume power.

From early October a 'contact group' consisting of members of seven political groupings had been meeting clandestinely to debate possible forms of dialogue with the political authorities. The groupings included: the Initiative for Peace and Human Rights, New Forum, Democracy Now, Democratic Awakening, the Social Democratic Party, the Green Party and the United Left. The invitation to the first sitting of the Round Table came from the Federation of Evangelical Churches.[10]

The pact between reform-minded sections of the old élites and the new élites was intended to fill the power vacuum and reduce the danger of violent internal unrest which had resulted from the insoluble contradiction of a political leadership prepared to negotiate and a floating mass unable to negotiate.

The following parties and groupings were represented at the central Round Table of the GDR: the Confederation of Free German Trade Unions (two representatives); the small splinter group United left (two); the Social Democratic Party (two); Democracy Now (two); New Forum (three); Green Party (two); the Initiative for Peace and Human Rights (two); Green League (two); the Independent Women's Association (two); Democratic Awakening (two); the SED-PDS (three); representatives of the Sorbian Round Table (the Sorbs are a small ethnic minority in eastern Germany — one); the Farmers' Mutual Aid Association (an organisation of cooperative farmers — two); CDU (three); DBD (three); NDPD (three); LDPD (three).[11] These representatives were joined at a later date by other groups.

Further Round Tables were set up at all levels of the state

hierarchy and in many non-state institutions. Negotiations at the central Round Table in Berlin were conducted under the business-like auspices of church representatives who did not eschew productive conflict. The early stages of negotiation revealed that the government, notwithstanding its many concessions, conceded little ground in a number of key points (economic reform, structural reform of the state apparatus, for example). Government acts did not reflect the declarations which accompanied the formation of the Modrow government.

After the extraordinary Party Congress in early December the SED–PDS put a temporary brake on the party's disintegration. This galvanised the government into loosening its ties with the Round Table. The representatives of the new political groupings and the people on the streets interpreted this as an attempt to restore the old positions of power of the SED — a suspicion confirmed by the attempt to preserve large sections of the State Security Service under a new name.[12]

The initial obstructive stance adopted by government representatives at the Round Table (not only on the question of the State Security Service), and its reluctance to undertake fundamental political and economic emergency measures, underlined the impression that the government and the party which supported it were only prepared to offer concessions when compelled to do so.

Further events undermined confidence in the government. One psychological turning point came with the mysterious desecration of the monument in honour of the Soviet Union in the Treptow district of Berlin in early January. It provoked an SED–PDS campaign against Fascism and 'anti-Sovietism' reminiscent of the 1950s. A steady flow of revelations of corruption, abuse of office and the general machinations of the State Security came to public attention. Economic crisis, mounting popular discontent and clear moves by the erstwhile 'Bloc Parties' (CDU, DBD, LDPD, NDPD) to jump the sinking ship of the SED fuelled a further intensification of the crisis.

Against this background the head of government expressed his willingness to address the Round Table. However, it was on 15 January that Hans Modrow finally spoke before its members. Only then were government representatives prepared to issue anything more than evasive answers to questions about the dissolution of the State Security Service. (On that evening a storming of the central headquarters of the State Security Ministry in the Normannenstrasse in Berlin took place.) Under intense public pressure the government yielded to the demand that the question of setting up a body 'to protect the constitution'

— seen as necessary by the Modrow government — should be decided by the *Volkskammer*. The dissolution of the 'Office for State Security' which the opposition movement considered vital to confidence-building was rejected for so long and with such vehemence that it appeared reasonable to assume that the old Ministry for State Security was, albeit in reduced form, to remain intact and that whole departments were to be transferred to other organs of state, such as customs, and thus to be reactivated at any time.

4.3 The 'government of national responsibility'

When he appeared before the Round Table on 15 January, Modrow offered the opposition a 'direct and responsible involvement in government by competent persons'.[13] He then called on the Round Table to collaborate in government commissions and legislation and invited representatives to accompany him on the visit he was about to make to the Federal Republic. A week later Modrow went a step further. The storming of State Security headquarters one week before and the rumours about an impending general strike or a planned coup by the State Security Service and sections of the army[14] demonstrated how volatile the situation was, how quickly it could turn violent and how fragile the pact between government and opposition actually was.

In these circumstances Modrow tried to grasp the initiative. He emphasised that as head of government he was responsible to the people, not a party, and announced a 'new chapter' in the process of 'revolutionary change'. He called on the Round Table to 'nominate persons who are willing to enter government as members of the Ministerial Council'.[15] At the same time he provided a government agenda for further legislation to be passed in the period leading up to the elections. This finally marked the transformation of the Round Table from a 'veto organ to an instance of government'.[16]

In his address to the *Volkskammer* on 29 January Modrow made what amounted to an admission of failure. He described the situation in the most pessimistic terms and admitted that the existing political structures could barely begin to resolve social tensions in the GDR. In several debates behind closed doors and already influenced by the coming election campaign the opposition groupings had persuaded themselves to participate in government.

In an attempt to avert the collapse of the political and economic order and the unforeseeable consequences it would have, the government agreed — again *in camera* — with representatives of the Round Table on 28 January to bring forward to 18 March the elections to the *Volkskammer* planned for 6 May. The rigging of the Communal elections in May 1989 which had greatly contributed to the popular protest later that year were rescheduled for 6 May 1990. Both the Round Table in its tenth session on 29 January and the *Volkskammer* consented to this proposal.[17]

On 5 February the new parties and movements entered the 'government of national responsibility' under Hans Modrow. Only the 'United Left' (VL) did not participate out of opposition to Modrow's advocacy of a confederal Germany. All other new groupings delegated ministers which brought the number of parties and political groups in government to thirteen.

Any assessment of this stage in the transition process can only be mixed. With Hans Modrow's election to the post of prime minister on 13 November, the government was to safeguard the changes introduced by the SED leadership under Egon Krenz and salvage what could still be saved. Measured against this objective the Modrow government failed.

The SED *Volkskammer* deputy, Jarowinski, expressed the view that this government which included, besides the SED, a higher proportion of representatives from the former 'Bloc Parties' was a 'democratic coalition government'.[18] His view must be emphatically refuted. The Modrow government was instead more of an attempt to exploit the 'Bloc Parties' for the purpose of a political opening within the framework of the existing institutional order. Only when it seemed that a total collapse of public order could not be averted was Modrow prepared to lift his 'blockade' of the Round Table. During this phase he proved himself a skilful political tactician by forcing the new political groupings to participate in his government.

The role of the *Volkskammer* between the revolution and the elections similarly appears in a mixture of light and shade. It provided the fractured reflection of change in GDR society. The *Volkskammer* was never a driving force but represented the individual and collective contradictions of personalities and institutions which in one way or another underpinned the old system. To this extent it is difficult to describe the *Volkskammer* as a parliamentary assembly[19]: it never possessed the legitimacy of a parliament, nor did it deserve to do so. Despite these shortcomings, the *Volkskammer* did play an important role in the first critical phase of transition: it assisted greatly in creating a public realm and brought the rulers of the past to public account. The fact that the Minister for State Security, Erich Mielke, was exposed as a nasty, senile old man[20] was more than just a marginal event — it was the symbolic moment in which the fairytale king stood naked before his former subjects.

The Round Table did play a constructive role in expediting and chanelling developments. It was not 'the' people but rather a transitory institution which made a major contribution in enabling the articulation of interests. To the extent that it was successful in fulfilling this role, the Round Table itself became a forum for the articulation of conflicts of interest between individual groups and — from mid-January — an effective stage for an election campaign now underway.

The campaigners, in particular the new political groups, had to learn the painful lesson that 'the people' soon went their own ways. In the initial phase dominated by the ultimate collapse of SED rule, particularly in its resolute stand against the retention of the State Security Service, the Round Table represented 'the people'. From the end of January, however, a paradoxical situation arose in which the Round Table and the government — for different reasons — acted as the representatives of an independent 'GDR identity' while the majority of the people had long wanted the quickest possible end of that very identity.

Notes

1 Juan J. Linz, 'Transitions to Democracy', *The Washington Quarterly*, Summer 1990, p. 151.
2 Ibid., p. 152.
3 Uwe Thaysen, *Der Runde Tisch oder: Wo Bleibt das Volk? Der Weg der DDR in die Demokratie*, Opladen, Westdeutscher Verlag, 1990, pp. 76–82.
4 'Sofortige Tagung der Volkskammer gefordert. Verfassungs- und Rechtsausschuss missbilligt Zögern des Präsidiums', *Neues Deutschland*, 8 November 1989, p. 1; cf. also the statement made by the president of the Volkskammer, Horst Sindermann, at the eleventh session of the *Volkskammer*, in Helmut Herles and Ewald Rose (eds), *Parlaments–Szenen einer deutschen Revolution. Bundestag und Volkskammer im November 1989*, Bonn, Bouvier, 1989, p. 158.
5 *Neues Deutschland*, 25 October 1989, p. 1.
6 Cf. Peter Joachim Lapp, 'Anspruch und Alltag der Volkskammer vor dem Umbruch 1989–1990, *Zeitschrift für Parlamentsfragen*, Vol. 21, 1990, No. 1, pp. 115–25.
7 'Diese Regierung wird eine Regierung des Volkes und der Arbeit sein' (statement by Prime Minister Hans Modrow), *Neues Deutschland*, 18–19 November 1989, pp. 3–5.
8 'Schritte zur deutschen Einheit. Dokumentation: Die deutschland-politische Konzeption Hans Modrows', *'DDR Journal 2. Die Wende*

der Wende', Frankfurt-on-Main, *Die Tageszeitung*, 1990, p. 72.

9 Karl-Heinz Arnold, *Die ersten hundert Tage des Hans Modrow*, Berlin (DDR), Dietz, 1990, p. 97.

10 On the debate about the form and sender of the invitation see in detail: Thaysen, *Der Runde Tisch*, op. cit., p. 25; a small detail illustrates the tricks the SED used to place itself at the head of the reform movement. It was reported in *Neues Deutschland* on 23 November 1989 that the Politburo 'in accordance with the Action Programme of the Party [had] proposed that the political parties united in the coalition government should join forces with other political forces [in the GDR] to create a "Round Table".'

11 Cf. Thaysen, *Der Runde Tisch*, op. cit.; Helmut Herles and Ewald Rose, *Vom Runden Tisch zum Parlament*, Bonn, Bouvier, 1990.

12 Cf. Thomas Falkner, 'Von der SED zur PDS. Weitere Gedanken eines Beteiligten, *Deutschland Archiv*, Vol. 24 (1991), No. 1, pp. 40–52.

13 Herles and Rose, *Vom Runden Tisch*, op. cit., p. 56.

14 Cf. the statement made by Hans Modrow to the Round Table on 22 January 1990 in Herles and Rose, *Vom Runden Tisch*, op. cit., p. 78.

15 Ibid., p. 81.

16 Cf. Thaysen, *Der Runde Tisch*, op. cit., p. 76.

17 Cf. 'Erklärung zur Demokratie und Rechtsstaatlichkeit', Herles and Rose, *Vom Runden Tisch*, op. cit., p. 102.

18 Herles and Rose, *Parlaments–Szenen*, op. cit., p. 73.

19 Ibid., p. 73.

20 Mielke's words ('But I love everyone, everyone!') were received with loud (liberated?) laughter in the Volkskammer; cf. Herles and Rose, *Parlaments–Szenen*, op. cit., p. 193.

5 Transition to democracy

5.1 'We are the people' — the citizens' movements

It had been becoming increasingly clear since spring 1989 that the
political system of the GDR was heading towards a crisis. The
Hungarian government's announcement that it would open its
borders and the rigged local elections of 7 May 1989 were only
the catalysts of a public rebellion the roots of which lay much
deeper. One of the architects of the opposition, Ehrhart Neubert,
described the situation in spring 1989 in the following, accurate
terms:

GDR society ceased to be a monolithic collective unified under the SED–
leadership. The centrifugal forces of the economy, international
developments and social contradictions brought concomitant changes to
the system. The thick-meshed organisational framework had lost its
socialising power.[1]

There was no single 'opposition' *per se* in the GDR. The situation there differed markedly from that in the other socialist countries. Although there had indeed been various informal groups
since the late 1970s meeting predominantly under the aegis of the
church, and a parallel 'public realm' of semi-legal and illegal
publications had emerged in the mid-1980s, there was no organised opposition comparable to Charter 77 in Czechoslovakia or
Solidarity in Poland. It is also interesting to note that there were
practically no points of contact between these groups and the
dissidents from the first three decades of the GDR. This is true
both in terms of personnel and in ideological terms.[2] Whereas
after the destruction of bourgeois political forces earlier opposition groupings had always been confined to 'deviants' from the
party line, these informal groups were strongly sub-cultural in
orientation and opposed to formal organisation.

The suggestion is not altogether implausible that these groups
were compelled by events outside the GDR (change in the Soviet
Union and the fundamental transition process underway in the
other socialist countries) to define and organise themselves as the

opposition. These groups broke out of the periphery of society with their appeal to boycott the elections in spring 1989. In addition, the obvious manipulation of election figures precipitated a collapse in loyalty — in this sense the groups made a decisive contribution to revolutionary change. Moreover, it could be said that the ecological, human rights and peace groups and the growing activism of church representatives undermined the cultural hegemony of the SED by the introduction of new and competing values and the reinterpretation of party principles.[3]

Another major difference between the GDR and other socialist countries can be found in the fact that socialist ideas and thinking had a formative influence even on oppositional circles. There had long been discussions in small groups about the need to conduct a root-and-branch reform of socialism — to produce a new, reformed, democratic socialism. The voices in favour of abandoning socialism as the guiding idea remained isolated.

One of the paradoxes which followed the downfall of the old system was that the most vehement critics of SED socialism were the most loyal adherents to the socialist idea.

Others adhered to socialism out of sheer opportunism. It was often those who later pronounced the harshest invective against socialism. None the less, until 1989 there had been a broad consensus about the fact that the historical and cultural roots of socialism, its contribution to anti-fascism and commitment to peace and in particular in its advocacy of equality in a political utopia would remain lasting components of a future political order in Europe.[4]

The above analysis describes accurately the point of departure from which the groupings undertook to make history in summer 1989. In the revolutionary events of autumn 1989 these small groups of opposition figures had become the beacon of hope for democratic renewal. The people on the streets were calling for democracy, free elections and the legalisation of 'New Forum'. Who were these groups?

Some months before October 1989, and in particular after the rigged local elections of May 1989, the 500 or so grassroots initiatives which for the most part had found refuge under the roof of the church had to decide if and how they could initiate the necessary process of change in the GDR. The massive exodus of late summer forced them to adopt a clear stance. In July the church group which called itself the 'Initiative for the Renunciation of the Principle and Practice of *Abgrenzung*' made an appeal for a broad social movement. A manifesto demanded an 'identifiable alternative' in the next *Volkskammer* elections scheduled for 1991.

The so-called political and moral unity shown by the rigged election results is more than ever before a fiction. Those who voted against or stayed away from the elections gave a signal that the nature of our society should become a matter of public concern. We need the kind of stability which is based on reconciling existing beliefs, on the courage and sense of responsibility of all individuals. Existing stability is based on fear and deepens the wounds of division in our society instead of healing them. The most important thing is a reform of electoral law so that it guarantees secret voting and provides the opportunity for exerting real influences on the composition of the representative bodies. The precondition for this is that independent interest groups should be legalised in accordance with the principle of the freedom of association provided in the constitution.[5]

It was no coincidence that in October–November 'New Forum' became the symbol for change and rebellion. Founded on 9 September 1989 by thirty representatives of various, predominantly church groups it was numerically the strongest opposition group. Founder members included the painter Bärbel Bohley, the widow of the renowned dissident, Robert Havemann, Katja Havemann, the defence lawyer Rolf Henrich who had written a book critical of the régime and had been expelled from the SED,[6] the physicist Sebastian Pflugbeil and the molecular biologist Jens Reich. The group launched an appeal in October 1989 which was quickly signed by more than 200,000 people. It was conceived of as a broad church of the opposition and as an association which would facilitate and initiate a 'democratic dialogue' about questions affecting the whole of society. The founding appeal contained the following statements:

If all these contradictions are to be acknowledged, opinions and arguments listened to and considered, if general interests are to be distinguished from particular interests then we need a democratic dialogue about the role of the rule of law, the economy and culture. We must think and talk about these questions publicly across the length and breadth of the country . . . . To this end, we hereby found a political platform for the whole GDR which enables people irrespective of profession, background, party or group to participate in the discussion of matters vital to GDR society. We have given this overarching initiative the name 'NEW FORUM'.[7]

On 12 September twelve people published an 'Appeal for Interference in Our Own Affairs'. They saw in the reluctance of state socialism to reform itself and to resolve the existing crisis the need to launch an appeal for the establishment of an alliance of all reform-minded people. 'We invite everyone who is interested in joining us to a discussion about the principles and vision of a

democratic transformation of our society.'[8] The founding
members of 'Democracy Now' included the co-founder of the
group 'Women for Peace', Ulrike Poppe, the church historian
Wolfgang Ullmann, the physicist and church synod member
Hans-Jürgen Fischbeck, and the film-maker Konrad Weiss. The
appeal published by the citizens' movement Democracy Now
had, in common with most comparable statements, been written
in a limited number of copies (readers were asked to make their
own copies and pass them on) and included 'ideas for a
democratic transformation in the GDR' which were introduced in
the following terms:

Our proposals aim to secure peace in our borders and thereby to serve
the cause of peace beyond these borders. We want to help create a
society based on solidarity and to democratise all spheres of life. At the
same time we must find a new relationship as partners of our natural
environment. We want to develop socialism further beyond the statism
in which it has become locked so that it can meet the challenges of the
future. We want to replace a custodial state ruled by a party which has
elevated itself to a position of governor and schoolmaster of the people
with a state based on the basic consensus of society which is accountable
to society and therefore becomes a public matter (*RES PUBLICA*) for
active citizens. Proven social achievements should not be jeopardised by
any reform programme.[9]

Democracy Now resulted from two opposition groups — the
Initiative for Peace and Human Rights and the Initiative for
the Renunciation of the Principle and Practice of *Abgrenzung*
with the participation of some Berlin intellectuals. Although this
group supported many of the views advanced by New Forum it
was established as a separate grouping — in the main because of
personal conflicts.

A third opposition group which acquired some importance in
the initial phase of the revolution was the group 'Democratic
Awakening'. In June 1989 an initiative of mostly church members
had come together. Among its founder members were the lawyer
from Rostock, Wolfgang Schnur (who was later prosecuted for
complicity in the State Security service), the pastor and later
defence minister of the GDR, Rainer Eppelmann, the Weimar
theologian, Edelbert Richter and a researcher with the GDR
Council of Churches, Ehrhart Neubert. After its founding
assembly had been prevented by the police the group established
itself as a party on 2 October 1989. One of the reasons behind its
foundation lay in dissatisfaction with the informal structure of the
opposition movement. Rainer Eppelmann is quoted as saying
that the founders of Democratic Awakening felt that it was time

to move 'away from spontaneity and toward action and established structures'.[10]

The Party Congress in mid-December was dominated by heated debate between its left and right wings in particular over matters concerning economic policy and German unity, and eventually this resulted in a split. A large number of prominent members joined the Social Democratic Party.

The citizens' movement had emerged at a time when any form of political activity outside the prescribed forms of 'socialist democracy' was blocked or suppressed by the state. This has been corroborated by reports from the Ministry for State Security (MfS) now made public. Reports from Autumn 1989 also display the state's unease in view of the mounting influence the ideas of these groups were having on the population.

A State Security report from June 1989 sent to the party leadership of the SED recorded concerted efforts at association by 'those people who seek the dilution and subversion of socialism and the political destabilisation and fundamental change of GDR society': approximately 150 grassroots church groups (peace circles, environmental groups, ecological groups, women's groups and human-rights groups) and ten alliances such as the Working Group for Church Solidarity, the Grass Roots Church, the Green-Ecological Network, Ark and the Initiative for Peace and Human Rights. The 'total potential' of these groups was estimated at about 2,500 people. Nearly 600 people were members of leading bodies whereas 'the so-called hard-core comprised a relatively small number of fanatical elements driven by a sense of mission, personal aggrandisement and political stature, many of them implacable enemies of socialism'. These people (roughly estimated at 60) included the pastor Rainer Eppelmann, Ulrike Poppe, Bärbel Bohley and Werner Fischer.[11] State Security reports also indicate that these groups had been systematically monitored by the Ministry of State Security.[12]

The citizens' groups had deliberately been founded as a forum. They sought to initiate a democratic dialogue about the many problems which had accumulated in the decades of a bureaucratic socialist dictatorship. They saw this as the precondition for the birth of a civil society.

The support for a broad and unrestricted dialogue was tantamount to sacrilege in the closed society of the GDR. In this society the party exercised a monopoly on information alongside which an informal communication network had emerged as the sole forum in which critical questions could be raised and problems identified. The new groups were an important part of this parallel public realm. However, their belief that a broad critical discussion was a long-term prospect was soon overtaken by reality. Their role as forums was soon exhausted and they had to make way for other forms of expression for political opinion and will: the mass demonstrations and the new parties. Their representation of 'the people' was strictly short lived. Opposition in the GDR differed markedly from that in the other countries of Soviet-type socialism in that it 'swam on the crest of the revolutionary process so that it seemed that it was at the forefront of the movement'.[13]

The dynamic of events meant that criticism of the existing order and defence against quite genuine attempts at restoration came to be overshadowed by the need to set up new, democratically legitimised institutions — first and foremost a parliament, a freely elected *Volkskammer*, in an attempt to avert the collapse of order and economic and social disintegration. Before they were ready, the new movements were faced with the choice between becoming a party or remaining a 'movement' with the organisation and decision-making forms the latter would imply.

The reluctance of New Forum, the citizens' movement Democracy Now and the Inititiave for Peace and Human Rights to reorganise as parties stemmed from the experiences of new social movements in the West that such a reorganisation would mean the gradual loss of identity as a movement and the danger of politics becoming an end in itself. However, this did not preclude participation in elections. Nevertheless, it cannot be ignored that the reluctance of these groups to form as parties quickly weakened their influence on the course of political events.

This did not prevent these three groupings — after an abortive attempt to form an electoral alliance in concert with the reformed Social Democrats and Democratic Awakening — from forging an alliance for the *Volkskammer* elections under the name of 'Alliance 90'. They defined themselves as political associations which would use their representatives in the *Volkskammer* and later in the district assemblies to wield concerted influence on parliamentary events.

During the 'dual rule' of the Round Table, these groups did have a decisive influence on political events — not only on the Modrow government via the central Round Table but at all levels and in a large number of social spheres including the mass media and the universities. The citizens' movements enjoyed particular success in articulating popular interest in the first phase of clearing away the rubble of the old system. As the elections approached, however, it became clear that despite their moral integrity the new groups could not secure a majority of votes. They represented minority positions in particular in their desire to seek an independent path for political reform.

Following the failure of the broad coalition of opposition groups, New Forum, the Initiative for Peace and Human Rights and Democracy Now joined forces to form 'Alliance 90' in February. The Alliance saw and sees itself still as a merger of groupings with a concern for the defence of individual and social rights informed by experience under a dictatorship. All three groups declared in their election statements the need to protect human and civil rights, the need for a society based on solidarity, the need for the guaranteed rule of law and the need to democratise the state and society. They also shared the belief that in the long term it would be possible to represent citizens' interests both inside and outside parliament without necessarily becoming a party.

The manifesto of Democracy Now includes the following statements, for example:

Wider democracy will be possible by means of citizens' movements which are open to everyone and do not require party membership. Citizens' movements can be parliamentary or extra-parliamentary. They open opportunities for direct democracy. They will mean that a spectator democracy can be replaced by a participant democracy.[14]

Disputes continued between New Forum and the other groups. The crux of the controversies lay in the position of the Alliance in the traditional right–left political spectrum and its forms of organisation. In keeping with its founding appeal, New Forum defined itself as a political grouping which was not on the left. It shared many points of contact with conservative value beliefs and rejected any form of party organisation.

Nevertheless the groupings continued to share beliefs beyond the election campaign and the *Volkskammer* elections. These shared beliefs dated back to the period before November 1989 when the rigidity of the SED and its public support for the reactionary régimes in Romania and China strengthened the likelihood of the violent suppression of any opposition and of growing repression in the GDR.

Despite major differences of opinion in the citizens' movements in the GDR, there remained broad agreement that they wanted to assist in the political building of the country. According to an appeal released in July 1990, they called upon *all* grassroots democratic groups in the GDR to support our initiative for a joint citizens' alliance. Our aim is to create an electable political association which could then conduct negotiations with the Greens about fielding joint candidates in the elections.[15]

In the summer it seemed for a short period that the alliance of citizens' movements, not least as a result of the debate about electoral law, would be defeated by the issue of its relationship with the Greens. The Greens expressed grave reservations about the process of German unification. Their admiration for the people who had taken to the streets in Autumn 1989 gave way to antipathy when the demonstrators started chanting 'We are *one* people'. The Greens criticised 'reunification fever' and warned of the rise of a 'Greater Germany' and a 'Fourth Reich'. The slogan 'Germany never again' became popular currency. Voters in the West rejected this escapist stance in the *Bundestag* elections, and the Greens failed to gain the 5 per cent of the vote they needed to gain parliamentary representation.

Following the collapse of the West German Greens, the eight *Bundestag* deputies of the Alliance 90–Greens pact laboriously pieced together for the elections faced a double dilemma: they had to act as sole representatives of the new ecological movement in parliament without sharing their experiences. They also saw their role as representatives of the interests of former GDR citizens, the majority of whom preferred direct material interests such as economic growth, job security, consumer durables and the Western lifestyle and gave no priority to post-material values. In the end they came to elicit the distrust of the West German Greens and members of the Green Party because they would not commit themselves to positions on the 'left'.

5.2 Forming a democratic party system

The official GDR had always set great store by the fact that one of the most important elements of the political system lay in the coexistence of several parties which enjoyed friendly cooperation. Despite this the system cannot be described as a working multiparty system since the Bloc parties amounted to little more than the smooth conduits of SED policy.

The abolition on 1 December 1989 of the key sentence in Article 1 of the Constitution enshrining the leading role of the party underwrote the end of a political era which had been dominated by the absolute hegemony of a self-proclaimed vanguard party. The 'trusting alliance' of the Marxist–Leninist Party and the parties of the 'Democratic Bloc' was also formally abandoned. All the Bloc parties left the 'National Front' and replaced their leaderships. (The only remaining incumbent was Manfred Gerlach who was chairman of the State Council and chairman of the LDPD until February 1990.)

All the parties drafted new manifestos which deleted the espousal of socialism. In so doing they hoped to submerge the fact that they too had to live with a trained past similar to that of the SED which had renamed itself the 'Party of Democratic Socialism' (SED–PDS) in December. Only a few months later, in the elections to the *Volkskammer*, these parties presented themselves with new party programmes. It is remarkable that — at least in external appearance — these parties were transformed into parties of the Western type. They ceased to see themselves as representatives of particular ideological views or as the advocates of selected social groups. Ideological thinking was suppressed and replaced by an attempt to cloak a tainted past with the rapid and inconspicuous adoption of the Western models of 'catch-all parties'[16] or 'people's parties'.

The people of the GDR had long been accustomed to a party system which guaranteed the leading role of the SED and conferred the status of reliable partners (or, more aptly, acolytes) on the parties of the Democratic Bloc — the Christian Democratic Union (CDU), Democratic Farmers' Party (DBD), Liberal Democratic Party of Germany (LDPD) and the National Democratic Party of Germany (NDPD). These parties had assured their unconditional support for the leading role of the SED in their programmes and statutes. Indeed, they continued to pledge such support even when the SED was in process of disbanding. However, whereas in November 1989 the LDPD and CDU successfully formulated the germ of an independent policy, comparable attempts by the DBD and the NDPD (artificially created by the SED in 1948) remained conspicuously ill-defined.

The new party system in the GDR was born in several phases. In autumn 1989 the Bloc parties freed themselves from the SED, and new political associations were founded which in the second phase in early 1990 were turned into parties.

The many efforts to establish new parties untainted by association with the *ancien régime* seemed more important than the reform of the old Bloc parties. These efforts were closely linked to the belief that a new political system could be created in the GDR which would then gradually unite with the Federal Republic. Even in the run-up to the *Volkskammer* elections — brought forward by the mounting popular pressure for re-unification — it was clear that these new parties would only be of a transitory nature.

Late 1989 and early 1990 witnessed the emergence of a large number of new parties and party groupings such as 'Democratic Awakening', the Social Democratic Party (SDP — renamed SPD in January 1990), the 'Greens', the 'Green Party in the GDR', the 'Green League' (a non-party umbrella group), the 'Democratic Association GDR 40', the 'Progressive New Party', the 'Free

German Union in the GDR', the 'Liberal-Socialist People's Party', the 'Independent People's Party', the 'German Forum Party' (an offshoot of New Forum), the 'European Home Party', the 'Nelken' (a Marxist party which sought to further the tradition of Karl Liebknecht and Rosa Luxemburg), the KPD which aimed to unite 'all honest communists' and the 'German Reunification Party', licensed at the end of January, which called for reunification in the boundaries of 1990.

Other new parties included the 'German People's Party' (DVP), the 'Christian Social Party of Germany' (CSPD) and CSU–GDR which later joined the 'German Social Union' (DSU), the 'Free German Union' (FDU), and the 'Party of Central German Democrats' (MNP) which displayed clear affinities with the neo-Nazi NPD in the West.

The third phase which took place against the background of the *Volkskammer* elections on 18 March is notable for attempts to found alliances and electoral pacts in order to prevent the fissuring of the party system. The Federal Chancellery in Bonn had been the meeting place on 16 January of political figures from the Western CDU and CSU. They had met to discuss how to create an 'Alliance against socialism'. Under the direct influence of and pressure from the West German CDU, and in particular Helmut Kohl himself, the 'Alliance for Germany' was formed on 5 February. It comprised, despite their differing views and internal conflicts, the CDU, the 'German Social Union' (DSU) closely linked to the Bavarian Christian Social Union (CSU) and 'Democratic Awakening – social + ecological' which had started as a citizens' movement. The LDP, FDP of the GDR and the 'German Forum Party' then formed a liberal alliance.

In total twenty four parties and associations fielded candidates for the *Volkskammer* elections. In addition, there were five joint lists:

1. Action Alliance United Left/Die Nelken — VL;
2. Alliance 90 (New Forum, Democracy Now, Initiative for Peace and Human Rights);
3. Alliance of Free Democrats – the Liberals (German Forum Party, Liberal Democratic Party, FDP);
4. Alliance of Socialist Workers (BSA) – German Section of the Fourth International;
5. Alternative Youth List (AJL), including the FDJ (Free German Youth);
6. Christian Democratic Union (CDU) – joint list with DA and DSU;
7. Christian League;
8. Communist Party of Germany (KPD);

9. Democratic Awakening – social + ecological (DA);
10. Democratic Farmers' Party of Germany (DBD);
11. Democratic Womens Alliance of Germany (DFD);
12. European Federalist Party – Europe Party (EFP);
13. Europe Union of the GDR (EU of the GDR);
14. German Beer Drinkers Union (DBU);
15. German Social Union (DSU);
16. Green Party + Independent Womens' Association;
17. Independent People's Party;
18. Independent Social Democratic Party (USPD);
19. National Democratic Party of Germany (NDPD);
20. Party of Democratic Socialism (PDS, successor party to the SED);
21. Social Democratic Party of Germany (SPD);
22. Spartakist – Workers Party of Germany (SpAD);
23. Union of Working Groups for Employment Law and Democracy;
24. Unity Now.

The unexpected victory of the former Bloc party CDU in the *Volkskammer* elections on 18 March 1990 accelerated the process of unification and the restructuring of the party system based on the model of the Federal Republic. This development determined the political debate in Summer 1990 and reached its conclusion in Autumn 1990 with the all-Germany party congresses of the CDU, SPD and FDP. Meanwhile, the PDS began organising itself in the west; only the Greens and the citizens' movements in the GDR insisted on independence.

The new parties, and more particularly the citizens' movements which had been so important in initiating revolutionary change, faced the problem of safeguarding their high moral authority and making it politically viable. The rapid collapse of state order had forced a dilemma on to groupings unprepared for it: whether they should reform as parties and thereby run the risk of forfeiting their identity as movements.

It is true for all parties that in the course of 1990 the influence of the Western parties became stronger and eventually dominant. Indeed, after the reunification of the two states the initiative rested entirely with the party leaderships in the West. From then on the parties in the East were the passive objects of further developments.

Commitment to a change of policy in a one-party centralised state is measured most clearly by the way in which the structures of the party are changed and its stranglehold on the state and economic apparatus released.

As a hegemonic party pervading all the spheres of GDR society the SED, with a membership of 2.3 million, possessed a far-reaching network of organisation and a corresponding influence on political representatives. A key element of any party reform would therefore have to be the transformation of the fundamental principles of organisation of such a 'Party of the new type' as laid down in the SED statutes of 1976. It is therefore not surprising that the extraordinary Party Congress in December 1989 was preceded by a large number of blueprints for new party statutes and a reformed party programme. These blueprints and the statutes promulgated by the party shared the view that the party should organise itself in future according to territorial boundaries — into district, local and municipal organisations. This implied a rupture with a party tradition which went back to the earliest days of the KPD. Unlike the Social Democratic parties, all the parties of the Communist International were organised in work cells. This break with the tradition of Leninist parties remained half-hearted, however.

The smallest party organisations were given the right to organise at the level of the workplace. However, this right was not extended to the state apparatus, the army and the police. It soon became clear that the attempt to maintain even a limited presence at workplace level failed when the workforce threatened to go on strike.

The same indifference was characteristic of the renaming of the party: a decision was made to try to reconcile two incompatibles. The name SED–PDS was an idle compromise intended to preserve the 'unity' of the party at almost any cost. The attempt to combine a party name accepted in the SED itself to be inextricably linked to Stalinism with an idea which was already occupied by Western social democracy and associated with a definite set of beliefs was tantamount to squaring a circle. Democratic socialism is indissolubly linked to parliamentary-democratic and economic-democratic ideas and has nothing to do with traditional Marxism–Leninism. The tradition of the SED, and therefore since 1948 at the latest that of a Leninist party, is irreconcilable with democratic socialism. With this name change the SED was gambling on trying to remain the strongest political force and thus indispensable to any prospective government. The gamble did not pay off.

Although the double name only survived for a short period of transition it could not conceal the vacillation in the SED between its past and future. The 'nostalgic, wavering line'[17] of a ruling triumvirate (Gregor Gysi, Hans Modrow and Wolfgang Berghofer) from different political and personal backgrounds played a major part in the future decline of the party.

Such indecision among other reasons helps to explain why before the end of January 1990 the party plunged into a crisis which threatened its very existence. The SED–PDS failed to adopt a clear stand on the question of German unity, which had been the key political issue since December 1989. Its manifesto committed the SED–PDS to reformist communism derived from Euro-communist ideas which had long since lost their lustre. The party apparatus had not had its powers radically curtailed. Instead, it used its power to restore the old order and more particularly for shady financial dealings which embroiled the party in further scandals. The desecration of the Soviet memorial to the fallen of World War II in the Treptow district of Berlin in early January and party reaction to this incident placed the future of the SED in jeopardy for the second time. Massive unrest followed and the apparatus tried to seize the opportunity to secure its position.[18]

For the second time a number of grassroots initiatives were mobilised. They comprised on the one hand 'platforms' ('Platform WF'; 'Platform for a Third Way'; 'Platform for Democratic Socialism')[19] and on the other members of the apparatus itself and minor functionaries who feared a decline in social position and sought to preserve their 'political home'.[20] A number of subsequent events made it clear that the broadly inexperienced party leadership (despite some exceptions) was largely dependent on the power of the apparatus. Leadership figures with experience both within and at the hands of the apparatus such as Modrow and Berghofer had reservations about a mobilisation of the party grassroots.

This attempt to save the old apparatus failed to arrest the party's decline. Before January 1990 disintegration had become so widespread that entire district groups disbanded. Prominent members of the technocratic reform wing like the vice-chairman Wolfgang Berghofer[21] or advocates of internal party transformation handed in their membership cards. The SED–PDS lost its most influential reformers. A large number of party intellectuals who had helped to mobilise the popular uprising in Autumn 1989 and had played a key role in galvanising the party into rebelling against its leadership left a party they no longer thought capable of fundamental reform.

Although the group led by Berghofer left for mainly pragmatic reasons, the declarations made by those who left the party reflect exactly the mood of the disappointed reformers:

The old SED and its leadership shamefully and irresponsibly ruined the GDR politically, economically and morally. As a result all party members, including critical voices prepared to reform, were brought into moral disrepute and deprived of their political home. Any attempt to steer a new course with a party so compromised by its past fuels the fears of many of a possible restoration of the SED. As active supporters of a radical renewal of the SED–PDS we cannot accept that the party has the political strength to undertake radical transformation and join forces with other democratic movements to resolve the deep crisis in which the GDR finds itself. We are deeply concerned about our country's future and as the undersigned submit our resignations from the SED–PDS.[22]

At its congress for the elections to the *Volkskammer* on 24–25 February the party completed the removal of the old name and renamed itself the 'Party of Democratic Socialism' (PDS). Its statutes describe it as 'a socialist party on German soil' which aims to create a humanistic democratic socialism in the 'tradition of the progressive German and international workers' movement.' 'It rejects ideological dogma.'[23]

The party was clearly trying to style itself as a form of popular movement for the salvation of the GDR based on the principles of 'democratic socialism'. The address of the party chairman contained the words:

The PDS is one of the political forces which vehemently opposes the absorption of the GDR by the FRG. All else is subordinate to this goal. We are ready to join a broad movement of all the patriotic forces on the left to guarantee the interests of GDR citizens . . . . We oppose West German annexation of the GDR because we want to safeguard peace, security and the interests of the people.[24]

The new programme adopted by the Party Congress reads like a warehouse catalogue for the left. It is an amalgam of political romanticism and nostalgia for the old GDR:

The PDS seeks to preserve
— the conscious commitment of the people to peace, anti-Fascism and solidarity;
— the best social relations where there is warmth and solidarity, not the law of the jungle;
— social security, including the right to work and secure housing provided by a large housing fund;
— the rights of woman as previously laid down in the constitution;
— a new role for the grassroots as brought about by the people's movement and the constitutional guarantee of plebiscites;
— a high degree of personal safety by preventing and combating crime;
— sufficient provision of places in kindergartens and day-nurseries; education irrespective of income or property;
— land reform and viable agricultural cooperatives.[25]

The PDS ran an astute election campaign with catchy slogans: 'Take it easy, take Gysi' and 'A strong opposition for the weak'. It did not oppose German unity outright but stressed that German reunification would create immense social problems. It played on enduring anticapitalist antipathy and popular concerns about 'Kohlonisation'.

In view of the heritage of the PDS the party did surprisingly well in the *Volkskammer* elections. It put itself in a position to be the major party of opposition in the first and last freely elected parliament in the GDR.

At first the CDU was even more afflicted with old-style thinking. It took until 26 October 1989 for the party newspaper to publish the so-called 'Weimar letter' of 10 September addressed to the party membership and the executives. The mass exodus had prompted some CDU members who performed functions in the Evangelical church to appeal to 'resist the distortion or suppression of social problems and the creation of taboos to justify inaction'. The authors, among them Martin Kirchner (later to be the general secretary of the CDU in the GDR), called for internal party democracy, an explanation of the role of the CDU in the Democratic Bloc and a determined approach to problems affecting the whole of society. First and foremost they sought to cultivate a culture of public opinion. They criticised SED media policy which encouraged 'suppression, silence and distortion'. The most far-reaching demand was for a change in the electoral system. 'We cannot accept that the coming elections to the *Volkskammer* and the regional assemblies will conform to the old system.'[26]

On 28 October 1989 the CDU party newspaper, *Neue Zeit*, published a declaration by the presidium of the main executive of the CDU which called for far-reaching reforms, a renewal of state and society and a 'fundamental change in public consciousness' based on the 'primacy of moral values and genuine democracy, strict adherence to the rule of law and unbiased media'. At the same time the CDU was painted as the 'party of socialism', peace, 'humanism and spiritual values' which was an independent member of the 'Bloc' and considered an alliance with the other parties as 'an invaluable prerequisite' for reaching common objectives.[27]

Only a few months had passed before the CDU then presented itself to the voters as a conservative 'popular party of the centre' which developed policy on the basis of ethical values. From early 1990 under the leadership of Lothar de Maizière (later to become the prime minister of the GDR), the CDU had been conducting a rapid renewal of its philosophy to which, after some initial hesitancy, the CDU in the Federal Republic lent its support. The GDR CDU was, however, no copy of its sister party: the eastern CDU attached particular emphasis to its social role and the importance of Christian values in politics.

It is the firm belief of the CDU that escalating world conflicts can only be resolved when Christian values such as admission of guilt, atonement, justice and solidarity are understood to be essential political values and they gain international recognition as such . . . . The CDU supports an effective market economy in which social welfare and the environment [can be] guaranteed . . . . It rejects command economics, the state monopoly of property and the party dictatorship. The CDU does not leave Marxism to claim sole ownership of the ideals of justice, freedom and equality associated with the word socialism but remembers their origins in Christian ethics.[28]

Reservations in the western CDU about its Eastern partner's past as a Bloc party were soon dispelled when the results to the *Volkskammer* elections in March 1990 showed that electors had 'forgiven' the party for its past. The decision to lend the full support to the CDU in the GDR was dictated by a number of factors: first, the Eastern party still had a considerable membership, large assets and above all a well-developed party organisation which would acquire especial importance in the forthcoming election campaigns. The CDU reaped further dividends from the fact that in summer 1990 the remaining members of the Democratic Farmers' Party were taken over. The all-German party was then able to absorb almost 200,000 new members.

In addition, the returns of the other two partners in the Alliance for Germany were sobering. The German Social Union (DSU), sponsored by the Bavarian CSU, failed to become the dominant conservative political force in the south of the GDR. Meanwhile, Democratic Awakening had declined to the point of irrelevance. None the less, the end of the Alliance prefigured disagreement among the conservative-democratic forces which was to continue unabated throughout the summer and culminated in a clear dwindling of importance for the CSU as a party in national terms after the *Bundestag* elections of 2 December 1990.

CDU successes in the GDR did not, however, mean that after merger with the Western CDU on 1 October 1990 it could exert any notable influence on the future direction of the party at national level — despite the fact that its membership figures lay at 200,000 compared to 680,000 in the Western *Länder*, or almost a quarter of the total membership. Observers of the merger congress discovered instead that fears held in some quarters of a 'left turn' in the CDU had proved unfounded.[29] Neither in election statements before the *Bundestag* elections in 1990 nor in the programme of the first post-reunification government could substantive evidence be found that the influence of Eastern CDU members had informed policy. The same applies to the Liberals and the Social Democrats.

Of all the parties in the old system the Liberals were the first to make a clear commitment to change. As early as summer 1989 the LDPD chairman, Manfred Gerlach, also a vice-chairman of the State Council, became the first and only leading political figure to commit himself publicly to *Glasnost* and *Perestroika* and call for a discussion of people's concerns. This brought him some credit in the first phase of the transition process. Nevertheless, even these tentative attempts to break free of the bunker mentality of the SED gerontocracy did not constitute a departure from old-style political thinking.

On 12 October 1989 Gerlach was still stating that the Russian Revolution had given the workers the 'historic initiative' and that historical reason called on the LDPD to see itself first as an alliance party. With this statement Gerlach was trying to concede a joint role to the new political forces in the country without calling into question the political principles which had obtained until then — most notably the leading role of the SED:

In reality we need to address the way in which the leading role of the SED and state power is exercised in the development of socialism in the GDR . . . . There must clearly be involvement from all the citizens' movements which despite the fact that they have not before been organised in parties or in the National Front wish to participate in dialogue in accordance with the Constitution. We distinguish between citizens who either publicly criticise or reject or call for reform of government policy and enemies of the state of workers and peasants. The first are to be involved in public discussion, the latter to be dismissed with the appropriate means.[30]

The exact nature of these appropriate means was not specified.

In October 1989 the LDPD did not question the leading role of the SED.

Notwithstanding all the developments, changes and rethinking we adhere to certain precepts. The LDPD is irrevocably a democratic party working inside and fostering socialism. Its members support this society and state . . . . The LDPD [remains] unwavering in its loyalty to the alliance of parties . . . and to socialism . . . . We Liberal Democrats recognise the leading role of the Marxist–Leninist party. We know (and this has been confirmed by recent world events) that the destiny of this country and socialism itself depend greatly on this leadership and its abilities.[31]

The Liberals developed in a way similar to that of the CDU. In early 1990 the LDPD had renamed itself the 'Liberal Democratic Party' (LDP). (The old name LDPD had, like the SED, DBD and NDPD, retained the title 'Germany' although the Honecker leadership in the 1970s had banished almost all public references to any claim to represent all of Germany.)

In March 1990 the Liberals presented themselves as a party with a 'liberal spiritual stance and vision' which saw the freedom of the individual as the cornerstone of all political aims. 'Man is the measure of all things. The state is to serve man, not vice versa. State despotism, bureaucracy and coercion are anathema to the liberal view.'[32] The LDP supported the rule of law and market economics and the fastest possible reunification of Germany as part of a European peace order.

The results of the *Volkskammer* elections in which the Liberals had gained only 5.3 per cent of the vote had given them food for thought. On 28 March the party leaderships of the LDP, FDP (East) and the German Forum Party agreed to merge their three parties. The new party was to retain the name 'Free Democratic Party — the Liberals'.

This plan was undone only a few days later by the rank-and-file members. Members of the German Forum Party (itself a product of the citizens' movements) were especially concerned that the LDP was too tainted by its past. After the failure of the merger the LDP joined ranks with the NDPD at the end of March under the name 'Alliance of Free Democrats — the Liberals'. They then entered into a joint parliamentary group with the FDP (East) in the *Volkskammer*.

The three liberal parties in the GDR were unable to unite before their fusion with the FDP (West) at a Party Congress in Hanover on 11–12 August 1990. With its 135,000 members the Alliance of Free Democrats, forged from the former Bloc parties LDPD and NDPD, would have dominated the FDP (East) with barely 2,000 members and the Forum Party, for which figures fluctuated between 500 and 3,000. The influx of new members was not however without its difficulties for the FDP (West) since it possessed only 67,000 members itself. A complicated selection procedure for party congress delegates was devised to ensure that Eastern German groups did not become preponderant. The chairmen of the Alliance of Free Democrats (the ex-LDP), Rainer Ortleb, and the FDP (East), Bruno Menzel, were elected deputy chairmen of the Federal FDP.

The Party Congress issued a policy declaration outlining the aims of the Liberals: 'The precepts of liberalism are the guarantee of inviolable basic rights, the free development of the personality, the protection of minorities, the division and control of state powers and the liberal state based on the rule of law.'[33]

The erstwhile Bloc parties CDU and LDPD forged their renewal in 'classical' conceptions of Christian and liberal politics. By contrast, the Democratic Farmers' Party and the National Democratic Party of Germany faced considerable problems in charting a new course. This meant that they ultimately ceased to exist as independent parties. They could not find the distinct home they could occupy in a democratic party system.

Both parties were created 'artificially' by the SED in an attempt to win over the rural population as well as former members of the *Wehrmacht* and minor Nazis to an alliance for the socialist transformation of society. They did not ever develop an independent identity yet possessed considerable assets which they brought with them when they merged with the CDU and LDP respectively.

By late March the party executive of the 80,000-strong NDPD decided to join the Liberals. At the end of June the DBD executive recommended that its members merge with the CDU.

5.3 New parties and electoral alliances

Social democracy was refounded illegally in early autumn 1989. It was then known as the 'Social Democratic Party in the GDR' (SDP). At its Berlin conference on 13 January 1990 the party adopted the name of the West German SPD and thereby claimed to be the successor of the SPD which had been forced to ally itself with the KPD to form the SED in 1946. The SPD in the GDR was quicker than the other parties to develop into an all-German party. In February 1990 Willy Brandt was elected its honorary president. The ideals of the SPD were largely informed by its founders who were members of the human-rights, peace and ecological movements in the GDR.

In its election manifesto the SPD described itself as a new party:

In the revolutionary awakening of Autumn 1989 the SPD joined the vanguard of the forces demanding political reform. But our party is not a new kind of party. From the outset it has deliberately placed itself in the long and established tradition of Social Democracy in Germany and the world. The SPD is committed to the guiding precepts of the social democratic movement: the democratic economic and social order which gives everyone a life in freedom, justice and solidarity.[34]

The identity of the reformed SPD in the GDR was derived from various traditions: the heritage of the workers' movement, humanism, Christian ethics and its role in the opposition movement during SED rule. Its self-definition as a broad democratic people's party with a political–ethical basis open particularly to the citizens' movements emerged more clearly than in the SPD in the Federal Republic. None the less, the practical politics of vote-winning soon diluted this commitment. (Before the end of January the SPD had revoked the planned electoral alliance with all the opposition groups.)

After the *Volkskammer* elections the SPD was plunged into deep crisis. Now in a Grand Coalition with the CDU, DSU and the Liberals it was faced with the difficulty of developing a distinct profile. Its claim to be the party of the workers and the 'ordinary people' was undone by the voters: workers had overwhelmingly voted CDU. Unlike the former Bloc parties the SPD had no working political apparatus. In many districts and localities it had no members. It proved unable to keep its election pledge never to enter into a coalition with the rightist-conservative DSU because the critical situation in the GDR called for a broad ruling coalition. The personal ambition of the party chairman, Markus Meckel, had secured the foreign ministry in the de Maizière cabinet, although it was obvious that the GDR scarcely had any room for manoeuvre. In domestic policy the SPD assumed the unenviable portfolios of the ministries of finance and employment and welfare. Internal party strife ensued between the 30,000-strong membership and the party leadership which had joined the Grand Coalition for reasons of national unity.

The Party Congress in June 1990 in Halle elected a new leadership which was able to curb these centrifugal tendencies without ever resolving the basic problem: in the difficult phase of transformation the SPD proved incapable of finding a distinct identity. It too became the object of West German party tactics in the months running up to unification.

The West German SPD's candidate for the chancellorship, Oskar Lafontaine, adopted an election strategy which played on the expected negative social and financial consequences of German unification. This strategy was not uncontroversial in the Western SPD. As subsequent events in the former GDR have shown, there was some justification in SPD claims that the Federal government saw unity only in terms of the state whereas Social Democrats understood unity to extend to equality in living standards.[35] However, this stance failed to take account of the prevailing mood in the GDR where it was seen as criticism of people's desire for rapid German unity.

The manifesto adopted by the unification Party Congress on 27

September 1990 in Berlin bore the title 'Toward the Restoration of the Unity of the Social Democratic Party of Germany'. It addressed the above problem in stating that 'the two parts of Germany will grow together more quickly the more the German people strive for greater social justice. For this reason we cannot and will not accept a division into first-and second-class Germans for years to come.'[36]

This commitment did not find its way into the internal party organisation. Notwithstanding the election of the last chairman of the Eastern SPD, Wolfgang Thierse, to the post of deputy party chairman of the all-German SPD, the unification of the two parties amounted in the end to absorption in the Western SPD. In view of the enormous gulf in membership figures (approximately 900,000 in the West as opposed to only 30,000 in the East), it would have been difficult anyway to achieve a stronger representation of Eastern members.

The German Social Union was founded on 20 January 1990 as an amalgam of about a dozen small Christian and conservative groupings and established a profile as the Eastern German equivalent of the Bavarian Christian Social Union (CSU). Initially the DSU inveighed against the 'Bloc party' CDU and could only be persuaded to enter the Alliance for Germany after great pressure had been applied. Whereas its founder, the Leipzig pastor Hans-Wilhelm Ebeling, conceived the DSU as the partner of the Western CDU and CSU, the populist wing around the later chairman, Hansjoachim Walter, favoured close ties only with the Bavarian CSU. In the election campaign the DSU acquired a reputation for being a party which opposed all forms of socialism and elevated the slogan 'Freedom, not Socialism' to a manifesto commitment as the following statement illustrates:

The DSU is a conservative party because it is committed to a durable system of values. It is a liberal party because it upholds the basic rights and freedoms of the citizens. And it is a social party because it lends special support to weaker people. Germany needs Freedom, not Socialism.[37]

From the outset the Alliance for Germany was seen as an alliance of expediency and it disintegrated immediately after the elections. The DSU left the Alliance in April while coalition negotiations were still in progress. The party leadership under the founding chairman Ebeling and the general secretary and later interior minister Peter-Michael Diestel was in effect toppled and the DSU adopted a rightist-populistic stance.

After the *Volkskammer* elections the Western CDU had severed almost all links with the DSU and concentrated instead on support for the Eastern CDU. There were tendencies within the DSU to establish itself on a long-term basis across the country. However, fusion with the CSU was precluded because this would have contravened an agreement that the CSU would restrict itself to Bavaria. Fusion would therefore *ipso facto* have brought to an end the joint parliamentary group of the CDU and CSU in the *Bundestag*. The DSU considered a number of options, however, including a merger with the Democratic Farmers' Party (DBD).

The case of the DSU clearly illustrates that German unification had considerable ramifications for all the parties and not only those in the Eastern regions. In summer 1990 in the run-up to elections to the *Bundestag* a bitter dispute broke out about electoral law. (The real root of the conflict actually lay in the question of the future structure of the party system.) As a party limited to one region (Bavaria), the CSU had derived its importance from its role in an important conservative bloc as partner of the CDU in the *Bundestag*. The addition of the new Eastern *Länder* considerably reduced this influence. This meant that the CSU was interested in finding a partner in the Eastern *Länder*. Since there were not yet any firm party alignments, the Western CDU must have had an interest in preventing a rightward shift among potential supporters in the GDR. The DSU appeared to have an offer ready for these voters. None the less, following its poor election results in the *Volkskammer* election and a halving of voter support in subsequent local elections, it became clear that an independent party to the right of the CDU would have no chance. As a result in the summer the DSU became a bargaining chip for the CSU in its quest to maintain national political influence.

5.4 Elections and voting behaviour

The revolutionary events in the GDR in late 1989 and early 1990 were understandably perceived in one particular light: the people had witnessed the collapse of a political and social system which all observers, despite clear signs of its crisis, had hitherto taken to be stable.[38] Following the collapse of the system, attention focused on the conflict between the political system and the people. It only gradually became clear that social reality was much more complicated. The SED bequeathed a society with deep social, cultural and regional differences. Deep cleavages have emerged in the society of the old DDR: between North and

South, between classes and social strata and between old and young. The impact on the GDR's citizens of a centralised state with neglected regions and a privileged capital was also translated into voting behaviour (see doc. 19).

The results in (East) Berlin clearly proved exceptional: here, the CDU gained less than half the votes it gained on average and only one-third of its share in the Erfurt region. Conversely, it was only in Berlin and the neighbouring region of Potsdam that the SPD managed to secure more than 30 per cent of the vote. In gaining 30 per cent of the vote, the PDS became the second strongest party. Berlin also provided the Liberals with their worst result and the citizens' movements their best. These results reflect the particular social structure of the former GDR capital with its high numbers of party cadres, state functionaries, scientific and cultural institutions and a traditionally well-organised workforce.

In the south of the GDR in the regions of Dresden, Karl-Marx-Stadt (which later reverted to its pre-1953 name of Chemnitz) and Erfurt the parties in the Alliance for Germany gained approximately 60 per cent of the vote.

The southern regions had suffered most from regional disparities during the exodus of 1989.[39] Most of those leaving the GDR came from the Erfurt, Suhl, Gera, Karl-Marx-Stadt and Dresden regions where social and environmental problems were most acute. It was here that the Alliance for Germany obtained its best results. By contrast, its results in the more northern regions were poor.

The SPD results were catastrophic when one considers that prior to the elections it had been widely expected to be the clear winner.[40] With the exception of the Berlin region it failed to pass the 30 per cent mark in any other area, and in Saxony and Thuringia it remained well below the 20 per cent mark.

The PDS secured its best results in Berlin and in the north where the SED had developed new industry in the last few decades. By contrast, the PDS vote in the traditionally industrial heartlands of the south crumbled. The party did gain strongholds in former regional capitals which retained administrative and political institutions typical of the old structures.

The socio-cultural causes for voting behaviour display some clear influences of GDR-specific factors. Unlike its Western sister the Eastern German CDU became the party of the working class, of which 55 per cent voted for the Alliance for Germany. It also gained majorities in all other population groups with the exception of the 'intelligentsia'.[41]

Only 22 per cent of workers voted for the traditional workers' party, the SPD. This result was only just above the SPD vote for the whole population. Similar levels of support came from the professional and clerical sector (20.6 per cent), the intelligentsia (22.7 per cent) and senior functionaries in the state, economy and 'social organisations' (21.6 per cent).

Setting aside the 4.7 per cent it gained from employees, the PDS obtained the second-worst result in workers' voting (11.9 per cent). It was most successful among leading functionaries (20.2 per cent) and the intelligentsia (31 per cent).

The basic pattern of voting behaviour repeated itself in the *Landtag* elections (to the regional assemblies) in October. The CDU gained 50 per cent of the workers' vote and remained the strongest party. The SPD secured only one in every four workers' votes, while the PDS's share fell to barely 6 per cent.

Based on the aforementioned peculiarities in GDR voting behaviour, observers after the *Volkskammer* elections said that voting patterns did not conform to party preferences and would undergo major change with the further rapid changes in economic and social circumstances introduced at the latest by the currency union in July 1990.

However, results in the local elections on 6 May, the *Landtag* elections on 14 October 1990 and the first all-German elections to the *Bundestag* on 2 December of the same year display remarkable continuity in voting behaviour.[42] Significant shifts did however take place. The local elections in particular revealed a number of peculiarities linked to regional problems.

A comparison of the three election results reveals little change. The CDU remains the dominant political force while only in Brandenburg (and then only in the *Landtag* elections) does the SPD become the strongest party. Here, as in Saxony where the CDU gained a convincing absolute majority in the *Landtag* elections, the results were heavily influenced by strong personalities running for regional prime minister: a leading church figure in the GDR, Manfred Stolpe, ran for the SPD in Brandenburg while Kurt Biedenkopf, one of the elders of the Western CDU, stood in Saxony.[43]

The PDS continued to lose support steadily in all the *Länder*. Unlike voter perception of the former Bloc parties, the CDU and FDP, the PDS was clearly seen as a party which represented the old GDR. This fact also helps to explain successes in (East) Berlin where the PDS succeeded in gaining 23.6 per cent of the vote (as opposed to the 30 per cent it obtained in the local elections in May) in the *Bundestag* elections and the elections to the Berlin regional parliament which were held at the same time. The party was even able to elect Gregor Gysi on a direct mandate to the *Bundestag*.

The results of the DSU are also significant. In the *Volkskammer* elections the party, modelled on and supported by the Bavarian CSU, gained 13.9 per cent of the vote in Saxony where the CSU had started a massive support campaign. However, it secured only 5.7 per cent of the vote in Thuringia and failed to make any significant impression on any of the other *Länder* it contested. In the October *Landtag* elections, the party's support collapsed in Saxony to only 3.6 per cent and in Thuringia to only 3.3 per cent. Overall, the DSU lost 237,000 voters to the CDU from which it gained only 81,000. Of the 6.6 per cent the DSU obtained in the *Volkskammer* elections, only 1 per cent remained after the *Bundestag* elections. The DSU experiment had failed.

The collapse of the West German Green vote in the *Bundestag* elections was not least due to the isolationism of its manifesto. While there had indeed been considerable scepticism in Alliance 90 about the form and speed of reunification, it principally concerned the means by which the people could be involved in decision-making. Wolfgang Templin, one of the co-founders of the Initiative for Peace and Human Rights, saw the reasons for the disastrous showing of the Greens and the poor results of the citizens' movements of the former GDR in the *Bundestag* elections in the incompatibility of their respective political positions: outright rejection of unification on the one hand and attempts to set a new agenda on the other. The unification process and the 'way in which it had been achieved' had 'upset and irritated' the Greens much more than Alliance 90.[44]

After four elections one can conclude that there have been no dramatic changes. For the time being, at least, majority political feeling is stable and liberal-conservative. The party system in the eastern *Länder* has broadly adopted the system of the old Federal Republic. There are, however, two exceptions: the PDS and Alliance 90. The PDS will never be able to escape its past. Moreover, it offers no credible political vision which would make it likely in the long term that it could establish itself as a socialist party to the left of the SPD. It also remains to be seen whether the eight *Bundestag* deputies of Alliance 90–Greens can succeed in forging a new type of party, a civil-rights party, in the German political system.

Nevertheless, the stability which has prevailed in voting behaviour in no way means that the parties' share of the vote will necessarily remain stable. It is clear that a number of reasons affected the way the people of the former GDR voted in the elections. To reduce these reasons to the truism that they wanted the Deutschmark and so voted CDU is an over-simplification. Of course voters in the East, like those in the West, credited the

CDU with greater economic competence. Of course, the SPD was too weak and too much of a 'pastor's party' to offer a credible alternative. Of course, the campaign of the SPD's candidate for the chancellorship confused a large number of voters in the GDR, and of course the majority wanted to vote for a quick end to the instability which had rocked daily life. Against this backdrop any prospect of an independent or even slower strategy — as propagated by the SPD and the citizens' movements — was considered dangerous.

It may be clear to experienced voters in the West, accustomed to treating the fulsome promise of politicians with some scepticism, that expectations of the abilities of political parties were too high. In the desolate world of a disintegrating GDR they must indeed have seemed like messianic tidings. Disappointment was quick to follow.

Notes

1 Ehrhart Neubert, 'Die Opposition in der demokratischen Revolution der DDR. Beobachtungen und Thesen', Detlef Pollack (ed.), *Die Legitimität der Freiheit. Politisch alternative Gruppen in der DDR unter dem Dach der Kirche*, Frankfurt-on-Main, Peter Lang, 1990, p. 209.

2 Hubertus Knabe, 'Politische Opposition in der DDR. Ursprünge, Programmatik, Perspektiven', *Aus Politik und Zeitgeschichte*, B 1–2/90, 5 January 1990, pp. 21–32; Helmut Müller-Enbergs, 'Die Rolle der Bürgerbewegungen in der Volkskammer', in Gert-Joachim Glaessner (ed.), *Eine deutsche Revolution. Der Umbruch in der DDR, seine Ursachen und Folgen*, Frankfurt-on-Main, Peter Lang, 1990, pp. 94–107.

3 Sigrid Meuschel, 'Wandel durch Auflehnung. Thesen zum Verfall bürokratischer Herrschaft in der DDR', Rainer Deppe, Helmut Dubiel and Ulrich Rödel (eds), *Demokratischer Umbruch in Osteuropa*, Frankfurt-on-Main, Suhrkamp, 1991, p. 41.

4 Ehrhart Neubert, *Eine protestantische Revolution*, Osnabrück, Kontext Verlag, 1990, p. 12.

5 'Wie viele müssen noch gehen . . . . Offener Brief an Christen und Nichtchristen in der DDR, *Die Tageszeitung*, 15 August 1989, p. 3.

6 Rolf Henrich, *Der vormundschaftliche Staat*, Reinbek, Rowohlt, 1989.

7 'Aufbruch 89. NEUES FORUM', *Oktober 1989. Wider den Schlaf der Vernunft*, Berlin, Verlag Neues Leben, 1990, pp. 18–19.

8 'Aufruf zur Einmischung in eigener Sache', *Demokratie Jetzt. Dokumentation des Arbeitsbereichs DDR—Forschung und–Archiv* (compiled by Helmut Müller-Enbergs), *Berliner Arbeitshefte und Berichte zur sozialwissenschaftlichen Forschung*, No. 19, Berlin, January 1990, Doc. No. 26.

9 'Thesen für eine demokratische Umgestaltung der DDR', *Aufruf zur Einmischung*, op. cit., Doc. No. 27.

10 Quoted in *Die Tageszeitung*, 18 October 1989.

11 'Information über beachtenswerte Aspekte des aktuellen Wirksamwerdens innerer feindlicher, oppositioneller und anderer negativer Kräfte in personellen Zusammenschlüssen, *Ich liebe euch doch alle! Befehle und Lageberichte des MfS Januar–November* 1989, Armin Mitter and Stefan Wolles (eds), Berlin, Basisdruck, 1990, pp. 46–50.

12 Cf. 'Information über die weitere Formierung DDR—weiter oppositioneller Sammlungsbewegungen', *Ich liebe euch doch alle!*, op. cit., p. 208.

13 Meuschel, *Wandel durch Auflehnung*, op. cit., p. 43.

14 *Politische Parteien und Bewegungen der DDR über sich selbst. Handbuch*, Berlin, Staatsverlag, 1990, p. 18.

15 'Offener Brief an alle Bürgerbewegten', *Die Tageszeitung*, 23 July 1990, p. 5.

16 Cf. Otto Kirchheimer, 'Der Wandel des europäischen Parteiensystems', *Politische Vierteljahresschrift*, **6**, 1965, No. 1. pp. 20–41.

17 Thomas Falkner, 'Von der SED zur PDS. Weitere Gedanken eines Beteiligten', *Deutschland Archiv*, **24**, 1991, No. 1, p. 35.

18 Ibid., p. 41.

19 Cf. Gregor Gysi and Thomas Falkner, *Sturm auf das grosse Haus. Der Untergang der SED*, Berlin, Edition Fischerinsel, 1990, pp. 122-30.

20 Ibid., p. 127.

21 An eye-witness fittingly describes Berghofer as a 'technocrat of power'. Cf. Falkner, *Von der SED zur PDS*, op. cit., p. 36.

22 '"Sozialdemokratisch" Dokumentation: Austrittserklärung der 40 SED—Mitglieder um Berghofer', *DDR Journal 2. Die Wende der Wende*, Frankfurt-on-Main, *Die Tageszeitung* 1990, p. 48.

23 Statute of the Party of Democratic Socialism. Adopted at the Election Congress of the PDS on 25 February 1990, *Wahlparteitag der Partei des Demokratischen Sozialismus PDS*, 24–25 February 1990, Berlin, PDS, 1990, p. 115.

24 Gregor Gysi, *Address to the Election Congress of the Party of Democratic Socialism, 24–25 February 1990*, Berlin, PDS, 1990, p. 15.

25 *Programme. Party of Democratic Socialism adopted at Election Congress*, 25 February 1990, Berlin, PDS, 1990, pp. 3–4.

26 'Brief aus Weimar an die Mitglieder und Vorstände der Christlich-Demokratischen Union Deutschlands, *Neue Zeit*, 26 October 1989, p. 3.

27 'Was wir wollen und brauchen: Reformen und Erneuerung — Vertrauen und neue Kraft. Entwurf zur Diskussion', *Neue Zeit*, 28 October 1989.

28 *Politische Parteien und Bewegungen der DDR über sich selbst*, op. cit., p. 12.

29 Peter Schmidt, 'Erster Parteitag der CDU Deutschlands in Hamburg', *Deutschland Archiv*, **22**, 1990, No. 11, pp. 1662–4.

30 Manfred Gerlach, 'Dem Fortschritt den Weg bahnen', *Der Morgen*, 13 October 1989.

31 Lutz Heuer, 'In diesen Wochen', *Der Morgen*, 30 September–1 October 1989, p. 5.

32 *Politische Parteien und Bewegungen der DDR über sich selbst*, op. cit., p. 55.
33 'Für ein liberales Deutschland', *Das Parlament*, No. 34–35, 17–24 August 1990, p. 10.
34 Quoted in: Helmut Müller-Enbergs, 'Volkskammerwahlen in der DDR 1990 — Synopse von (Wahl-) Programmen 15 kandidierender Parteien', *Berliner Arbeitshefte und Berichte zur sozialwissenschaftlichen Forschung*, No. 28, Berlin, March 1990, p. 11.
35 'Eine eminente Fehlentscheidung,' interview mit Oskar Lafontaine, *Der Spiegel*, No. 22, 28 May 1990, pp. 26–29.
36 'Zur Wiederherstellung der Einheit der Sozialdemokratischen Partei Deutschlands', *Vorwärts*, No. 10, 1990, p. 14.
37 Quoted in Müller-Enbergs, *Volkskammerwahlen*, op. cit., p. 6.
38 Cf. Gert-Joachim Glaessner (ed.), *Die DDR in der Ära Honecker. Politik — Kultur — Gesellschaft*, Opladen, Westdeutscher Verlag 1988.
39 Cf. Siegfried Grundmann, 'Aussen- und Binnenimmigration der DDR 1989. Versuch einer Bilanz', *Deutschland Archiv*, 22, 1990, No. 9, pp. 1422–32; Siegfried Grundmann and Ines Schmidt, Wanderungsbewegungen in der DDR 1989, *Berliner Arbeitshefte und Berichte zur sozialwissenschaftlichen Forschung*, No. 30, Berlin, April 1990.
40 This was caused by problematic opinion polls conducted in the run-up to the elections. Cf. Wolfgang G. Gibowski, 'Demokratischer (Neu-) Beginn in der DDR. Dokumentation und Analyse der Wahl vom 18. März 1990', *Zeitschrift für Parlamentsfragen*, 21, 1990, No. 1, pp. 5–22; Matthias Jung, 'Parteiensystem und Wahlen in der DDR. Eine Analyse der Volkskammerwahl vom 18. März 1990 und der Kommunalwahlen vom 6. Mai 1990', *Aus Politik und Zeitgeschichte*, B 27/90, 29 June 1990, pp. 3–15; *infas–Report Wahlen DDR 1990. Wahl der Volkskammer der DDR am 18. März 1990*. Analysen und Dokumente, Bonn-Bad Godesberg, March 1990.
41 In past GDR terminology the 'intelligentsia' included all 'graduates of universities and technical colleges' or employees in equivalent positions in industry.
42 This does not mean that in the long term the number of floating voters in the eastern *Länder* cannot be higher than in the West. Cf. Gibowski, *Demokratischer (Neu-) Beginn*, op. cit., p. 21.
43 'Forschungsgruppe Wahlen, Wahl in den neuen Bundesländern. Eine Analyse der Landtagswahlen vom 14. Oktober 1990', *Berichte der Forschungsgruppe Wahlen Mannheim*, No. 60, 14 October 1990.
44 Wolfgang Templin, 'Eine bittere Lektion', in *Bündnis 2000. Forum für Demokratie, Ökologie und Menschenrechte*, 1, 1990, No. 1, p. 7.

6 Political controversy at home

The unexpected election results of 18 March 1990 coupled with the parlous state of the GDR economy placed political parties under enormous pressure. Their aim was to form workable parliamentary majorities in the *Volkskammer* and a government. However, the Grand Coalition led by Lothar de Maizière functioned properly for only a few weeks. After this time the parties were engaged in a permanent election campaign.

In an agreement struck on 12 April the coalition partners (CDU, DSU, Democratic Awakening, Liberals, German Forum Party, Alliance of Free Democrats, FDP and SPD) made a commitment to the accession of the GDR to the Federal Republic under the terms of Article 23 of the Basic Law. The coalition saw its role as furthering the 'process of German unification with parliamentary participation'.

6.1 The controversies surrounding the new East German constitution

On 1 December 1989 the *Volkskammer*, nominally the GDR parliament, voted with five abstentions to change Article 1 of the 1974 version of the Constitution. The article stated that the GDR was a 'socialist state of workers and peasants' and represented the 'political organisation of the working people in the towns and on the land under the leadership of the working class and its Marxist-Leninist party'. (In the 1968 version the GDR was described as a 'socialist state of the German nation'.) The *Volkskammer* deleted the half-sentence which read 'under the leadership of the working class and its Marxist-Leninist party'.

A short but instructive scene from this session demonstrates that it was not merely a question of deleting declarations. A CDU deputy proposed on behalf of his party dropping the description 'workers and peasants' so that the article would have read 'The German Democratic Republic is a socialist state'. The CDU argued that if the country wanted to give a new signal it would have to be clear that it was a state for everyone. In a brief but emotional debate the president of the Writers' Union, Hermann Kant, felt obliged to point out that the workers and peasants did in fact constitute a majority of the population. By an overwhelming majority the *Volkskammer* rejected the CDU motion[1] and in so doing demonstrated that it no longer wished to accept the right of one party always to play the leading role. It was a symbolic act which all other parliaments in the socialist countries emulated.

The Volkskammer debated another change to the Constitution six weeks later. In anticipation of a completely new constitution the debate focused on this occasion on altering articles which impeded the establishment of joint ventures with Western firms and private companies in the GDR. These alterations were the first step toward the fundamental transformation of the social system of the GDR. For the first time the dominance of state property was put in question, private investment was allowed and efforts were made to integrate the GDR economy into the international division of labour by means of joint ventures.

These changes to the Constitution represented a tentative move to shed the role of the Constitution inherent in Marxism–Leninism. The SED had always rejected liberal-bourgeois constitutions because they were seen to be an expression of the class interests of the bourgeoisie. The cession of certain specific rights of formally equal individuals to the society was seen to be in the sole interest of increasing private property and securing the old property relations.[2]

Marxist–Leninist constitutional theory denied that liberal constitutions with their social and political compromises could create the preconditions for individual freedoms and greater social equality. In this sense the 'socialist Constitution of the GDR' was incompatible with the democratic revolution in late 1989 and early 1990. Even step-by-step improvements to the old Constitution would not be enough to underpin the process of democratic change. As a result, in its first session on 7 December 1989 the Round Table included a working group which would be charged with drafting a new constitution.[3] This working group presented a draft constitution for the GDR in spring of the following year. All the parties in the Round Table had contributed to it.

Originally conceived as a constitution for a democratic GDR the draft also provided a template for a future all-German constitution or for an improved and updated Basic Law for the Federal Republic. The draft constitution envisaged a comprehensive range of basic rights, proposed constitutionally enshrined state objectives such as the right to employment or environmental protection and provided for the use of plebiscites.[4] Since the revolution in the GDR had been 'peaceful', the overemphasis placed on representation in the Basic Law of the Federal Republic (which stemmed from the historical distrust of parliament in the sovereign) seemed obsolete. The draft constitution proposed by the Round Table underlined the notion of direct civil participation in the working of government. The freely elected *Volkskammer* had then to decide if it would endorse the draft. Certainly the new political groupings saw it as an aim of the events of Autumn 1989 to prepare the legal basis for a democratic reformation of the GDR.

Nevertheless, the *Volkskammer* rejected the proposal. Although in its first sitting it had symbolically deleted the preamble of the old Constitution which contained a commitment to the 'developed socialist society', it failed to agree on the Round Table draft or indeed on a new draft constitution.

Under the terms of the coalition accord of the CDU, DSU, SPD and the Liberals, it would still be possible to work out a new constitution. It was to enshrine as the inviolable rights of the individual the right to employment, to a home and to an education. If they failed to produce a new constitution, these aspects were to be incorporated into the Basic Law of the Federal Republic. The coalition agreed to 'organise swiftly and responsibly' the process of unification. This necessitated principles based on the rule of law which were to be introduced by transitional arrangements which would take account of elements of the old GDR Constitution of 1949 and the draft proposed by the Round Table.[5] However, the pace of unification defeated this process.

In its fifteenth session on 17 June 1990 the *Volkskammer* promulgated guidelines for a new constitution which would annul the legal regulations of the GDR committing individual citizens and state institutions to socialism, the 'socialist rule of law' and 'democratic centralism'. In order to smooth the way for the economic, social and currency union, the basic foundations of these constitutional guidelines stipulated that the sovereign rights of the GDR could be transferred to joint German institutions and institutions of the Federal Republic. The GDR was described as a 'liberal, democratic, federal, socially and ecologically conscious state based on the rule of law' which would guarantee the independence of local government. The basic principles guaranteed free collective bargaining, freedom of economic activity, private ownership, an independent judiciary and the protection of the environment.[6] They also created the necessary legal framework for negotiations on the two most important documents for the practical realisation of German unification: the 'State Treaty on Currency, Economic and Social Union' signed on 18 May 1990 and the 'Unification Treaty' of 31 August 1990.

6.2 The State Treaty on Currency, Economic and Social Union

The freedom to set a budget is a prerequisite for the autonomy of any polity. In early summer 1990 the economic and social situation in the GDR had come so perilously close to the abyss, politicians were left with little alternative other than a *de facto* renunciation of sovereignty by ceding responsibility for financial policy to the Federal Republic. The basic constitutional principles carried by the *Volkskammer* had created the necessary legal parameters for the State Treaty with the Federal Republic which resulted in a Currency, Economic and Social Union on 1 July 1990.[7] In fact preliminary talks on this union had taken place as early as 20 February under the Modrow government. At the time debate included possibilities of a currency system and a confederation.

However, in the intervening months tens of thousands had continued to leave the GDR for the better economic prospects and social opportunities of the Federal Republic. The abolition of the GDR currency and introduction of the West German mark was intended to staunch the haemorrhage and create the conditions for economic recovery in the GDR. It was also a signal that German unity was to be achieved without delay. In effect it meant the end of the GDR and was understood as such by most of the population. Addressing the *Volkskammer*, the GDR finance minister, Walter Romberg, said that the surrender of sovereignty over currency implied the loss of a major part of 'economic sovereignty and consequently of political sovereignty'.[8] The introduction of the West German mark thus became the 'trademark of the unification process'.[9]

Several legal regulations from the Federal Republic took immediate effect in the GDR. Old GDR laws were annulled and the *Volkskammer* was required to pass new laws which would regulate transitional arrangements.[10] Even before the completion of formal unification the authorities could cooperate 'in accordance with internal law', legal protection became possible and a joint government commission for the introduction of the State Treaty was set up.

The State Treaty was explicitly intended as the first step toward the unification of the two German states. According to the preamble the parties to the treaty resolved 'without delay [to] bring about in freedom the unity of Germany in a European peace order'.[11]

The treaty brought to an end any debate about retaining certain elements of the social and economic order of the GDR. It describes the 'Social Market Economy' as the 'common economic order' of the two states and offers a definition of this order: 'It is based primarily on the right to private ownership, competition, the freedom to set prices and the full freedom of movement of labour, capital, goods and services.' It was only the intervention of the GDR government which expanded this definition by stating that the 'legal permission for particular forms of economic ownership by public authorities or other lawful bodies [was] not excluded provided this would not discriminate against private individuals'.[12]

The GDR representatives also succeeded in incorporating into the treaty the words 'the Social Union and the Currency and Economic Union form one whole'. According to the original wording the 'social community' merely 'supplemented' the currency and economic union.[13] These modifications only acquired true political significance in so far as a number of measures were envisaged which would cushion the impact of an immediate conversion to the market economy. These measures included first and foremost special employment regulations in eastern Germany which would continue to have effect after the completion of formal unification.

The State Treaty was the cause of controversial debate in the *Volkskammer*. Alliance 90 and the PDS in particular criticised the government for the failure of the treaty to secure the equal participation of the GDR people and for the simple transposition of the political and social system of the Federal Republic. In the *Volkskammer* debate on the State Treaty one Alliance 90 deputy, Tschiche, said that the GDR was merely being 'absorbed by the Federal Republic and subjected to the dominance of the social system of the West'.[14] By contrast, the governing coalition extolled the opportunities the treaty would create. In view of the catastrophic economic situation in the *Länder* of the old GDR, the expectations of Günther Krause, the chief negotiator for the de Maizière government and later federal transport minister, seem excessively sanguine:

The State Treaty created the necessary parameters for a speedy transition from the socialist command economy to the social market economy in all areas of the economy . . . . Structural change in the economy and in agriculture will bring about rapid improvements in the enterprises and will offer the people up-to-date, secure and above all safe employment.[15]

At the signing of the State Treaty GDR Minister President de Maizière made a statement much quoted since which displays the hope of *naïveté* with which he and his colleagues saw the introduction of the market economy: 'No one will be worse off than he has been. Quite the contrary!' The Federal Chancellor Helmut Kohl stressed that no one would be 'subjected to unacceptable hardship'.[16]

The parties in the de Maizière coalition agreed that there was no political alternative to the currency union. However, there was some deep disagreement about how it would be possible to prevent negative social costs. The Finance Minister, Walter Romberg (SPD), repeatedly emphasised the precarious state of the public budget and the minister for welfare warned of mass unemployment. At the same time the SPD parliamentary leader believed that there was no danger of long-term mass employment but only of a 'prolonged search for work'.[17] These optimistic expectations drew criticism not only from opposition forces in the *Volkskammer* and the *Bundestag*. Prominent economic specialists, among them members of the Bundesbank, had expressed concern that the East German economy would not be able to withstand the shock of a sudden exposure to market forces and that the consequences for the economic performance of the Federal Republic would be incalculable.[18] These fears were to be confirmed shortly after completion of the currency and economic union: expected investment from Western companies did not materialise; the removal of politically subsidised prices for GDR produce on the Western market meant that these companies were no longer competitive and Comecon collapsed.

The factual discussion of such problems was made all the more difficult because the question of the social consequences of the currency union and the 'costs of unity' dominated an election campaign already underway. It was only at the end of February 1991 long after the GDR had been consigned to history and the dust of several election campaigns had settled that the economic and social plight of the new *Länder* could be seen without prejudice. Only at this point did the government and opposition seriously reflect on the consequences if the division into two states were to be followed by long-term social and economic division. In a government statement Helmut Kohl insisted that the achievement of equal standards of living in east and west was the priority for the coming years. His appeal had been central to the election campaign of the SPD one year before.[19]

Germany's neighbours saw the State Treaty not only as a legal treaty containing certain economic and social accords. They quite justifiably saw it as the first and decisive step toward the restoration of the unity of Germany as a single state. It is therefore not surprising that the question of Germany's border with Poland was raised before state unity had been realised. While there was great controversy in the Federal Republic, and the government forfeited much credibility by its reticence on the matter, there was unanimity among Eastern German political forces that the Polish western border was to remain inviolable. With the conclusion of the State Treaty both the *Volkskammer* and the *Bundestag* issued a 'resolution on the German-Polish border' which offered future guarantees on the inviolability of the border and an undertaking that all territorial claims would be dropped.

6.3 The Unification Treaty

The fragility of the political situation in the GDR in the summer of 1990 is documented by a *Volkskammer* sitting. On 17 June, symbolic as the anniversary of the suppression of the East German uprising of 1953, the DSU tabled a motion to declare without delay the accession of the GDR to the Federal Republic. For different reasons Konrad Weiss, a prominent Alliance 90 deputy, argued in the same vein.[20]

Although the State Treaty had brought about the *de facto* annulment of GDR sovereignty, the state continued to exist in international law. The State Treaty on the one hand was formally an internationally binding treaty between the Federal Republic and the GDR and on the other hand a constitutionally binding treaty[21] which revoked many key parts of GDR law. In order to prevent the planned accession of the GDR to the Federal Republic from amounting to an *anschluss* or annexation a second state treaty would have to enshrine the basis for a regulated accession.

After long and arduous public debate about the form and timing of the accession, the *Volkskammer* of the GDR issued a declaration on 23 August which foresaw the date of accession as 3 October 1990. Various preconditions would have to be met if accession were to proceed: the second state treaty, known as the 'Unification Treaty', would have to have been completed; the '2 + 4 talks' held by the two German states and the four victorious powers of World War II would have had to have reached a stage in which the aspects of external and defence policy pertaining to German unity could be finalised and the creation of new *Länder* in the GDR would have had to have progressed far enough to enable *Landtag* elections on 14 October.

The Unification Treaty was signed on 31 August 1990. On 23 September 440 deputies in the *Bundestag* (forty-seven against, three abstentions) and 299 deputies in the *Volkskammer* (eighty against, one abstention) voted in favour of the Unification Treaty. The *Bundesrat* had already endorsed the treaty unanimously on 21 September.[22]

Unlike the first State Treaty with its emphasis on reform of the economic system, the Unification Treaty related to all other legal spheres such as the Constitution, administrative law, penal law, EC law and international law, In roughly 900 pages of typescript almost everything was regulated: from the law governing parties, scrutiny of State Security files of the old GDR to the regulation that a registrar in registry district 1 in Berlin (West) was now registrar of the registry district 1 for the whole of Berlin, even to the articles of a law governing the use of seed in agriculture.

It soon became clear, however, that the industry of German administrative officials contained serious flaws. For example, local districts were scarcely covered by the treaty. This is all the more curious since local government autonomy was one of the cornerstones of the political system in the old Federal Republic. As a result these omissions created major problems, and in early 1991 most local districts in the new eastern *Länder* were facing bankruptcy.

The Unification Treaty also failed to ensure the speedy development of an operational administrative system in the GDR. This is explained not only by lack of funds but also by the absence of qualified officials. By force of circumstance some administrative sectors still operate with the old employees briefed and monitored by western advisers. Administrators from the old Federal Republic have little interest in moving east where there are lower salaries and lower standards of living in the towns and local districts. The training of new administrators will take time.

The Federal government believed that it would be able to finance the costs arising from German unity by means of a specially designated fund for 'German Unity'[23] which would raise money on the financial markets. In consequence the government laid down special regulations for the financing of the new *Länder*. This involved taking the new *Länder* out of the system in the old federal order of the Federal Republic which sought to ensure that there were no great disparities between poorer and more prosperous regions (known as the *Länderfinanzausgleich*).

The government hoped to cushion the financial burden of the citizens of the old Federal Republic and trusted to luck that the people of the former GDR would be content with a gradual improvement in living standards. These and other miscalculations in late February 1991 led to a revision of the Unification Treaty in order to prevent lasting damage to the social and economic future of the eastern *Länder*.

In the view of the prime minister for the Land of Brandenburg, the Unification Treaty had made a 'cardinal error' in 'consciously or unconciously underestimating the financial requirements of the new *Länder* and local districts'.[24] It was felt that this had only been belatedly recognised.

The reason for the underestimation of the financial needs of the new *Länder* stemmed — as soon became clear — from the unrealistic assumption that the economy in the east would soon experience a boom. The opposite was the case. So fraught with difficulty did the transition from a centrally planned economy to the market economy prove that it induced a radical change in the existing policies of the Federal government in early 1991. The possibility of prescribing economic regulations from the centre in the Unification Treaty proved illusory. The success of the completion of state unity must be measured in terms of the economic and above all social equality of living standards guaranteed by the Basic Law.

In order to prevent the division of Germany being replaced by a long-term social division new and comprehensive political decisions are needed which will be unprejudiced by the interests of the electorate and party sympathisers. These decisions will also change life in the old Federal Republic fundamentally. The unity of Germany as a state may have been achieved, but the process of the unification of two fundamentally different German social systems has only just begun.

Notes

1 Mitschrift der 13. Sitzung der Volkskammer, 1 December 1989.
2 *Wörterbuch zum sozialistischen Saat*, Berlin, Dietz, 1974, p. 373.
3 Helmut Herles and Ewald Rose, *Vom Runden Tisch zum Parlament*, Bonn, Bouvier, 1990, p. 24.
4 Cf. Entwurf, *Verfassung der Deutschen Demokratischen Republik. Arbeitsgruppe 'Neue Verfassung der DDR' des Runden Tisches*, Berlin, Staatsverlag, 1990.
5 *Informationen*, Bundesminister für innerdeutsche Beziehungen (ed.), No. 8, 1990, supplement.

6 Cf. 'Verfassungsgrundsätze', *GB1 I*, Nr. 33, 22 June 1990, pp. 299–300.

7 Cf. Vertrag über die Schaffung einer Währungs-, Wirtschafts- und Sozialunion zwischen der Bundesrepublik Deutschland und der Deutschen Demokratischen Republik vom 18 May 1990 (BGB1. II, p. 537), *Die Verträge zur Einheit Deutschlands*, Munich, Beck 1990, pp. 1–23 (hereafter referred to as Staatsvertrag).

8 'Volkskammer der Deutschen Demokratischen Republik, 10. Wahlperiode', 8, *Tagung* (Sondertagung), 21 May 1990, p. 211.

9 Karl Otto Pöhl, 'Das Diktat der Stunde liess längeres Warten nicht zu. Zur Währungsunion — Die Sicht der Bundesbank', *Frankfurter Rundschau*, 4 July 1990, p. 6.

10 See appendices in Staatsvertrag.

11 Staatsvertrag preamble.

12 Ibid., Art. 1,3.

13 Ibid., Art. 1,4. 'Zum Entwurf eines Staatsvertrages der Bonner Koalitionsparteien vom 24 April' cf., 'Wie die Bundesrepublik sich einen Vertrag mit der DDR vorstellt. Das ''Arbeitspapier''' über die Währungsunion, Wirtschafts- und Sozialgemeinschaft, *Frankfurter Rundschau*, 26 April 1990, pp. 16–18.

14 'Volkskammer der Deutschen Demokratischen Republik, 10. Wahlperiode, 16', *Tagung*, 21 June 1990, p. 576.

15 Ibid., p. 568.

16 The speeches made by Helmut Kohl and Lothar de Maizière on the signing of the State Treaty are reprinted in *The Unification of Germany in 1990. A Documentation*, Press and Information Office of the Federal Government (ed.), Bonn, 1991.

17 Cf. 'Volkskammer der Deutschen Demokratischen Republik, 10. Wahlperiode, 8'. *Tagung* (Sondertagung), 21 May 1990, p. 218.

18 Karl Otto Pöhl, 'Das Diktat der Stunde liess längeres Warten nicht zu', loc. cit. One year later Pöhl described the results of the currency union as a 'disaster'.

19 Cf. 'Regierungserklärung und Bundestagsdebatte', *Das Parlament*, 41, 1991, No. 7–8; 'Eine eminente Fehlentscheidung', Spiegel–Gespräch mit SPD–Kanzlerkandidat Lafontaine über die Währungs- und Wirtschaftsunion mit der DDR', *Der Spiegel*, No. 22, 28 May 1990, pp. 26–29.

20 Cf. 'Volkskammer der Deutschen Demokratischen Republik, 10, Wahlperiode, 15', *Tagung* (Sondertagung), 17 June 1990, pp. 535–42.

21 Ingo von Münch, *Einführung zu: Die Verträge zur Einheit Deutschlands*, op. cit., pp. XV–XVI.

22 Vertrag zwischen der Bundesrepublik Deutschland und der Deutschen Demokratischen Republik über die Herstellung der Einheit Deutschlands — Einigungsvertrag —, 31 August 1990, BGBl. II, p. 889, *Die Verträge zur Einheit Deutschlands*, op. cit., pp. 43–569.

23 Cf. 'Gesetz über die Errichtung eines Fonds ''Deutsche Einheit''', 25 June 1990, BGB1. II, p. 518.

24 Manfred Stolpe, 'Wir fordern nur das Notwendigste zum Überleben', *Frankfurter Allgemeine Zeitung*, 18 February 1991, p. 17.

7 Political culture in transition — a new society and its heritage

The 200th anniversary of the birth of Johann Wolfgang von Goethe fell on 28 August 1949. His work was celebrated by two German writers — Thomas Mann, who had returned from American exile to Switzerland, and Johannes R. Becher, who had returned from exile in Moscow to become the president of the *Kulturbund* for the democratic renewal of Germany and later the minister for culture of the GDR. Both writers pondered the impact of Goethe on post-war Germany and the lessons which might be drawn from his work. Thomas Mann entitled his speech 'Goethe and Democracy' while Becher spoke of Goethe the 'liberator'.[1] Both Mann and Becher concerned themselves with the relationship between intellectual (*Geist*) and political power (*Macht*) and the position of Germany in Europe.

For Mann the failure of 'European democracy' to acquire any firm foothold in Germany was one of the reasons for 'the German catastrophe' — the 'German-dominated Europe' and the 'megalomania of German nationalism' which had forced him to flee the country. A European Germany by contrast would be a democratic Germany, a Germany

one can live with, which does not provoke fear but affection in the world because it is a participant in the democratic religion of humanity which ultimately defines moral life in the Occident and is implied when we say the word 'civilisation'. Misfortune had it that such European democraticism never gained enough political power in Germany, that power never wanted to join forces with it; instead, unlike for other peoples, this same idea became historically almost synonymous with German powerlessness.[2]

It was the 'European spirit *à l'allemand*' which Thomas Mann longed for and which he believed would offer the hope of a reconciliation between intellect and political power. This would presuppose the kind of 'democratic pragmatism' which had hitherto eluded the German people and which alone could help to safeguard the rights of society against political power.

A reconciliation between intellect and power was also the central theme of the speech delivered by Becher. He rejected the 'doomed mind of Frederick the Great', his 'dangerous and epigonal imitators' and the 'Prussified Germany' which represented the 'defencelessness of the German mind and the triumph of the barrack drill and the goose-step'.[3] Becher called for no more and no less than a 'classical German politics' which had been buried with the failure of the German democrats in 1848. Now, with the emergent German Democratic Republic, Becher thought that these politics were nearing realisation.

In the immediate post-war the 'other Germany' in the East seemed to offer a suitable home for many intellectuals. Despite the visible and mounting repression of the free spirit, they witnessed first in the Soviet Occupation Zone and then in the GDR fundamental social and political change in progress. After the catastrophe of Nazism it seemed like the only solution. Many shared Becher's view that the ideology of crude individualism impeded the true freedom of the individual. What was needed was a new definition of freedom — according to Becher, 'freedom is harmony'.[4] Hopes of a new Germany were soon to prove deceptive, however.

Conservative, romanticist, nationalistic and even racial antipathy towards the free citizen and the plural society were to be replaced by the leading role of the party which was teleologically legitimised. The Socialist Unity Party saw its role as a power of order above society and as the self-appointed guarantor of the laws of history. Ostensibly the unity of intellect and power had been achieved: the rulers and the ruled were subject to the same laws although their understanding was the sole preserve of a small élite — the avant-garde. Propaganda was used to conceal the discrepancy between social reality and the level of social development according to party ideology. Hannah Arendt has described what resulted as the 'emancipation of thought from a knowing and knowable reality'.[5]

7.1 Authoritarian political culture

It was a widely held belief in the political mainstream of the Federal Republic that the SBZ or Soviet Occupation Zone (as it was known in West Germany until as recently as the 1960s) had abandoned the traditions of humanism. The GDR was seen as other, as alien and as a secular challenge to a culture rooted in the traditions of the West and Christianity. The fact that communist movements and systems shared the same parentage as the democratic societies of the West in the Enlightenment and that communism was a secular promise which had not yet been fulfilled[6] were long ignored.

Many people in the old Federal Republic are only today becoming aware that in the forty-five years for which the SBZ–GDR existed, an independent political culture had evolved whose repercussions will long be felt in the political climate in Germany. If culture is taken to be a wide-ranging expression of human relations and actions, then it is a socially mediated process. The relationship between culture and social system is mirrored by the relationship between political culture and political system. If the definition of political culture fails to take account of the social system and the general cultural context which the social system provides, then it is reduced to vacuity. When discussing political culture, the political realm is more than just the functioning of certain structures; it also comprises a subjective sphere which differs according to political system and country and determines the collective action of citizens *vis-à-vis* politics.[7] Political culture refers to the sum of the attitudes, feelings and views which influence and direct political behaviour.

A significant aspect of all political cultures, but in particular of those which have not emerged in a democratic polity, lies in the fact that no society exhibits one single 'dominant' political culture.[8] There are always political subcultures some of which are more and some less evident. The people who dictate rules because they hold power cannot always be sure that these rules will be heeded. Inherited beliefs are at work in all societies and have proved extremely resistant to the demands of modern society and its rapid political and social change. In addition, in all societies the various social strata possess their own norms and value systems. Those groups in society which are disadvantaged and excluded by political authority often develop a remarkable resilience and form their own culture.[9]

The ideology of the official GDR portrayed political culture as a 'central element of socialist democracy and the socialist way of life'. The reference to the 'socialist way of life' encompassed all the attitudes, behaviour and actions of its citizens in all social spheres, in the workplace and in their leisure, in public and with the family, in politics and with friends.[10] This concept contained central axioms of the political and social understanding of the SED which dictated official political culture:

— the self-appointed leading role of the working class and its 'Marxist–Leninist party' in the state and in society;
— the right of the party to direct and plan society as a whole according to its will;
— the conviction that socialist society is capable of realising gradually equal life opportunities for all;
— the emphasis on work as the centre of all life;
— the planned raising of the 'material and spiritual–intellectual standard of life' as an objective of state and party policy;
— the political participation and mobilisation of citizens in the framework of the existing complex of institutions and organisations in accordance with the principles of 'democratic socialism';
— the linking of socialist life with SED military policy and the 'protection of the socialist homeland'.[11]

Any attempt to analyse the traditions of political culture in the GDR faces an obvious contradiction: an authoritarian political system invoked traditions in political culture which had been unable to set roots at any time in German history. From 1945–6 the SED undertook to safeguard the traditions of political and social movements which had proclaimed their aim as the abolition of exploitation and oppression, of social want and political intimidation. The SED portayed itself as the executor of the ordinary people in their social and political struggles: the poor peasants of the Peasant Wars in the early sixteenth century, the German Jacobins, the democratic bourgeoisie in the 1948 revolution and the German workers' movement. It was claimed that in its short life the GDR had done more to provide a better and more meaningful existence and a high material and cultural standard of living to its citizens than previous centuries of German history.[12]

The two German states which were founded with different conceptions of socio-economic and political order needed to establish a new political culture. After 1945 the GDR had embarked on the road of 'anti-Fascist-democratic transformation' and made a radical break with German political tradition. Root-and-branch social and economic changes, most notably land reform, expropriation of major industries and the restructuring of the education system, opened the door in 1948 for a new stage in the evolution of a socialist society which was to be modelled on the Soviet Union. The words of one political slogan of the time ran 'learning from the Soviet Union means learning to win'. This radical rupture with the past concealed the fact that many ties with traditional German political culture persisted — despite the 'revolution from above'. These traditions survived until the end of the GDR and appear likely to inform the future.

The political culture of the GDR rested essentially on four traditions:

1. There was a distinct reform of the traditional authoritarian state. The *Obrigkeitsstaat* had been particularly prominent in Germany — a country without established democratic traditions.
2. The political system of the GDR had absorbed elements of the old workers' culture and incorporated them into the dominant political culture.
3. The SED assumed the right to exercise power as a movement committed to cultural revolution. It also aimed to bring about a communist society.
4. The political culture of the 'socialist' GDR was always informed by national specifics and differed greatly from that of other countries in the 'socialist camp'.

A further significant factor was at work: the GDR had long been confronted with the cultural and political beliefs articulated by the 'new' social movements in the West. They derived from the tradition of fundamentally different historical protest movements which the SED dismissed variously as anti-progressive, *petit-bourgeois*, romantic or radical leftist. These influences played a key role in facilitating the emergence of a protest movement in the GDR.

Authoritarianism had exerted a formative influence on German political culture. It established the principle of the division of state and society, the notion of the neutrality of the state conceived not as the result of a social contract but as the highest expression of authority and an independent instance endowed with its own undelegated power, the notion of the state servant who is neutral in matters of party interest and the political virtues of the subject, deference, obedience and political absenteeism.[13]

The GDR had indisputably achieved a radical break with many of these beliefs. State and society were seen as a unit, society was organised by and through the state and its future was formed by central state planning. The state was not neutral but the instrument of the party. It was empowered by the historical mission of the party to build socialism and communism. State servants were not 'neutral' but party cadres who defended party interests in the state administration. Lastly, citizens were to make a full contribution to the construction of socialist society.

Notwithstanding these differences three central aspects of the authoritarian state remained in place. They were reformed to serve the political objectives of the Marxist-Leninist party, the SED: the formation and legitimation of the state did not come about by means of consensus with the citizens. Although state and society did form a unit the people had no voice in determining the aims and functions of state and society. On the contrary, they were subordinate to the supreme authority of the state. The fact that its power was as the instrument of the party was of subordinate importance for the relations between citizens and the state.

Political absenteeism was not perceived as a virtue but as a transgression against the moral code of socialist society. However, it was not replaced by civic participation in social and political matters; instead it was superseded by the mobilisation of the people in the service of the aims of party and state. Criticism would lead to sanctions imposed by either party or state.

When the people of the GDR went to the polls in March 1990, they were participating in a truly free election for the first time in almost sixty years. Only octogenarians could remember political democracy in their own lifetime. Political culture was characterised by an almost uninterrupted transition between two dictatorships fundamentally different yet similar in their rejection of liberal democracy. The democratic revolution of 1989 cannot hide the extent to which the people of the GDR had internalised authoritarian character traits:

Thinking was the most dangerous thing of all here. That is obviously because of the almost seamless transition from one totalitarian system to another. We have lived under totalitarianism for fully three generations now which means that much of what is fundamental and natural to free society was simply lost . . . . The whole society here suffers from a cancer: it stands to attention and carries out orders at any price.[14]

In a remarkable way the political and social system was dictated by a legacy of behaviour patterns which owed more to Prussian authoritarianism than to the socialist tradition. In his aptly named critique of 'real socialism' *Der vormundschaftliche Staat* (the custodial state) published in 1989, Rolf Henrich writes:

It is still seen as morally permissible behaviour to fulfil unerringly duties imposed from above even if this goes against one's own inner beliefs. People still applaud perfect organisation, Prussian obedience etc. and fail to see the dangers of such organisation and the lack of personality. As a social formation state socialism unscrupulously exploits these facets of the German social character which derive from the Prussification of Germany.[15]

State socialism furthered the tradition of organisational-military thought which had informed the communist movement since Lenin and his admiration for the organisational success of the German postal service and Trotzky's War Communism.

The political and social structures in the GDR and, despite national differences, in the other socialist countries reflected the belief that society could be rationally and scientifically planned and that there was a privileged group — the vanguard — and its Marxist-Leninist party, which possessed knowledge of the laws of history and was able to act as the executor of the laws of history and society. The eminent German philosopher Hannah Arendt has pointed to the contradiction which from the outset lay between these aims and reality: a group of people was ostensibly convinced of its ultimate objective and invoked this objective — the execution of the laws of nature or society — to crush underfoot freedom and human dignity. Totalitarian ideology always pretends 'to have found the key to history or the solution to the riddles of the universe'.[16]

Since they proclaimed putative certainties, these beliefs offered the people the opportunity to identify with them. They also met with interest in pluralistic democracies fundamentally alien to them. Historical experience and the obvious failure of the socialist countries has robbed these ideas of their fascination.

In common with the other socialist countries the GDR was a political-goal culture which had broadly lost sight of its goals. After a long period of remarkably dynamic social and political development, the GDR was for years faced with the need to secure and preserve its achievements. Daily experience was governed not by utopian socialism and the goal of communism but by social behaviour and political attitudes forged by socialism. Both the political leadership and its citizens had begun to accommodate themselves to the here and now.

In the long term, however, this could not work: the institutional structures of the old system blocked the path of the new lifestyles now emerging. The structures for social and political planning and leadership remained in place; in addition, the legitimation model of a political movement which prosecuted its aims from above by means of the socialist state and coercion (including the deployment of terror in the first years of its rule) remained intact. The institutional system and the officially proclaimed norms and value system had outlived the demise of utopian objectives.

The SED disliked the notion of the *citoyen* as the dominant social type in the 'developed socialist society'. Official political culture rested on a hierarchical and authoritarian conception of society which imposed strict constraints on the free development and independent organisation of social groups and individuals. It dictated that individual life experience was to be interpreted in accordance with prescribed paradigms. By contrast everyday consciousness and the attitudes, feelings, beliefs and political behaviour of the citizens were subject to manifold influences which ran increasingly counter to the official political culture of Marxism–Leninism, acceptable behaviour and the powers of the institutions.

7.2 The Leninist heritage

A second tradition in the political culture of the GDR was the culture of the workers' movement which has its roots in pre-industrial, peasant, craft and urban-plebeian popular cultures. The workers' movement displayed the many attempts at organisation undertaken by the organised-labour movement which not only involved the political and social organisation of workers in parties or unions but included leisure organisations, choirs, sports clubs, cycle clubs, cultural organisations and cooperatives. Only recently has the importance of the regional, parochial and religious workers' traditions for the emergence and consolidation of a distinct workers' culture been recognised.[17] Here, workers' culture can be seen as a subculture endowed with countercultural elements. As a subculture it was a response to the proletarian way of life; the attempt to improve workers' living conditions by means of self-help and independent organisation in what was seen as the hostility of the outside world. Workers' culture was a counterculture in so far as it was the culture of a political and social movement which was convinced of one aim: that contemporary society was historically moribund and that the future belonged to socialism.

However, the SED had appropriated only certain aspects of this tradition. Whereas in the Social Democratic wing of the workers' movement the certainty of a socialist future was steadily dissipating, the KPD and its successor, the SED, continued to adhere to their role as the guarantor and executor of the laws of the historical process. With this conviction, the democratic traditions of the workers' movement were curtailed. The working class on whose behalf the SED claimed to act was reminded that its role was not to help formulate but to fulfil the objectives prescribed by the party.

For all that it cannot be denied that under the changed social and political conditions in the GDR, traditional forms of solidarity fostered by the workers' movement in its struggle for political and social rights lived on. This was particularly visible in the workplace. A large number of employment rulings and the emphasis placed on the work ethic and the importance of traditions of work were both a reflection of a deliberate attempt to cultivate central elements of the culture of the workers' movement and to develop further such traditions and tailor them to changed social circumstances. In the 1940s and 1950s the notion of the 'worker's honour' was politically curtailed and instrumentalised. It later came to mean the development of a new understanding of the leading class in a socialist society of science and technology.

For over two decades emphasis had been placed on the importance of the role of the sientific-technological intelligentsia. At the same time the party disseminated the belief that the working class would increasingly be assimilated into the intelligentsia, and the process of rationalisation and automation would free workers from heavy labour and monotonous work. When it became clear that this vision of the future could not be realised, the SED forfeited more of its legitimacy. The workers in the GDR had been deprived of another collective and individual hope — the hope that they could rise (higher) socially with education and professional training. How then could an individual reconcile himself psychologically to a society which proclaimed 'your workplace is the battlefield for socialism' when there was no attendant relief from daily misery.

The GDR placed itself in the tradition of the world communist movement which had emerged as a cultural-revolutionary movement. This movement did not confine revolution to the transformation of a socio-economic system but extended it to the very transformation of existing culture. The communist revolutions which have reached their objectives were the revolutions of a minority — a revolutionary élite whose vision of the future of society were shared only in exceptional cases (and then only briefly) by the majority of the population. In order to establish these visions a didactic dictatorship was required which would overcome the traditionalism of the 'masses'. The new socialist being was to be forged by education and not by his own social experience. More than seventy years after the Russian Revolution in 1917 and more than forty years after the socialist transformation of the SBZ and later GDR, the horizons of the revolutionary élites had approached that of the citizens. Although references were still made to the distant goal of a future communist society, the leaderships were more concerned with the resolution of the many economic, social and cultural problems for which the party could no longer offer any solutions. Instead, it sought refuge in the ritual invocation of the bold aims and ideals of socialism without being able to offer a way out of an escalating economic, environmental, social and cultural crisis. When the conflicts became more acute, the party felt a cold draught: the new guise of communism was a fiction.

7.3 The Federal Republic as a model

Unlike in the other socialist countries political culture in the GDR was always informed and influenced by the peculiarity of its national situation. By seeking to define itself by ideological and political demarcation (*Abgrenzung*) from the Federal Republic, the SED and the state it had created unintentionally underpinned the criteria by which East Germans commonly judged their country: how did they compare with the Federal Republic?

Political and everyday life in the GDR was influenced and often distorted by permanent comparison with the Federal Republic. The political leadership never tired of stressing the security in which GDR citizens could live and that there was no unemployment or material poverty[18] and that the country was spared many of the maladies of capitalist society such as crime and drug addiction.

Many if not in fact the majority of East Germans tended to compare their situation with the Federal Republic rather than with other capitalist countries. In turn this narrowed their perspective. Very few had the opportunity to make a true comparison. Travel restrictions for GDR people other than pensioners had been tangibly relaxed only in the last few years. About two million visitors could then gain their own impression of what life was like in the West. The vast majority based their comparisons on the presumed and only indirectly experienced reality in the other German state conveyed by the Western mass media. When East Germans could make their own comparisons after 9 November 1989, the result was like a collective shock.

While the East Germans enjoyed the highest standard of living in Comecon, their unattainable political, economic and cultural model was always the Federal Republic. Its image was ever present in television and yet out of reach. At the same time, their view was distorted by ideological slogans, a party disinformation policy and the closed borders of the GDR. The GDR remained a social order isolated from the outside — and particularly the Western — world. Apart from radio and television broadcasts, its people had only limited and regulated access to international culture and science.

This is one of the reasons which explain why the image of the West and the Federal Republic remained remarkably rigidified even for those who had criticised or rejected SED hegemony and the realities of socialism. (For the sake of balanced argument it should be noted that Manichean views of the world are also prevalent in the Federal Republic.)

One example of this distortion is provided by the 'Appeal for an independent GDR' published on 26 November 1989. Its first signatories included the renowned writers Volker Braun, Christa Wolf and Stefan Heym, the Evangelical Bishop Günter Krusche and other prominent representatives of the opposition such as Sebastian Pflugbeil, Ulrike Poppe, Friedrich Schorlemmer and Konrad Weiss. The signatories were figures with the most diverse political positions who agreed in their advocacy of an independent GDR. Their goal was to 'develop solidarity in a society which guarantees peace and social justice, the freedom of the individual, the freedom of movement for all and the preservation of the environment'. Either this way out of the country's crisis could be taken in the aim of developing a socialist alternative to the Federal Republic or a less attractive option could be taken which would involve 'accepting the beginning of the sell-out of our material and moral values through the economic pressure and intolerable conditions which influential economic and political circles in the Federal Republic attach to their aid and [accepting] that sooner or later the German Democratic Republic will be absorbed into the Federal Republic'.[19]

In an interview in December 1989 Manfred Lötsch, a well-known GDR sociologist, put the deep-seated uncertainty at the heart of this position in the following terms:

You know, this for-or-against appeal was of course — shall we say — a very simplified, euphemistic offer of alternatives, I'd agree there. What made me sign . . . was more a kind of political activism, the desperate need for a straw to hold onto. It's as simple as that. Perhaps in the secure, private knowledge that it didn't exist, that's possible. It's the desperate idea of a somehow different, socialist society — a society different from the society of the Federal Republic . . . . I believe that perhaps somewhere among the bankrupt enterprise that was socialism there are assets worth saving.[20]

It is not a question of assessing the reality of one or other of the claims of predictions — some events did in fact follow a remarkably similar course; at issue is the Manichean world view of Good and Evil which this appeal articulates — of pure utopia against crude reality. This appeal reflects a sensibility not untypical of GDR society in the process of change.

Notes

1 Thomas Mann, 'Goethe und die Demokratie', *TM, Politische Schriften und Reden*, Vol. 3, Frankfurt-on-Main, Fischer, 1968, pp. 212–33; Johannes R. Becher, 'Der Befreier', *JRB, Von der Grösse unserer Literatur, Reden und Aufsätze*, Leipzig, 1971, pp. 303–43, (authors translation).

2 Mann, *Goethe*, op. cit., p. 214.

3 Becher, *Der Befreier*, op. cit., pp. 320; 308.

4 Ibid., p. 333.

5 Hannah Arendt, *The Origins of Totalitarianisam*, New York, Harcourt Brace Jovanovich 1973, p. 352.

6 Cf. Richard Löwenthal, *World communism: the Disintegration of a Secular Faith*, Oxford, Oxford University Press, 1964.

7 Cf. Sidney Verba, 'Germany: the Remaking of Political Culture', in Lucian Pye and Sidney Verba (eds), *Political Culture and Political Development*, Princeton, Princeton University Press, 1965.

8 Cf. Barbara Jancar, 'Political Culture and Political Change', *Studies in Comparative Communism*, **17**, 1984, No. 1, pp. 69–82; Lowell Dittmer, 'Comparative Communist Political Culture', *Studies in Comparative Communism*, **16**, 1983, No. 1–2, pp. 9–24.

9 Cf. Oskar Negt and Alexander Kluge, *Geschichte und Eigensinn*, Frankfurt-on-Main, Zweitausendeins, 1981.

10 Cf. *Lebensweise und Lebensniveau im Sozialismus*, Berlin (DDR), Verlag Die Wirtschaft, 1977.

11 *Wörterbuch des wissenschaftlichen Kommunismus*, Berlin (DDR), Dietz, 1982, p. 354.

12 Erich Honecker, 'Würdiges Jubiläum Berlins, das heute den Namen "Stadt des Friedens" trägt', *Konstituierung des Komitees der Deutschen Demokratischen Republik zum 750jährigen Bestehen von Berlin am 7. February 1985*, Berlin (DDR), Dietz, 1985, p. 8.

13 Cf. Martin Greiffenhagen, 'Vom Obrigkeitsstaat zur Demokratie: Die politische Kultur in der Bundesrepublik Deutschland', in Peter Reichel (ed.), *Politische Kultur in Westeuropa. Bürger und Staaten in der Europäischen Gemeinschaft*, Frankfurt-on-Main, Campus, 1984, pp. 52–65.

14 'Denken war das Allergefährlichste. Die in West—Berlin lebende russische Journalistin Sonja Maraolina unterhielt sich mit der in Ost—Berlin lebenden russlanddeutschen Wissenschaftlerin Jelena Schmidt über die DDR: Wie sie war und wie sie wird', *Die Tageszeitung*, 30 September 1990, p. 15.

15 Rolf Henrich, *Der vormundschaftliche Staat. Vom Versagen des real existierenden Sozialismus*, Reinbek, Rowohlt, 1989, p. 92.

16 Cf. Arendt, *The Origins of Totalitarianism*, op. cit., p. 457.

17 Cf. Gerhard A. Ritter (ed.), *Arbeiterkultur*, Königstein/Ts., Anton Hain, 1979; Albrecht Lehmann, *Studien zur Arbeiterkultur. Beiträge der 2. Arbeitstagung der Kommission 'Arbeiterkultur' in der Deutschen Gesellschaft für Volkskunde, 8–12 May 1983*, Munich, F. Coppenrath, 1984.

18 The following verbally vouchsafed anecdote illustrates how this can lead to an abstruse situation: GDR television had filmed scenes of a free meal provided in a welfare institution; the film was not broadcast because bananas — a scarce commodity in the GDR — were being served as a dessert.

19 'Aufruf für eine eigenständige DDR vom 26. November 1989', in Charles Schüddekopf (ed.), *Wir sind das Volk! Flugschriften, Aufrufe und Texte einer deutschen Revolution*, Reinbek, Rowohlt, 1990, p. 240.

20 'Das Scheitern des real existierenden Sozialismus in der DDR. Ein Gespräch', *Deutsche Studien*, **28**, March 1990, No. 109, p. 11.

8 Revolt and resignation: the painful farewell to socialism

Observers of political and economic developments in the GDR had long observed a manifest contradiction between official political culture with its antiquated rituals and sloganeering and the culture of everyday experience.[1] The Federal Republic's first Permanent Representative in the GDR, Günter Gaus, coined the phrase *'Nischengesellschaft'* (niche society) to describe how people evaded the intrusions of the state by withdrawing into their private worlds.[2]

From the early 1980s a growing number of people were prepared to commit themselves to various humanitarian causes under the protection of the church.[3] However it is important not to romanticise: until summer 1989 these groups were marginalised in GDR society. Only a little more than six months later they were to be marginalised again.

Two new developments occurred in the summer and autumn of 1989. With the opening of the Austro-Hungarian border, tens of thousands of mostly young people left the GDR. At the first available opportunity they withdrew their loyalty to 'their' state. When it emerged that the régime could only stand by helplessly in the face of events, at first a few hundred and then a growing number took to the streets.

For years the SED had tried to politicise every sphere of life in the GDR. 'Production battles' and 'harvest battles' and competitions were organised. If the official statements are to be believed, then the policies of the party operated always as a catalyst for everyday acts. Workers at the petrochemical combine in Schwedt (on the Polish border) assured the General Secretary of the SED, Erich Honecker that:

the continuity and the pioneering scientific leadership style of the Central Committee of the SED and your personal example radiate on the performance, initiative and creativity of the working people to a great extent. The profound harmony between the advantages of socialism we experience from day to day and the interests of the working people and their families is a source of indomitable strength to our combine and enables us to . . . meet strategic challenges.[4]

The results of such politicisation were in fact symptoms of fatigue. Under the surface of a totally politicised society grew the 'political culture of a non-political society'.[5]

The basic facets of political culture which had developed over a number of years collapsed within a few weeks and months in the summer and early autumn of 1989. They were replaced by a mass culture of political resistance, and until mid-1990 the situation was dominated by the tens of thousands who made their exit and hundreds of thousands who stayed and voiced their rights on the streets.

In summer 1989 the exodus had increased dramatically. It was a reaction to accumulating social and political problems[6] and at the same time a reaction to and catalyst for the political and social eruption which was to bring about the end of the GDR a few months later. Above all it was the at times panic-stricken nature of the exodus which demonstrated the fragility of the situation and encouraged many to voice their feelings openly and publicly.

In addition to the weekly demonstrations in Leipzig, Dresden and many other East German towns and cities and the major hundred-thousand-strong demonstration on 4 November in Berlin (estimates vary from 500,000 to one million), the party grassroots of the SED in November and December 1989 went almost every day in their thousands to put their demands to the party headquarters. The initiative had passed to the street demonstrators and the once all-powerful SED could do nothing to stop them. In his address to the Berlin demonstration, the writer Stefan Heym said it was 'as if someone had opened the window after years of stuffiness and stale air, of empty slogans and bureaucratic arbitrariness, of official myopia and deafness'.[7]

The mass demonstrations were notable for the political maturity and creativity they displayed as the following banners indicate: 'Egon [Krenz] — what do you say about China now?'; 'You preached water for forty years and drank wine!'; 'You don't need bananas when it comes to the crunch'; 'My proposal for the first of May — the people see the leaders' parade'; 'You can't pay for forty years of frustration with only four weeks of dialogue'; '1789–1989'; 'Passports for all and red cards for the leaders'.

In the revolutionary euphoria of autumn 1989, many in the GDR believed that the seeds of a completely new political culture were beginning to bear fruit: the 'desire for justice, democracy, peace and the protection and preservation of nature' was the motivation behind New Forum — a wish which it wanted to see fulfilled in all areas in the coming transformation of society.[8] Similarly, the founding appeal launched by Democracy Now called for the people to 'think together about our future, about a society based on solidarity and in which social justice, freedom and human dignity are guaranteed to all'.[9]

The end of the GDR brought in its wake the collapse of the institutional structure of official political culture. The people heaved a liberating sigh of relief and believed that they had rid themselves of everything which had oppressed them for so long. They only gradually realised that they could not get rid of their past quickly and that they had been more profoundly influenced by the old system than they had previously thought.

In the *Eighteenth Brumaire of Louis Bonaparte*, Karl Marx used a poetic image to describe the lasting influence of inherited beliefs in a society which had set about building something altogether new and unique in history:

The tradition of all the dead generations weighs like a nightmare on the brain of the living. And just when they seem engaged in revolutionising themselves and things, in creating something that has never yet existed, precisely in such periods of revolutionary crisis they conjure up the spirits of the past to their service and borrow from them names, battle-cries and costumes in order to present the new scene of world history in this time-honoured disguise and this borrowed language.[10]

Although the majority of East Germans wanted the end of the old system (as was evident not least in the election results on 18 March 1990), they now face obvious difficulties in relinquishing it for good. This can scarcely be cause for surprise since the people in the old GDR were transposed unprepared into a new social reality which they knew only from hearsay but which had always been held up as an ideal.

None the less, there were those who believed that the GDR offered an opportunity for the creation of a new, socialist society. Despite decades of disappointment, hope for an alternative to capitalism was stronger in the GDR than in the other socialist countries. The collapse of 'real socialism' again nurtured the hope that this goal could now at last be reached.

Both reform-minded SED members and members of the citizens' movements were left clutching one straw. They now hoped to realise a long-cherished or newly emerging wish. Both groups sought to build a genuine socialism, a truly just society on the rubble of socialism. But their view of the Federal Republic shared indisputable similarities with the view propagated by the Marxist–Leninists whom they had never believed.

Others succumbed to the illusion that by adopting the Western economic order the major problems would be rapidly if not immediately resolved. On 18 March 1990 the voters elected for rapid change — which meant more than getting their hands on the Western Mark as many Western observers remarked with a mixture of ignorance and arrogance frequently visible as the process of unification developed. Their decision represented the hope of expediting a radical break with the political, economic, social and cultural past and living a life in political freedom and economic prosperity like the Germans in the West. It was only later that many people recognised the risks that this would involve, for example for the obligation of the state to protect people from all the risks of life, as was taken for granted in the GDR.

Citizens of the former GDR only gradually realised that they had pledged themselves to the radical transformation of their entire lives. Like many dictatorships before it, the authoritarian welfare state of Erich Honecker protected the population from the vicissitudes of world economic developments by means of demarcation (*Abgrenzung*) and the ruthless exploitation of natural and human resources. The price paid in terms of the near total destruction of the industrial infrastructure, the destruction of any industrial future for the country and the exploitation of the natural world came to light only after the fall of the SED. Even without revolutionary change in the long term, the concealed economic and environmental crisis would ineluctably have precipitated social crisis. The fact that it now accompanies the process of democratisation and the integration of the GDR into a market economic order is not without its problems. It is often too readily forgotten that the process of transition from authoritarianism to democracy is not the cause of the crisis. By the same token, the initially naïve trust in the power and will of politics can all too easily turn into disappointment, resignation or apathy.

The hopes of spring 1990 were quickly dispelled and the great expectations disappointed. When in the summer and early autumn of 1990 the economic situation again became grave and the currency union did not produce the anticipated short-term improvements but an escalation of the crisis instead, the initial mood of optimism gave way to deep resignation. There was a danger of regressing into old attitudes, summed up in saying 'things are taking their socialist course': in other words it was not worth getting involved, it only created difficulties. It will take years before these deep-seated beliefs and behaviour patterns are overcome.

A growing sense of insecurity has resulted. All the opinion polls demonstrate a high level of anomie. The old system of norms and values has collapsed, old institutions are being disbanded and the economic and social situation is unstable. The new legal norms and institutions are not yet working properly, and new economic and administrative structures must be developed. Even the simplest facets of everyday life — from health insurance to job hunting, childcare and leisure activities — need to undergo complete reorganisation. In the past these activities would have been carried out by the 'custodial state'.

There is a widespread feeling among the people in Eastern Germany that the dependency of the past has been replaced by another. This is not unusual in the context of transitions from dictatorship to democracy. However, in the case of the coexistence of the German people in one united policy, this feeling does assume a problematic dimension: the new order is inherited from the West; it has not been developed by the people of the East, its representatives are rarely versed in the circumstances and sensibilities of the former GDR and its people and all too frequently conceal their own ignorance under arrogance and sanctimoniousness.

The politically prudent if not (in view of the international political situation) imperative choice of accession under Article 23 of the Basic Law has produced some serious side effects: it inevitably means that familiar experience cannot be preserved and that alien experience must be adopted. The preservation of familiar experience does not mean salvaging the old political and economic structures. It means instead that overnight entirely new norms, procedures and modes of behaviour prevail. (This distinguishes the process of transition in the GDR from that in Eastern Europe or from the replacement of dictatorship which had not changed the capitalist order.) As a result, life experience, behaviour codes, social forms and qualifications are invalidated *en masse* and replaced by new ones which cannot be learned overnight in crash-course fashion. An entire society must return to school, must learn what its colleagues and teachers in the West have known for a long time. The fact that this society's own experience could usefully be used without injury does not occur to these teachers or most of their colleagues. The former GDR Prime Minister Lothar de Maizière alluded to this problem in introducing his government's programme in spring 1990. He said: 'Where we became used to the custody of the state and passivity we shall have to grow up as a society — independently and actively. This holds for every citizen as it holds for the parliament, government and the entire life of society.'[11]

A new social character is indeed required in the new German *Länder* which is fundamentally different to that in the old GDR. There, both party and state expected unwavering obedience in return for social security and modest prosperity.

The writer Jurek Becker points to the fragility of the interrelationship between the rulers and the ruled in the GDR in an essay published in the weekly *Die Zeit* in August 1990. A member of the State Security Service is here quoted as saying: 'They could finish us off with a snap of the fingers. Just a hard shake and they'd be rid of us. But they're too afraid to do it. We control them and they *let themselves* be controlled. It takes two to spy.'[12]

In marked contrast to the political cultures of other socialist countries, the political culture of the GDR was marked by a lack of conflict. Becker goes on:

If the official absence of contradiction lasts long enough, at some stage it can be taken for agreement; it was easy to make this mistake in the GDR and a major part of the party leadership — probably the biggest section — succumbed to it . . . . Real existing socialism was the joint effort of the party leadership, its cronies and servants. This is not changed by the fact that it prospered against the will of some and in accordance with the will of others; everyone involved helped to mould its face.[13]

There is a widespread tendency in the former GDR to suppress this interrelationship. The continuing exposure of the all-pervasive character of the instruments of repression appears to confirm the simple image that a ruling phalanx oppressed an entire society. It is not necessary to cite the numbers of the many people who played a role in such oppression (the number of active informal members of the State Security Service in 1989 alone runs into hundreds of thousands) in order to question this Manichean picture. The official ideology and the world view propagated by the SED had a far deeper effect on the thoughts and actions of East Germans than many are now prepared to admit. With some resignation the writer Peter Schneider drew an historical parallel with this situation:

Today we can see that hardly anyone in the GDR had his heart or at least his fist in communism. The whole GDR must have been a day clinic for ideologically abused adults. And we can now see that the SED and the other Bloc parties — just like the NSDAP in its time — were training grounds for clandestine resistance fighters who in fact worked with such secrecy that hardly anyone noticed anything until the end . . . . The exercise I describe is by no means restricted to the GDR. It is passionately pursued on both sides of the border.[14]

The collective suppression of the past cannot succeed. It resists either in the form of new documents which reveal either complicity of individuals or several politicians in the injustices of the past or in the form of the inherited norms and behaviour patterns of former citizens of the GDR who, despite efforts to conform, remain incompatible with their citizens in the West. Peculiarities remain; only the collapse of the communist system revealed that there was something approaching an independent social character in the GDR.

The longer the SED-dictated politico–social system remained in place, the greater the success the SED had in implanting its propagated vision of a society of relative equality. In comparison with Western societies the GDR was indeed a society with, in relative terms, egalitarian social structures. By contrast, the country now faces a marked 'polarisation in incomes, circumstances and risks — possibly even more profound than in the old Federal Republic'.[15] With the impact of mass unemployment — reliable estimates now predict that mass unemployment will reach between 30 and 50 per cent of the workforce — the new prosperity, especially among the middle class and the new administrative élites, will stand opposite new poverty — with unforeseeable ramifications for social stability and the collective consciousness.

By comparison, the GDR did constitute an egalitarian society. Nevertheless, closer inspection shows that this 'society of equals' was little more than an ideological construct. The data of a 'social report' published after the revolution demonstrate that differences in income, social circumstances, working conditions, between town and country and in the individual regions of the GDR had been widening since the early 1970s.[16] The various social strata — workers, clerical and professional employees, farmers, the 'intelligentsia', urban and rural, north and south, young and old — each had their own experiences and followed these experiences in everyday life and not the ideological proclamations that everyone was equal. If people were too expressive of their individualism they were looked upon with suspicion. Wherever people wavered in their unstinting support for the policies of the party and the state, social and political sanctions were not far off.

The unequal distribution of power was of greater significance, however. 'In its administration' SED rule was reminiscent of 'a patrimonial rule operating in the realms of free, traditional despotism' — a form of rule which the German sociologist Max Weber called 'sultanistic rule'.[17]

Until September 1989 there had been no indications that the

party patrimony[18] of the SED could be a colossus on clay feet. In consequence it is not surprising that the majority of people in the old GDR led a double life: a public life in which they adhered unerringly to the dictates of party and state and a private life in which they sought to fulfil their own understanding of individuality. It is not easy to break with modes of behaviour in which people have been drilled over a number of decades.

At the same time there are signs of attempts to withstand the difficulties of the transition process reminiscent of countries which have undergone similar experience: as problems multiply a sense of nostalgia is cultivated; people start saying: it wasn't so bad after all under Hitler, Stalin, Franco, Breznev, Ulbricht, Honecker. This 'GDR nostalgia', even among those who a few months previously had called for a rapid end to the GDR, was born of memories of a difficult but predictable time. This feeling of uncertainty and anxiety was expressed in a letter, written by an elderly woman from Erfurt: 'A woman in the shop said recently: soon we won't have any home anymore and she's not entirely wrong. You could put it another way: we'll soon have no say in our home. Even if we have never experienced a situation like this it does remind you a little of 1945 — unconditional surrender.' It should be added that this woman from the bourgeoisie never believed in any socialism let alone the 'real' variety.

The process of transition in all the former socialist countries is accompanied by an extreme modernisation crisis. Not only did the political, social and economic reality of the old system produce rigid authoritarian patterns of thought and behaviour; its failure to modernise[19] also meant that the social qualifications vital to a modern society such as flexibility, innovation, performance and mobility could only be inadequately developed.

The concomitants of modern society were selectively filtered. Although social reality was influenced by industrial society, its political isolationism prevented it from fully realising its progressive role and served to emphasise many of its negative side-effects. These were in turn cushioned by the presence of the authoritarian welfare state. Sociologists and writers noted the growing mechanisation and rationalisation of work and life, growing pressure of time and performance in the fight for daily needs, rising social aggression, monotony at work and at leisure, anonymity in the new high-rise housing complexes, growing alienation between the generations, inflated divorce and suicide rates and the double burden of childcare and employment which befell women.

Few of these social experiences were shared by people in the

Federal Republic, and they were heavily informed by the peculiarities of a distinct social system. Now at breakneck speed two social orders with antagonistic political, economic and social systems but a common history and culture are growing (or ruling) together. Only now are people beginning to realise that in both parts of Germany highly diverse and fundamentally different social characteristics have developed which cannot simply be merged by laws or with the assistance of the Bundesbank.

One could say polemically that the events of 1989 have brought Germany state unity and social division. Until 9 November 1989 the majority of the German people were convinced that only politics were preventing them from living in a common polity. There was great reluctance to admit that forty years of division had produced social and cultural separation. Only those who had — in the main involuntarily — crossed between East and West had a sense born of bitter personal experience of the deep divisions which separated both societies and of the completely different mentalities in East and West.

Notes

1 Irma Hanke, *Alltag und Politik. Zur politischen Kultur einer unpolitischen Gesellschaft. Eine Untersuchung zur erzählenden Gegenwartsliteratur in der DDR in den 70er Jahren*, Opladen, Westdeutscher Verlag, 1987.

2 Günter Gaus, *Wo Deutschland liegt. Eine Ortsbestimmung*, Hamburg, Hoffmann und Campe, 1983.

3 See for example Detlef Pollack (ed.), *Die Legitimität der Freiheit. Politisch alternative Gruppen in der DDR unter dem Dach der Kirche*, Berlin, Peter Lang, 1990; Jörg Swoboda (ed.), *Die Revolution der Kerzen. Christen in der Umwälzung der DDR*, Wuppertal and Kassel, Onkenverlag, 1990.

4 *Neues Deutschland*, 27 January 1986, p. 3.

5 Cf. Hanke, *Alltag und Politik*, op. cit.

6 Cf. Siegfried Grundmann, 'Aussen- und Binnenmigration der DDR 1989. Versuch einer Bilanz', *Deutschland Archiv*, **22**, 1990, No. 9, pp. 1422–32; Siegfried Grundmann and Ines Schmidt, 'Wanderungsbewegungen in der DDR 1989', *Berliner Arbeitshefte und Berichte zur sozialwissenschaftlichen Forschung*, No. 30, April 1990.

7 cit. *Wir treten aus unseren Rollen heraus. Dokumente des Aufbruchs Herbst '89*, Berlin, Zentrum für Theaterdokumentation und -information 1990, p. 219.

8 Gründungsaufruf: 'Eine politische Plattform für die ganze DDR', Gerhard Rein (ed.), *Die Opposition in der DDR. Entwürfe für einen anderen Sozialismus*, Berlin, Wichern, 1989, p. 14.

9 *Aufruf zur Einmischung in eigener Sache*, ibid., p. 59.

10 Karl Marx, *The Eighteenth Brumaire of Louis Bonaparte*, in: Karl Marx and Friedrich Engels, *Collected Works*, Vol. 11, London, Lawrence and Wishart, pp. 103–4.

11 'Volkskammer der Deutschen Demokratischen Republik, 10. Wahlperiode, 3', *Tagung*, 19 April 1990.

12 Jurek Becker, 'Zum Bespitzeln gehören immer zwei. Über den Umgang mit der DDR-Vergangenheit', *Die Zeit*, 3 August 1990, pp. 35–6.

13 Ibid., p. 36.

14 Peter Schneider, 'Man kann ein Erdbeben auch verpassen', *German Politics and Society*, Issue 20, Summer 1990 (Special issue: *Germany: From Plural to Singular*), p. 2.

15 Gerhard Bäcker, 'Sozialpolitik im vereinten Deutschland. Probleme und Herausforderungen, *Aus Politik und Zeitgeschichte*, B 3–4/91, 11 January 1991, p. 7.

16 Cf. Sozialreport. *Daten und Fakten zur sozialen Lage in der DDR*, Gunnar Winkler (ed.), Berlin, Verlag Die Wirtschaft, 1990.

17 Max Weber, *Wirtschaft und Gesellschaft*, Tübingen, Mohr, 1972, p. 134.

18 Cf. Gert-Joachim Glaessner, *Bureaucratic Rule: Overcoming conflicts in the GDR*, Cologne, Index, 1986.

19 Cf. Gert-Joachim Glaessner and Fred Klinger, 'The three cultures, — Social Forces and Socialist Modernisation in the GDR', *Studies in GDR Culture and Society* 9, Lanham, University of America, 1989, pp. 1–10.

Bibliography

Ackermann, Anton, 'Gibt es einen besonderen deutschen Weg zum Sozialismus?', *Einheit*, **1**, No. 1, 1946, pp. 22–32.

Andert, Reinhold and Herzberg, Wolfgang, *Der Sturz. Erich Honecker im Kreuzverhör*, Berlin, Aufbau, 1990.

Arendt, Hannah, *The Origins of Totalitarianism*, New York, Harcourt Brace Jovanovich, 1973.

— *On Revolution*, New York, Harcourt Brace Jovanovich, 1963.

Bahr, Egon, 'Das Gebot staatlicher Einheit und das Ziel Europa im Widerspruch', *Frankfurter Rundschau* (Dokumentation), 13 December 1988, p. 10.

— *Sicherheit für und vor Deutschland. Vom Wandel durch Annäherung zur Europäischen Sicherheitsgemeinschaft*, Munich, Hanser, 1991.

Bahro, Rudolf, *Die Alternative. Zur Kritik des real existierenden Sozialismus*, Cologne and Frankfurt-on-Main, Bund-Verlag, 1977.

Bálla, Balint, *Kaderverwaltung. Versuch zur Idealtypisierung der 'Bürokratie' sowjetisch-volksdemokratischen Typus*, Stuttgart, Enke, 1972.

Barzel, Rainer, 'Zur Deutschlandpolitik der neuen Bundesregierung', *Texte zur Deutschlandpolitik*, Bundesministerium für innerdeutsche Beziehungen (ed.), Reihe III, Bd.1, Bonn, 1985.

Bauer, Tamas, 'Reforming or Perfecting the Economic Mechanism', *Social Research* **55**, 1988, No. 4, pp. 715–46.

Belwe, Katharina, *Psychosoziale Befindlichkeit der Menschen in den neuen Bundesländern nach der Wende im Herbst 1989*, Pressespiegel, Gesamtdeutsches Institut (eds), Bonn, 1991.

Benda, Ernst, '"Königsweg" oder "Holzweg". Professor Ernst Benda über verfassungsrechtliche Fragen der deutschen Vereinigung', *Der Spiegel*, No. 18, 30 April 1990, p. 75.

— 'Das letzte Wort dem Volke. Auch die ost-deutschen Bürger müssen sich unsere Verfassung zu eigen machen', *Die Zeit*, No. 38, 14 September 1990, p. 13.

'Bericht der Bundesregierung zur Lage der Nation im geteilten Deutschland', *Bulletin*, Presse- und Informationsamt der Bundesregierung (ed.), No. 123, 9 November 1989, p. 1059.

Beziehungen der Deutschen Demokratischen Republik zur Bundesrepublik Deutschland, Dokumente 1971–1988, Berlin, Staatsverlag, 1990.

Boveri, Margret, *Der Verrat im 20. Jahrhundert, I. Für und gegen die Nation. Das sichtbare Geschehen, II. Für und gegen die Nation. Das unsichtbare Geschehen*, Hamburg, Rowohlt, 1956.

Brandt, Peter and Ammon, Herbert (eds), *Die Linke und die nationale Frage. Dokumente zur deutschen Einheit seit 1945*, Reinbek, Rowohlt, 1981.

Brandt, Willy, 'Deutsche Wegmarken', *Der Tagesspiegel*, 13 September 1988, p. 9.

Bruns, Wilhelm, 'Die Regelung der äusseren Aspekte der deutschen Frage', *Deutschland Archiv*, **22**, 1990, No. 11, pp. 1726–32.

— *Von der Deutschland-Politik zur DDR-Politik? Prämissen, Probleme, Perspektiven*, Opladen, Leske & Budrich, 1989.

Bürger, Ulrich, *Das sagen wir natürlich so nicht! Donnerstag-Argus bei Herrn Geggel*, Berlin, Dietz, 1990.

'Christlich-demokratische Perspektiven zur Aussen-, Sicherheits-, Europa- und Deutschlandpolitik', *Frankfurter Allgemeine Zeitung*, 19 February 1988, p. 4.

Dahrendorf, Ralf, *Reflections on the Revolution in Europe*, London, Chatto and Windus, 1990.

Das deutsch–deutsche Treffen am Werbellinsee. Dokumentation zum Treffen des Bundeskanzlers der Bundesrepublik Deutschland, Helmut Schmidt, mit dem Generalsekretär des ZK der SED und Vorsitzenden des Staatsrates der DDR, Erich Honecker, vom 11. bis 13. Dezember 1981, Bundesministerium für innerdeutsche Beziehungen (ed.), Bonn, 1982.

Davy, Richard, 'Grossbritannien und die deutsche Frage, *Europa Archiv*, **45**, 1990, No. 4, pp. 139–44.

DDR. Gesellschaft Staat Bürger, 2. Aufl., Berlin (DDR), Staatsverlag, 1978.

Demokratie Jetzt. Dokumentation des Arbeitsbereichs DDR-Forschung und — Archiv (compiled by Helmut Müller-Enbergs), Berliner Arbeitshefte und Berichte zur sozialwissenschaftlichen Forschung, No. 19, Berlin, January 1990.

Deppe, Rainer, Dubiel, Helmut and Rödel, Ulrich (eds.),*Demokratischer Umbruch in Osteuropa*, Frankfurt-on-Main, Suhrkamp, 1991.

Der Besuch von Generalsekretär Honecker in der Bundesrepublik Deutschland. Dokumentation zum Arbeitsbesuch des Generalsekretärs der SED und Staatsratsvorsitzenden der DDR, Erich Honecker, in der Bundesrepublik Deutschland im September 1987, Bundeministerium für innerdeutsche Beziehungen (ed.), Bonn, 1988.

Dittmer, Lowell, 'Comparative Communist Political Culture', *Studies in Comparative Communism*, **16**, 1983, No. 1–2, pp. 9–24.

'"Eine eminente Fehlentscheidung". Interview mit Oskar Lafontaine', *Der Spiegel*, No. 22, 28 May 1990, pp. 26–8.

Ein Erfolg der Politik der Vernunft und des Realismus. Offizieller Besuch des Generalsekretärs des Zentralkomitees der Sozialistischen Einheitspartei Deutschlands und Vorsitzenden des Staatsrates der Deutschen Demokratischen Republik, Erich Honecker, in der Bundesrepublik Deutschland vom 7. bis 11. September 1987, Berlin (DDR), 1987.

Einführung in die marxistisch–leninistische Staats- und Rechtslehre, Akademie für Staats- und Rechtswissenschaft der DDR (eds.), 2. vollst. überarb. Aufl., Berlin (DDR), Staatsverlag, 1986.

Eisenmann, Peter, 'Die Jugend in den neuen Bundesländern. Sozialistische Bewusstseinsbildung und ihre Folgen', *Aus Politik und*

Zeitgeschichte, B 27/91, 29 June 1991, pp. 3–11.

'Erklärung der CDU–CSU-Bundestagsfraktion zur aktuellen Lage der Berlin- und Deutschlandpolitik in Berlin (West) am 19. Januar 1988', *Informationen*. Bundesministerium für innerdeutsche Beziehungen, (ed.), No. 2, 1988, Dokumentation, pp. 19–20.

Erste Beratung der Ostverträge im deutschen Bundestag am 23, 24, und 25. Februar 1972. Mit dem Bericht der Bundesregierung zur Lage der Nation, Presse- und Informationsamt der Bundesregierung (ed.), Bonn, 1972.

Falkner, Thomas, 'Von der SED zur PDS. Weitere Gedanken eines Beteiligten', *Deutschland Archiv*, **24**, 1991, No. 1, pp. 30–51.

Forschungsgruppe Wahlen, 'Wahl in den neuen Bundesländern. Eine Analyse der Landtagswahlen vom 14. Oktober 1990', *Berichte der Forschungsgruppe Wahlen, Mannheim*, No. 60, vom 14. October.

Friedrich, Carl Joachim (ed.), *Revolution*, New York, Atherton, 1966.

Fritsch-Bournazel, Renata, *Europa und die deutsche Einheit*, Bonn, Europa Verlag, 1990.

Fröhlich, Stefan, 'Umbruch in Europa. Die deutsche Frage und ihre sicherheitspolitischen Herausforderungen für die Siegermächte', *Aus Politik und Zeitgeschichte*, B 29/90, 13 July 1990, pp. 35–45.

Gasteyger, Curt, *Die beiden deutschen Staaten in der Weltpolitik*, Munich, Piper, 1976.

Gauck, Joachim, *Die Stasi-Akten. Das unheimliche Erbe der DDR*, Reinbek, Rowohlt, 1991.

Gaus, Günter, *Wo Deutschland liegt. Eine Ortsbestimmung*, Hamburg, Hoffmann und Campe, 1983.

Geiger, Wolfgang, '''Die Konturen des neuen Deutschland sind alles andere als klar . . .''. Frankreich und die Wiedervereinigung', *Die Neue Gesellschaft/Frankfurter Hefte*, **37**, 1990, No. 3, pp. 210–15.

— ''' Wenn Deutschland erwacht . . .''. Die deutsche Frage aus französischer Sicht, *Die Neue Gesellschaft/Frankfurter Hefte*, **37**, 1990, No. 1, pp. 63–8.

Geissler, Rainer, 'Soziale Ungleichheit zwischen Frauen und Männern im geteilten Deutschland', *Aus Politik und Zeitgeschichte*, B 14–15/91, 29 March 1991, pp. 13–24.

Gibowski, Wofgang G., 'Demokratischer (Neu-) Beginn in der DDR. Dokumentation und Analyse der Wahl vom 18. März 1990', *Zeitschrift für Parlamentsfragen*, **21**, 1990, No. 1, pp. 5–22.

Glaessner, Gert-Joachim, *Herrschaft durch Kader. Leitung der Gesellschaft und Kaderpolitik in der DDR am Beispiel des Staatsapparates*, Opladen, Westdeutscher Verlag, 1977.

— *Sozialististische Systeme. Einführung in die Kommunismus- und DDR-Forschung*, Opladen, Westdeutscher Verlag, 1982.

— 'Ende der Reformen? Bedingungen und Grenzen der Wandlungsfähigkeit sowjet-sozialistischer Systeme am Beispiel der DDR, *Deutschland Archiv*, **15**, 1982, No. 7, pp. 700–9.

— (ed.), *Die DDR in der Ära Honecker. Politik — Kultur — Gesellschaft*, Opladen, Westdeutscher Verlag, 1988.

— 'Vom ''realen Sozialismus'' zur Selbstbestimmung'. Ursachen und Konsequenzen der Systemkrise in der DDR, *Aus Politik und*

Zeitgeschichte, B 1–2/90, 5. January 1990, pp. 3–20.

— (ed.), *Eine deutsche Revolution. Der Umbruch in der DDR, seine Ursachen und Folgen*, Frankfurt-on-Main, Peter Lang, 1991.

— and Scherer, Klaus-Jürgen, *Auszug aus der Gesellschaft. Gemeinschaften zwischen Utopie, Reform und Reaktion*, Berlin, Verlag Europäische Perspektiven, 1986.

Gleserman, G. J., *Klassen und Nation*, Berlin (DDR), Dietz, 1975.

Glotz, Peter, 'Renaissance des Vorkriegsnationalismus?', *Die Neue Gesellschaft/Frankfurter Hefte*, **37**, 1990, No. 1, pp. 40–6.

Grundmann, Siegfried and Schmidt, Ines, *Wanderungsbewegungen in der DDR 1989*, Berliner Arbeitshefte und Berichte zur sozialwissenschaftlichen Forschung, No. 30, 1990.

— 'Aussen- und Binnenmigration der DDR 1989. Versuch einer Bilanz, *Deutschland Archiv*, **22**, 1990, No. 9, pp. 1422–32.

Gwertzman, Bernhard and Kaufman, Michael T. *The collapse of Communism*, New York, Random House, 1990.

Gysi, Gregor and Falkner, Thomas, *Sturm auf das grosse Haus. Der Untergang der SED*, Berlin, Edition Fischerinsel, 1990.

Habermas, Jürgen, *Die nachholende Revolution. Kleine politische Schriften VII*, Frankfurt-on-Main, Suhrkamp, 1990.

Haltzel, Michael H., 'Amerikanische Einstellungen zur deutschen Wiedervereinigung, *Europa Archiv*, **45**, 1990, No. 4, pp. 127–32.

Handbuch Deutsche Demokratische Republik, Lexikonred. d. VEB Bibliographisches Institut (ed.), Leipzig, 1984.

Hanke, Helmut, 'Kulturelle Traditionen des Sozialismus', *Zeitschrift für Geschichtswissenschaft*, **33**, 1985, No. 7, pp. 589–604.

Hanke, Irma, *Alltag und Politik. Zur politischen Kultur einer unpolitischen Gesellschaft. Eine Untersuchung zur erzählenden Gegenwartsliteratur in der DDR in den 70er Jahren*, Opladen, Westdeutscher Verlag, 1987.

Hanrieder, Wolfram F., *Deutschland, Europa, Amerika. Die Aussenpolitik der Bundesrepublik Deutschland 1949–1989*, Paderborn, Schöningh, 1991.

Havemann, Robert, *Dialektik ohne Dogma. Naturwissenschaft und Weltanschauung*, Reinbek, Rowohlt, 1964.

Hefty, Paul, 'Die Drohung des Artikels 146', *Frankfurter Allgemeine Zeitung*, No. 222, 24 September 1990, p. 1.

Hegedüs, Andràs, *Sozialismus und Bürokratie*, Reinbek, Rowohlt, 1981.

Henrich, Rolf, *Der vormundschaftliche Staat. Vom Versagen des real existierenden Sozialismus*, Reinbek, Rowohlt, 1989.

Herles, Helmut and Rose, Ewald (eds.), *Parlaments-Szenen einer deutschen Revolution. Bundestag und Volkskammer im November 1989*, Bonn, Bouvier, 1989.

— *Vom Runden Tisch zum Parlament*, Bonn, Bouvier, 1990.

Huntington, Samuel, *Political Order in Changing Societies*, New Haven, Yale University Press, 1968.

Ich liebe Euch doch alle! Befehle und Lageberichte des MfS Januar–November 1989, Armin Mitter and Stefan Wolles (eds.), Berlin, Basisdruck, 1990.

infas-Report Wahlen DDR 1990. Wahl der Volkskammer der DDR am 18. März 1990. Analysen und Dokumente, Bonn–Bad Godesberg, 1990.

Jancar, Barbara, 'Political Culture and Political Change', *Studies in*

Comparative Communism, **17**, 1984, No. 1, pp. 69–82.

Janka, Walter, *Schwierigkeiten mit der Wahrheit*, Reinbek, Rowohlt, 1990.

Jung, Matthias, 'Parteiensystem und Wahlen in der DDR. Eine Analyse der Volkskammerwahl vom 18. März 1990 und der Kommunalwahlen vom 6. Mai 1990', *Aus Politik und Zeitgeschichte*, B 27/90, 29 June 1990, pp. 3–15.

Just, Gustav, *Zeuge in eigener Sache. Die fünfziger Jahre*, Berlin, Buchverlag Der Morgen, 1990.

Kaiser, Karl, *Deutschlands Vereinigung. Die internationalen Aspekte*, Bergisch Gladbach, Bastei Lübbe, 1991.

Kielmansegg, Peter Graf, 'Entscheiden muss die Politik. Die Verfassung kann kein Regierungsprogramm sein, sie bestimmt nur die Regeln für den demokratischen Meinungsstreit', *Die Zeit*, No. 20, 10 May 1991, p. 8.

Kimmel, Michael S., *Revolution. A Sociological Interpretation*, Cambridge, Polity Press, 1990.

Kirchheimer, Otto, 'Der Wandel des europäischen Parteiensystems', *Politische Vierteljahresschrift*, **6**, 1965, No. 1, pp. 20–41.

Klages, Helmut, *Überlasteter Staat — verdrossene Bürger? Zu den Dissonanzen der Wohlfahrtsgesellschaft*, Frankfurt-on-Main, Campus, 1981.

Klaus, Georg, *Kybernetik und Gesellschaft*, Berlin (DDR), Deutscher Verlag der Wissenschaften, 1964 (3. bearb. u. erw. Aufl. 1973).

— *Kybernetik — eine neue Universalphilosophie der Gesellschaft?*, Berlin (DDR), Akademie-Verlag, 1973.

Kleines Politisches Wörterbuch, 4. Aufl., Berlin (DDR), Dietz, 1983.

Knabe, Hubertus, 'Politische Opposition in der DDR. Ursprünge, Programmatik, Perspektiven', *Aus Politik und Zeitgeschichte*, B 1–2/90, 5 January 1990, pp. 21–32.

Korbonski, Andrzej, 'The Politics of Economic Reforms in Eastern Europe: the Last Thirty Years', *Soviet Studies*, **XLI**, 1989, No. 1, pp. 11–19.

Kosing, Alfred, *Nation in Geschichte und Gegenwart. Studie zur historisch-materialistischen Theorie der Nation*, Berlin (DDR), Dietz, 1976.

Krenz, Egon, *Wenn Mauern fallen. Die Friedliche Revolution: Vorgeschichte — Ablauf — Auswirkungen*, Vienna, Paul Neff, 1990.

Krockow, Christian Graf von, *Nationalismus als deutsches Problem*, Munich, Piper, 1976.

Lange, Gerhard, 'Zur moralisch-politischen Erneuerung im Einigungsprozess', *Aus Politik und Zeitgeschichte*, B 19/91, 3 May 1991, pp. 11–20.

Lange, Klaus (ed.), *Aspekte der deutschen Frage*, Herford, Busse Seewald, 1986.

Lapp, Peter Joachim, 'Anspruch und Alltag der Volkskammer vor dem Umbruch 1989–90', *Zeitschrift für Parlamentsfragen*, **21**, 1990, No. 1, pp. 115–25.

Lehmann, Albrecht, *Studien zur Arbeiterkultur. Beiträge der 2. Arbeitstagung der Kommission 'Arbeiterkultur' in der Deutschen Gesellschaft für Volkskunde in Hamburg vom 8. bis 12. Mai 1983*, Münster, F. Coppenrath, 1984.

Leicht, Robert, 'Königsweg zur Einheit. Das Saarland als Beispiel: Wie ein abgestufter Beitritt zur Bundesrepublik gelang', *Die Zeit*, No. 10, 2 March 1990, p. 7.

Liebert, Ulrike and Merkel, Werner (eds.), *Die Politik zur deutschen Einheit. Probleme. Strategien. Kontroversen*, Leverkusen, Leske & Budrich, 1991.

Linz, Juan J., 'Totalitarian and Authoritarian Regimes', in Nelson Polsby and Fred Greenstein (eds.), *Handbook of Political Science*, Vol. III, Reading, Mass., Adison Wesley Press, 1975.

―――― 'Transitions to Democracy', *The Washington Quarterly*, Summer 1990, pp. 143–64.

'Löst sich die CDU von ihrer bisherigen Deutschlandpolitik?', *Frankfurter Allgemeine Zeitung*, 15 February 1988, pp. 1–2.

Löwenthal, Richard, *World Communism: the Disintegration of a Secular Faith*, Oxford, Oxford University Press, 1964.

Ludz, Peter Christian, *Parteielite im Wandel. Funktionsaufbau. Sozialstruktur und Ideologie der SED-Führung. Eine empirisch-systematische Untersuchung*, 3. Aufl., Cologne and Opladen, Westdeutscher Verlag, 1970.

Maaz, Hans-Joachim, 'Psychosoziale Aspekte im deutschen Einigungsprozess', *Aus Politik und Zeitgeschichte*, B 19/91, 3 May 1991, pp. 3–10.

Mann, Thomas, 'Goethe und die Demokratie', *Politische Schriften und Reden III*, Frankfurt-on-Main, Fischer, 1968.

Meier, Helmut and Schmidt, Walter, *Erbe und Tradition in der DDR. Eine Diskussion der Historiker*, Berlin (DDR), Akademie-Verlag, 1988.

Meinel, Reinhard and Wernicke, Thomas, *Mit tschekistischem Gruss. Berichte der Bezirksverwaltung für Staatssicherheit Potsdam 1989*, Potsdam, Edition Babelturm, 1990.

Mengel, Hans-Joachim, 'Keine Zeit für eine neue Verfassung? Der Einigungsprozess mit der DDR erschöpft sich im Transfer eines wirtschaftlichen Systems', *Frankfurter Rundschau*, No. 155, 7 July 1990, p. 5.

Meuschel, Sigrid, *Legitimation und Parteiherrschaft. Zum Paradox von Stabilität und Revolution in der DDR 1945–1989*, Frankfurt-on-Main, Suhrkamp, 1992.

Mitscherlich, Alexander and Margarete, *Die Unfähigkeit zu trauern. Grundlagen kollektiven Verhaltens*, Munich, Piper, 1977 (1st edition, 1967).

Modrow, Hans, *Aufbruch und Ende*, Hamburg, Konkret Literatur Verlag, 1991.

Müller-Enbergs, Helmut, 'Volkskammerwahlen in der DDR 1990 ― Synopse von (Wahl-)Programmen 15 kandidierender Parteien', *Berliner Arbeitshefte und Berichte zur sozialwissenschaftlichen Forschung*, No. 28, Berlin, 1990.

―, Schulz, Marianne and Wilgohs, Jan, *Von der Illegalität ins Parlament. Werdegang und Konzept der neuen Bürgerbewegungen*, Berlin, Links-Druck, 1991.

Müller-Gangloff, Erich, *Mit der Teilung leben. Eine gemeindeutsche Aufgabe*, Munich, List, 1965.

Negt, Oskar and Kluge, Alexander, *Geschichte und Eigensinn*, Frankfurt-on-Main, Zweitausendeins, 1981.

Neubert, Ehrhart, 'Protestantische Kultur und DDR-Revolution', *Aus Politik und Zeitgeschichte*, B 19/91, 3 May 1991, pp. 21–9.
— *Eine protestantische Revolution*, Osnabrück, Edition Kontext, 1990.
Neumann, Sigmund, 'The International Civil War', *World Politics*, **3**, 1949, No. 1, pp. 333–50.
New German Critique. Special Issue on German Unification, No. 52, Winter 1990.
Politische Parteien und Bewegungen der DDR über sich selbst. Handbuch, Berlin, Staatsverlag, 1990.
Pöhl, Karl Otto, 'Das Diktat der Stunde liess längeres Warten nicht zu. Zur Währungsunion — Die Sicht der Bundesbank', *Frankfurter Rundschau*, 4 July 1990, p. 6.
Pollack, Detlef (ed.), *Die Legitimität der Freiheit. Politisch alternative Gruppen in der DDR unter dem Dach der Kirche*, Frankfurt-on-Main, Peter Lang, 1990.
Pradetto, August, 'Zusammenbruch des "Realsozialismus", deutsche Einheit und europäische Integration', *Europäische Rundschau*, **13**, 1990, No. 4, pp. 45–62.
Preuss, Ulrich K., 'Auf der Suche nach der Zivilgesellschaft. Der Verfassungsentwurf des Runden Tisches', *Frankfurter Allgemeine Zeitung*, 28 April 1990.
— 'Grundgesetz-Chauvinismus oder . . .', *Die Tageszeitung*, 3 March 1990, p. 2.
— *Revolution, Fortschritt und Verfassung. Zu einem neuen Verfassungsverständnis*, Berlin, Wagenbach, 1990.
Probst, Lothar, 'Bürgerbewegungen, politische Kultur und Zivilgesellschaft', *Aus Politik und Zeitgeschichte*, B 19/91, 3 May 1991, pp. 30–5.
Przybylski, Peter, *Tatort Politbüro. Die Akte Honecker*, Berlin, Rowohlt, 1991.
Pye, Lucian and Verba, Sidney (eds), *Political Culture and Political Development*, Princeton, Princeton University Press, 1965.
'Regierungserklärung von Bundeskanzler Willy Brandt am 2. Oktober 1969', *Bulletin*, Presse- und Informationsamt der Bundesregierung (ed.), No. 132, 1969.
Reichel, Peter (ed.), *Politische Kultur in Westeuropa. Bürger und Staaten in der Europäischen Gemeinschaft*, Frankfurt-on-Main, Campus, 1984.
Rein, Gerhard (ed.), *Die Opposition in der DDR. Entwürfe für einen anderen Sozialismus*, Berlin, Wichern, 1989.
Ritter, Gerhard A. (ed.), *Arbeiterkultur*, Königstein/Ts., Anton Hain, 1979.
Roggemann, Herwig, 'Die Verfassungsentwicklung der deutschen Staaten auf dem Wege in die gesamtdeutsche Föderation, *Juristische Rundschau*, No. 7, 1990, pp. 265–72.
Saña, Heleno, *Das Vierte Reich. Deutschlands später Sieg*, Hamburg, Rasch und Röhrig, 1990.
Schabowski, Günter, *Das Politbüro. Ende eines Mythos. Eine Befragung*, Reinbek, Rowohlt, 1990.
Schelsky, Helmut, *Der Mensch in der wissenschaftlichen Zivilisation*, Cologne/Opladen, Westdeutscher Verlag, 1961.

Schmidt, Helmut, 'Einer unserer Brüder. Zum Besuch Erich Honeckers', *Die Zeit*, No. 31, 24 July 1987, p. 3.
— 'Was ist der Deutschen Vaterland? Ein endgültiger Verzicht auf die Einheit würde nur das Misstrauen unserer Nachbarn in Ost und West verstärken', *Die Zeit*, No. 29, 14 July 1989, p. 4.
Schmidt, Peter, 'Erster Parteitag der CDU Deutschlands in Hamburg', *Deutschland Archiv*, **22**, 1990, No. 11, pp. 1662–4.
Schmidt, Walter, *Nation und deutsche Geschichte in der bürgerlichen Ideologie der BRD*, Frankfurt-on-Main, Verlag Marxistische Blätter, 1980.
Schumann, Michael, 'Sozialistische Ideologie und Politik in unserer Epoche', *Staat und Recht*, **37**, 1988, No. 3, pp. 195–203.
Schüddekopf, Charles (ed.), *Wir sind das Volk! Flugschriften, Aufrufe und Texte einer deutschen Revolution*, Reinbek, Rowohlt, 1990.
Schütze, Walter, 'Frankreich angesichts der deutschen Einheit', *Europa Archiv*, **45**, 1990, No. 4, pp. 133–8.
Seifert, Jürgen, 'Ein blosser Beitritt wird der DDR nicht gerecht'. Verfassungsfragen der deutschen Einigung, *Frankfurter Rundschau*, 20 March 1990, p. 16.
Simon, Helmut, '''Vom deutschen Volk in freier Selbstbestimmung . . .'' Die geeinte Nation braucht ihre Verfassung', *Die Zeit*, No. 29, 13 July 1990, pp. 8–9.
Skocpol, Theda, *States and Social Revolutions*, New York, Cambridge University Press, 1979.
Sodaro, Michael J., *Moscow, Germany, and the West from Khrushev to Gorbachev*, Ithaca and London, Cornell University Press, 1990.
Sommer, Theo, 'Quo vadis, Germania? Eine Standortbestimmung der Bundesrepublik nach dem Besuch von Bush und Gorbatchow', *Die Zeit*, No. 26, 23 June 1989, p. 3.
Sozialismus und Nationen, Berlin (DDR), Dietz, 1976.
Starck, Christian, 'Das Grundgesetz für Deutschland — Schritt für Schritt. Beitritt der DDR oder ihrer Länder — die schonende Lösung der deutschen Frage', *Thüringer Tageblatt*, 3 May 1990, p. 4.
Stasi intern. Macht und Banalität, Bürgerkomitee Leipzig (ed.), Leipzig, Forum Verlag, 1991.
Statut der Sozialistischen Einheitspartei Deutschlands, Berlin (DDR), Dietz, 1976.
Stojanov, Christo, 'Das '' Immunsystem'' des ''real existierenden Sozialismus''', *Aus Politik und Zeitgeschichte*, B 19/91, 3 May 1991, pp. 36–46.
Strauss, Franz Josef, 'Die moralische Substanz der Nation bleibt erhalten. Beitrag von Franz Josef Strauss beim Münchner Podium 84 ''Reden über das eigene Land: Deutschland''', *Frankfurter Rundschau* (Dokumentation), 2 January 1985, p. 16.
'Der Streit der Ideologien und die gemeinsame Sicherheit', *Vorwärts*, No. 35, 29 August 1987, pp. 31–3.
Swoboda, Jörg (ed.), *Die Revolution der Kerzen. Christen in der Umwälzung der DDR*, Wuppertal and Kassel, Onkenverlag, 1990.
Synopse zur Deutschlandpolitik 1941–1973, Werner Weber and Werner, Jahn, (eds), Göttingen, Otto Schwartz, 1973.
Templin, Wolfgang, 'Eine bittere Lektion', *Bündnis 2000. Forum Für*

Demokratie, Ökologie und Menschenrechte, **1**, 1990, No. 1, pp. 7–9.

Texte zur Deutschlandpolitik, Bundesministerium für innerdeutsche Beziehungen (ed.), Reihe III, Bd. 5, 1987; Bd. 6, 1988.

Thaysen, Uwe, *Der Runde Tisch. Oder: Wo bleibt das Volk? Der Weg der DDR in die Demokratie*, Opladen, Westdeutscher Verlag, 1990.

Thies, Jochen and van Well, Günther (eds.), *Auf der Suche nach der Gestalt Europas. Festschrift für Wolfgang Wagner*, Bonn, Verlag für internationale Politik, 1990.

Ullmann, Wolfgang, 'Das Volk muss entscheiden. Das vereinte Deutschland braucht eine neue Verfassung', *Die Zeit*, No. 22, 24 May 1991, pp. 5–7.

Valance, Georges, *France – Allemagne. Le Retour de Bismarck*, Paris, Flammarion, 1990.

Vertrag zwischen der Bundesrepublik Deutschland und der Deutschen Demokratischen Republik über die Herstellung der Einheit Deutschlands — Einigungsvertrag — Bulletin Presse- und Informationsamt der Bundesregierung (ed.), No. 104, 6 September 1990, pp. 877–1120.

Die Verträge zur Einheit Deutschlands, Munich, Beck, 1990.

Weber, Max, *Wirtschaft und Gesellschaft. Grundrisse der verstehenden Soziologie*, 5. rev. Auflage, Tübingen, J.C.B. Mohr, 1972.

Weidenfeld, Werner (ed.), *Die Deutschen und die Architektur des Europäischen Hauses. Materialien zu den Perspektiven Deutschlands*. Cologne, Verlag Wissenschaft und Politik, 1991.

Weston, Charles, 'Die USA und der politische Wandel in Europa', *Aus Politik und Zeitgeschichte*, B 49/90, 30 November 1990, pp. 28–36.

Wickert, Ulrich (ed.), *Angst vor Deutschland?*, Hamburg, Hoffmann und Campe, 1990.

Wilms, Dorothee, 'Deutschlandpolitik im Rahmen der europäischen Einigung' (Rede vor dem Institut Francais des Relations Internationales am 25. Januar 1988 in Paris), *Texte zur Deutschlandpolitik*, Bundesministerium für innerdeutsche Beziehungen (ed.), Reihe III, Bd. 6, 1988, Bonn, 1989, pp. 22–36.

— 'Probleme und Perspektiven der Deutschlandpolitik' (Rede vor dem deutschlandpolitischen Forum der Friedrich-Ebert-Stiftung in Bonn am 24. Januar 1989), in *Informationen*, Bundesministerium für innerdeutsche Beziehungen (ed.), Nr. 3/1989, Dokumentation.

Wingen, Max, 'Familien im gesellschaftlichen Wandel: Herausforderungen an eine künftige Familienpolitik im geeinten Deutschland', *Aus Politik und Zeitgeschichte*, B 14–15/91, 29 March 1991, pp. 3–12.

Winter, Martin, 'Ein ostpolitisches Godesberg auf Raten. Heiner Geissler, die CDU und die Formulierung christdemokratischer Deutschlandpolitik', *Frankfurter Rundschau*, 19 February, 1988, p. 3.

Wir treten aus unseren Rollen heraus. Dokumente des Aufbruchs Herbst '89, Berlin, Zentrum für Theaterdokumentation und -information, 1990.

Wörterbuch des wissenschaftlichen Kommunismus, Berlin (DDR), Dietz, 1982.

Wörterbuch zum sozialistischen Staat, Berlin (DDR), Dietz, 1974.

Wuttke, Carola and Musiolek, Berndt (eds), *Parteien und Politische Bewegungen im letzten Jahr der DDR*, Berlin, Basis Druck, 1991.

Documents

Sources

Doc. 1–8: *Oktober 1989. Wider den Schlaf der Vernunft*, Berlin, Neues
Leben/Temperamente 1990, Elefanten Press Verlag, 1989.
Doc. 9: Programme of the Party of Democratic Socialism adopted at the
Election Party Congress, 25 February 1990.
Doc. 10: Charter of Paris for a new Europe, Paris, 1990.
Doc. 11: *Europäische Zeitung*, December, 1989.
Doc. 12–18: *The Unification of Germany in 1990. A Documentation*,
published by the Press and Information Office of the Federal Govern-
ment, Bonn, 1991.
Doc. 19: Various newspapers.

The citizens' movements

Document 1 Awakening 89

NEW FORUM

In our country there is a clear breakdown in communication between state and society. This is confirmed by widespread disaffection and retreat into the private sphere or mass exodus. Refugee movements on this scale are usually caused by want, starvation and violence. That clearly cannot be true of the GDR.

The damaged relationship between state and society paralyses the creative forces of our society and prevents solutions being found to the problems we face at local and global level. We squander our energies in bad-tempered passivity when we have more important things to do for our lives, our country and humanity. The reconciliation of interests between groups and social divisions in state and the economy is not working properly. In addition, public communication about the situation and personal interests is repressed. In private, everyone readily offers a diagnosis and discusses the most important measures to be taken, but their wishes and efforts differ widely and are neither weighed up rationally nor assessed for their practicability. On the one hand we want a broader choice of goods and a better supply; on the other we see the social and environmental costs of these measures and call for an end to unrestrained growth. We want scope for economic initiative without this degenerating into a rat-race. We want to hold on to what has been successful while creating space for renewal so that we can live less wasteful and environmentally destructive lives. We want ordered relations but not state diktat. We want free, confident people who also act with a sense of community. We want to be protected against violence without having to face a society of henchmen and informers. Idlers and armchair heroes should be driven from their privileged positions without placing the socially weak and defenceless at a disadvantage. We want an effective health system for all, but no one should be allowed to feign illness at the expense of others. We want to export and participate in international trade without becoming either the debtor or servant of the leading industrial nations or the exploiter and creditor of the economically weaker ones.

If we are to recognise all these contradictions, listen to and assess opinions and arguments and distinguish general from particular interests, we need a *democratic dialogue* about the role of the rule of law, the economy and culture. We must carefully consider and debate these questions publicly, *together*, the *length and breadth of the country*. The readiness and will to achieve this will depend on our ability to find a way out of the present critical situation in the foreseeable future. In the circumstances of current social developments we need

— the participation of more people in the process of social reform,
— the pooling of the many individual and group efforts.

To this end we hereby found a *political platform* for the whole of the GDR which will enable people from all professions, backgrounds, parties and groups to play a role in the discussion and resolution of social problems which is vital to this country. We choose to give this overarching initiative the name NEW FORUM.

We shall place the activities of NEW FORUM on a legal basis in accordance with the basic right enshrined in Article 29 of the Constitution of the GDR to articulate our political interest by common action as an association. We shall register the creation of such an association with the responsible organs of state of the GDR in accordance with the Constitutional Order of 6 November 1975 (*Legal Gazette I*, No. 44, p. 723).

Any effort to give NEW FORUM expression and a voice is based on the quest for justice, democracy, peace and the protection of our natural world. It is this impulse we wish to see fulfilled in all areas in the coming transformation of society. We appeal to all the citizens of the GDR eager to participate in a transformation of society to join NEW FORUM. The time is ripe.

September 1989

Document 2 Appeal for intervention in our own affairs

Democracy Now

Friends, citizens and affected parties:

Our country lives in internal discontent. Some people grieve over prevailing relations and others resign themselves. The country at large is losing its faith in what had historically developed in the GDR; many are no longer able to accept the fact that they are here; many are leaving because conformism has its limits.

As recently as a few years ago 'real existing' state socialism was seen to be the only possible variety. It is characterised by the monopoly power of a central state party, state ownership of the means of production, a society made uniform by an all-pervading state and the regimentation of a great many citizens. Despite its undoubted achievements in terms of social security and justice, it is now clear that the era of state socialism is nearing its end. It needs a peaceful, democratic renewal.

Gorbachev's personal initiative has introduced and encouraged the Soviet Union, Hungary and Poland to pursue the path of democratic transformation. They face enormous economic, social, environmental and ethnic problems which could lead this transformation to catastrophe with grave consequences for the entire world. The efforts of the socialist workers' movement in social justice and solidarity are at stake. Socialism must now discover its true, democratic form if it is not to be lost forever. It cannot be allowed to disappear because humanity, faced with its own extinction and in the search for lasting forms of coexistence, needs alternatives to Western consumer society whose prosperity is paid for by the rest of the world.

Contrary to propaganda the political, economic and environmental signs of the crisis of state socialism are plain to see — even in 'the colours of the GDR'. But nothing has suggested that the SED leadership is prepared to reconsider. Instead, it seems to be speculating about the collapse of the reform process in the Soviet Union. But the objective is to help achieve this democratic transformation.

The political crisis of state socialism became especially clear in the local elections of 7 May 1989. The doctrine of the 'moral and political unity of Party, State and People', which was taken to justify the exemption of the all-powerful SED from a due election process, could be protected from exposure by ballot-rigging. Between 10 and 20 per cent of the population in big cities openly refused to vote for the candidate of the National Front. There can be no doubt that the number would have been much higher in secret elections.

The National Front no longer represents so many people. In fact, they now have no political representation in society. The support felt by many citizens for a democratisation of the relationship between state and society still cannot be stated in openly in the GDR. For this reason we now call for the creation of the

Citizens' Movement 'DEMOCRACY NOW'.

We appeal to everyone who is affected by the plight of this country. We invite all initiatives with similar aims to come together. In particular we want an alliance of Christians and critical Marxists. Let us think together about our future, about the solidarity of a society in which

— social justice, freedom and human dignity are guaranteed to all,
— social consensus is sought through public dialogue and achieved through the just reconciliation of different interests,
— the free and creative efforts of our citizens create a living pluralism in our society,
— internal peace is secured by the rule of law and the upholding of that law,
— economy and ecology are brought into harmony,
— prosperity is no longer accumulated at the cost of the poor countries,
— people can fulfil their lives through community spirit and creativity for the common good can be explored and realised.

We invite everyone who is interested in participating to a dialogue about principles and ideas for a democratic transformation of our country. In January or February 1990 we intend to invite interested participants to a meeting of representatives which would agree on a statement of principles and elect the speakers who could introduce this programme into the dialogue of all social forces so urgently needed.

We hope to be able to draw up our own lists of candidates for the forthcoming elections to the *Volkskammer.* (extract)

Berlin, 12 September 1989

Document 3 Democratic Awakening — social, ecological (DA)
Association of Democratic Initiatives

With the following statement of aims the association Democratic Awakening — social, ecological (DA) puts forward a basis for political agreement among its members. This declaration of political will is at the same time a public invitation to a debate about the objectives of a social reorientation of the German Democratic Republic. The DA sees itself as part of the broad and non-violent reform movement for democracy in the GDR and appeals to all reformist forces for solidarity. Democratic Awakening will align itself with other reformist forces irrespective of their ideological and religious origins and irrespective of their political stance provided basic agreement in democratic, social, ecological and non-violent principles can be achieved. The diversity of the reformist movement is in keeping with the programme of Democratic Awakening and is seen as an important part of the democratisation now underway. For this reason the high degree of cohesion sought within the DA and reflected in its internal form of democratic organisation does not preclude the formation of factions.

The political demands and aims of Democratic Awakening are irrevocably linked to profound hopes for the creation of a Common European Home, a European peace order and a more just world. At the same time the DA accepts the specific historical circumstances which apply to the GDR. At present this means emphasising the inviolability of frontiers in Central Europe, GDR membership of the Warsaw Treaty and a number of other international commitments. In addition the DA views disarmament policy, the CSCE process and the reform movements in the other socialist countries as political instruments which could secure for the GDR its deserved place in the world community and also determine the political culture and practice within our own frontiers.

In view of the special relationship of the GDR towards its Eastern neighbours, forged by wartime and post-war history, Democratic Awakening is committed to anti-Fascism and anti-militarism. In the context of the reform process in Eastern Europe, anti-Stalinism has also become clearer. By its activities, the DA would like to help to ensure that relations with our Eastern neighbours not only take place at government or opposition level but that they also lead to a widespread meeting of peoples.

The DA attaches particular significance to the special relationship with the Federal Republic which results from a shared German history and culture. In addition the DA takes account of the ties of family and friendship which link millions of citizens across borders. However, any potential confederation of the two German states can only come about in the context of a European peace order'

Although 'Democratic Awakening' takes a critical view of much in real existing socialism, this does not mean that it rejects in principle the vision of a socialist social order. But the DA distinguishes between the lasting values, just motives and viable theories of socialism and the undemocratic claims of the Socialist Unity Party in the name of socialism to possess a monopoly of trans-historical truth and immutably correct policies.

For this reason the genuine and successful socialist achievements in the GDR must be discussed, upheld and further developed. For the sake of an active political polity, banal and sanctimonious criticisms must be avoided. But Democratic Awakening holds the SED and its uncritical allies publicly responsible for the dangerous political, economic, social and environmental situation in the GDR. These crises have led to a crisis of credibility in 'socialism' and harmed the reputation of the GDR abroad.

Therefore Democratic Awakening joins other reformist forces in the GDR in assuming the role of a democratic opposition. The political objective is a democratic, social and ecological society which furthers the socialist tradition.

1. Democratic society requires:
1.1 The separation of state and party/ies!
   The state and the state apparatus must be de-ideologised as far as possible. State organisations, institutions, administration and organs and bodies of public law cannot be exposed to the unaccountable influence of party or parties. This is particularly true for schools and the entire training system, for the security forces, the military and the economy.
1.2 The development of a free public domain and unimpeded access for all to this domain.
   All forms of public expression (media, art, religion etc.) cannot be subject to state control. Their institutional independence must be guaranteed. The public domain must become a social and moral means by which society can control and evaluate itself.
1.3 The free formation of will and the public expression of political will by political means!
   The creation of parties, independent trade unions and other associations must be made possible. There must be free and unimpeded preparation for and execution of free and secret elections as a basic principle of political democratisation.
1.4 Control of the state and its administrative organs!
   Executive and legislature must be separated at all levels. In addition, the system of administrative courts must be completed. New constitutional courts must be set up.
1.5 Administrative reform!
   The natural and historically inherited regions of the GDR must once again become administrative units (for example Saxony, Thuringia, Berlin etc.). A constitution based on a federal state (based for example on the Austrian, Swiss or West German model) is to be created.
1.6 Respect for the independent minds of citizens!
   Conditions must be created for all individual rights and opportunities for the development of the individual. (Cf. CSCE accords and Marx and Engels' *Communist Manifesto*: '. . . the free development of the individual [is] the condition for the free development of

all . . ./MEW Bd. 4, S. 482). Permanent rules are required in particular for the right to freedom of movement and unimpeded exit and entry from the country.

The citizens can longer be dictated to. Bureaucracy must be rolled back in all areas.

1.7 Development of political self-organisation at every level (local, regional, national)!

Citizens' initiatives, political-group activities in the workplace and the neighbourhood and forms of direct democracy such as referenda must become a part of the democratic system.

2. A truly social society requires:

2.1 Priority given to the value of equality in the socialist tradition!

In its promotion of individual and collective performance, society must be understood to be an unshakeable community of solidarity. Equality is a goal for the whole of society and a constant objective. Accordingly, the distribution of material goods and services must be democratised. The different and hierarchical distribution system (Intershop, Delikat, Exquisit, normal consumption, consumer privileges for party cadres) must be abolished. This means that a product-based distribution system must give way to a people-based social system (higher pensions and a minimum wage).

2.2 Expansion of the welfare system!

We cannot allow the emergence of a 'new poverty' caused by weak performance. The standardised state provisions must be complemented by an additional system for individual self-help. The socially weak (so-called 'asocial persons') would no longer be viewed as criminals.

2.3 A social basis for property!

The proliferation of different forms of ownership should be promoted in terms of sociability, that is towards the greater effect of the participation of many in profit and ownership. State-owned means of production must give way to socially owned means of production, and for all forms of property ownership forms of codetermination are to be developed.

2.4 Expansion of house-building!

Social communication must be improved by widening the range of housing standards available. The building of new socially owned housing must be expanded. The renovation of old cities and a reappraisal of urban and rural planning and building is to proceed with the objective of increased opportunity for communication.

2.5 Development of the health system!

The assessment of sickness or health must not be determined by ability to pay. Wider socio-psychological criteria are to be considered here. Motivation for employment in nursing must be enhanced by reversing the in-built advantages of industry and administration over the health system. The development of non-technological procedures for diagnosis and therapy must be accelerated.

2.6 Reorganisation of penal courts!

The basis for a reform of the penal justice system must be formed by overcoming the demands of state and society for atonement. Instead, integrative models should predominate as a higher form of 'justice' and 'punishment' per se should be severely limited.

2.7 Promotion of independent social organisation!

Effective independent social organisation should be evolved by the promotion of self-help groups, social integration initiatives, interest communities, professional associations, and trade unions.

In the context of independent social organisation, flexible forms of resistance against new forms of rule in industrial society must be tested (for example data protection).

3. An ecological society needs:

3.1 A step-by-step restructuring of industrial society!

Unit production costs must include environmental costs (social costs). This will also bring pressure to bear on greater product and process innovation and open up new markets. Good products and good technologies are environment and consumer friendly.

3.2 Saving energy and resources!

In addition to special technologies, renewable energy sources and structural changes in the economy dealing with the closed circulation of raw-materials will also lead to environmental gains. For this reason small and medium-sized economic units (decentralisation of agriculture and energy production) should be redeveloped with the environment in mind.

3.3 Changes in consumer habits!

Public and private consumption originate with value beliefs, which are changeable and which require spiritual and cultural awareness. For example, a reduction in the high meat consumption dangerous to health and the environment can be achieved through appropriate information campaigns and improved opportunities for a vegetarian diet. Public consumption should be subject to democratic control.

3.4 Reduction and conversion of armaments and the military!

The production of armaments and the maintenance of an army should be viewed as the destruction of labour and material. By means of disarmament and the systmatic conversion to defensive strategies, social and environmental savings can be made.

3.5 Promotion of independent environmental organisations!

The urgency of environmental restructuring has already galvanised a large number of private and collective initiatives. They should be encouraged and supported. All environmental questions should be treated with the highest possible degree of public openness.

September 1989

Document 4 Joint declaration

The citizens' movement Democracy Now
Democratic Awakening
The Group of Democratic Socialists
Initiative for Peace and Human Rights
Initiative Group for a Social Democratic Party in the GDR
New Forum
and representatives of peace groups

On 4 October 1989 representatives of the above groups met to discuss the possibilities for joint political action.

We welcome the growing diversity of initiatives as a sign of an awakening and of a growing courage to voice independent political ideas in public. We share the will to achieve a democratic transformation of state and society. We need to end a situation in which citizens of this society do not have the opportunities to exercise their political rights in the way demanded by the United Nations Convention on Human Rights and CSCE documents.

We declare our solidarity with all those who have been persecuted for their support of these aims. We call for the release of prisoners, repeal of past sentences and a stop to inquiries underway.

We believe it is imperative to start a debate in this country about the minimum conditions which must be met before democratic elections can take place: They must offer a range of different candidates. They must be secret (voters must use a booth). They must be free: no one must be pressurised into making a particular decision.

The next elections should take place under the auspices of the UN. We want to work with observers and see how we can form an electoral alliance with our own joint candidates.

Political change in our country requires the participation and criticism of everyone. We appeal to all the citizens of the GDR to participate in the process of democratic renewal.

Angelika Barbe (Initiative Group SDP); Marianne Birthler (Initiative for Peace and Human Rights); Ibrahim M. Boehme (Initiative Group SDP); Rainer Eppelmann (Democratic Awakening); Martin Gutzeit (Initiative Group SDP); Barbara Haenchen (Peace Circle Pankow); Heinz Kuechler (Democracy Now); Kathrin Menge (New Forum); Rudi Pahnke (Democratic Awakening); Sebastian Pflugbeil (New Forum); Gerd Poppe (Initiative for Peace and Human Rights); Ulrike Poppe (Democracy Now); Werner Schulz (Peace Circle Pankow); Dr Wolfgang Ullmann (Democracy Now); Reinhard Weidauer (Democratic Awakening) and a representative of the Group of Democratic Socialists

Berlin 4 October 1989

Document 5 Resolution

of a meeting of Berlin stage workers and guests from all other GDR theatres on 15 October 1989 in the Deutsches Theatre, Berlin. Adopted with 700 signatures.

We, the participants of the meeting of Berlin theatre workers, condemn in the strongest possible terms the unlawful and inhumane treatment by the police of hundreds of citizens who were rounded up on 7, 8 and 9 October. They were forced to stand to attention for hours with their faces to the wall, some of them undressed. They were denied sleep by threat of force. They were verbally abused. Some sustained injuries.

This treatment wholly contravenes the norms of the socialist rule of law. In addition, it bears no relation whatsoever to the alleged reasons for the round-up which in almost every case resulted in either a fine or release without charge. We call for a public inquiry into these events. We demand a statement from the Minister of the Interior and the Minister of State Security and punishment of those responsible.

We call on the union to support the rights of the people involved, some of whom are our colleagues.

Berlin, 15 October 1989

Document 6 Speeches by Joachim Walther and Volker Braun at a demonstration in Berlin

When, eighteen years ago, smoke rose from the chimney of the Great House we were granted a new General Secretary and I was twenty-eight. Many people wanted be believe the new man. He encouraged free expression, but it soon became clear that he did not really mean what he had said: public criticism remained unwelcome. He proclaimed that from now on there would be no taboos for art and literature, but we still faced bans, censorship and gagging. He spoke of the bond between art and the people, fidelity to real life, realism in politics and liked to view his people from platforms as, carefully drilled, they 'spontaneously' cheered when passing. He boldly promised the citizens an accessible bureaucracy, but this was a verbal squaring of the circle because every bureaucratic rule tends towards leading a life of its own and because the word 'secretary', for instance, comes from the Latin *secretus* which means isolated or secret. In the end he retreated into spheres where the people, that vulgar herd, also known as 'the masses', could not follow him; and while he added three elastic paragraphs to the penal code, he smugly reminded his people that they had never before breathed so freely as they were doing here and now under his leadership. We have, he went on, already had democracy — the socialist one — and gave the example of kitchen commissions. The statistics produced growth figures which swelled quickly at the top, while the real shortcomings stayed at the bottom and grew. Banners instead of openness; slogans, not solutions. All this is history, but is also part of our lives.

When on Wednesday of last week smoke rose from the chimney of the Great House, we were granted a new General Secretary and I was forty-six. The new man speaks of truthful media, of dialogue without taboos and realism in politics. Not yet enough, but some things are better, especially one point: a great many are eighteen years the wiser. This time they don't just want to have to believe the new man, don't only want to be allowed to hope, they do not request, they demand freedom of opinion, freedom of information, free elections. And they are quick to distrust empty phrases like: more effective development of socialist democracy. *More* effective: as if to say it had already existed. The old apparatus reaches for the powder puff and rejuvenates its grey cheeks. But this time we can see that many are not prepared to be appeased by cosmetics but ask questions: about the structure of the State. They ask peacefully on the streets and doggedly in discussion so that in future they can do more than simply believe or hope. They want to exercise control and no longer simply trust; they want to choose — which presupposes selection and dismissal. And in so doing they demonstrate to the once all-powerful patriarch what he is without his children who have long grown up and found their own minds: a lonely and powerless *homo hierarchicus*. Now he has the opportunity to get off his throne and change from a rigid skeleton into a living being. Down here, we stand ready to offer him a warm welcome.

Joachim Walther, Berlin, 4 November 1989

Author's note — Joachim Walther (b. 1943), poet, novelist. 1990 deputy chairman of the writer's union of the GDR.

Volker Braun

Against the sleep of reason, first I'll read a poem.

Awoken from dogmatic slumber,
You used the night,
I trained in the expectation, of which,
You too know that sweet pain, The unknown are loving,
The unknown fact, how, what are you saying,
My veins almost exploded in my flesh,
How weary am I of crossing the Markus Square,
You dream don't you, you dream with resolve and on the streets
    openness lives.

I wrote the following short texts in commemoration of the Prague Spring and in the expectation of change.

Yesterday the Spring was a scandal. Today the Summer is just right. Once the river ran into sand, now the floods enter our sight. The *Wende* — that unexpected offshore breeze in the corridors of smashed writing desks, the blood which the newspapers and the glory and hunger vomit, and history turns on a peg, for a moment decided.

Change of Decoration*
The administration explains to me that it has long completed rebuilding quite unnoticed, but the house is no roomier, the staircase uncomfortable. And are the small rooms any brighter? And why are people moving out and not in?

Eurasian Teachings
When the Great Wall stood the people began to walk.
The peasant to his ox seventy years after October: Exalted one, you have filled my stable with shit. Your strength is no longer my gain, now I will slaughter you for a tractor.

The Sound Warriors
From the bunkers under Tiananmen Square the armoured cars drive into the crowd. The age-old practice of the age-old party.

Volker Braun, Berlin, 4 November 1989

Author's note — Volker Braun (b. 1939), poet, playwright, novelist, essayist. Collected works published by Suhrkamp Verlag and Mitteldeutscher Verlag 1990–1. * *Tapetenwechsel*. When questioned about *Glasnost* and *Perestroika* in an interview in 1987 the then ideology secretary of the SED, Kurt Hager, compared changes in the Soviet Union with redecoration. He added that such redecoration in itself did not require the GDR to follow suit.

Declarations by the new parties

Document 7 The Social Democratic Party in the German Democratic Republic (SDP)

Fellow citizens of the GDR,

On 7 October 1989 in Schwante in the Oranienburg district we took our rightful place in the political life of our country. We believe that changes in our circumstances can only be achieved by the citizens themselves. Our aim is to create an environmentally minded social democracy.

— **Environmental** because the preservation of our natural environment is the sole basis for our future development.
— **Social** because true freedom is possible only among equals, and social wealth must therefore be justly distributed.
— **Democratic** because we are convinced that a polity can only survive if all its citizens are equally entitled to help create a peaceful political life.

We want to establish a state based on the rule of law

— in which no citizen need be afraid to express publicly his own opinion,
— in which no cunning system of reward and punishment trains people to be loyal subjects,
— which exists from the right of its citizens to decide for themselves.

With these aims we remain faithful to the traditions of democratic socialism. We call for an economic order that promotes not hinders people's initiative and performance. To this end we seek economic reforms in which private and public forms of ownership coexist and in which fair competition strengthens performance.

Fellow citizens, We will welcome anyone who hears an echo of his or her own political aims here. If there is not yet any local SDP in your area get in touch with the nearest contact address. If there really is no local party yet, form your own with likeminded people. Suggestions about organisation are enclosed in the statutes.

What should the local association do?

They should:

— create a democratically elected leadership structure;
— list regional problems and seek possible solutions;

— look for practicable solutions together as a local SDP;
— seek contact with neighbouring local parties or assist in their formation.

We believe that politics will be changed by the contribution of many; for this reason we shall soon meet in public at our first full Party Congress.

Executive of the SDP, Berlin, 14 October 1989

Document 8 Initiative to set up a Green Party in the GDR

The transformation of our destroyed environment is fundamental to the renewal of our society. But it is not only the environment which is contaminated; our consciousness is contaminated to a much greater degree by the utopian view that continually rising prosperity and therefore permanent economic growth can be made objective of social development. Such a utopia implies that human beings can move about at will in the life system we call earth. It even makes the arrogant presumption that we can subject the earth to our will.

This is linked to the belief that performance and its reward are the central measurement of human existence. The arrogance of this presumption drives the weak to the very edge of their existence. In fact, it increasingly pushes them over that edge. Thus, it is irrelevant if they die without dignity and company in a nursing home or if they are shovelled into the mass graves of the Third World or become exhibits in a museum for extinct plant and animal species. This kind of contaminated consciousness has now logically introduced the potential destruction of all life, a possibility for the first time in history.

We are therefore acting out of pure self-preservation when we put an end to the process and this consciousness we have all helped to create. For this reason the Green Party will give our ecological worldview political force in GDR society by making it the unconditional basis for all our efforts.

As an initiative we have passed the following FOUNDING AIMS FOR THE GREEN PARTY IN THE GDR: The Green Party in the GDR sides with all the forces which advocate democracy and freedom by far-reaching reforms in our country. This party is ecological, feminist and non-violent.

THE MAIN AIMS OF THE GREEN PARTY ARE:

A systematic ecological reform of our country as part of a radical renunciation of growth based on environmental destruction and the squandering of raw materials and the Stalinist treatment of people, the economy and the environment. Immediate action must be taken in the environmental disaster zones in the Leipzig – Bitterfield – Halle, Dresden – Karl-Marx-Stadt and Cottbus areas and in rescuing many historical old towns, countryside and castles, for example in Mecklenburg.

The final safeguarding of peace by general and complete disarmament. The dissolution of the two military blocs, reduction of the NVA to the lowest necessary defensive level and the abolition of military exclusion zones is a compelling need for peace and the environment. We reject violence, national chauvinism and racism and are resolute in our anti-Fascism.

The unqualified equality between women and men at all economic and political levels — from local peoples' assemblies to the composition of the State Council which continue to constitute overwhelmingly patriarchal institutions. Here, women as mothers shall enjoy preferential status.

The natural world is to be protected for its own sake from the unrestricted development of human beings. Only in this way can it become the basis for human community and culture. In consequence in each economic activity we should ask ourselves: where, for whom, why?

The GREEN PARTY subscribes in principle to LASTING DEVELOP-MENT.
First and foremost we want to prevent the current movement for renewal in our country from succumbing to the pressure of irrational, shortsighted and material compensation and becoming a free-for-all society of waste with a throwaway mentality.

We consider an ecological orientation at all levels of education to be an urgent necessity, for example the introduction of environmental and peace studies. Acting on the basis of the existing GDR constitution we advocate constitutional reform.

We demand that the activities of the GREEN PARTY in the GDR shall not be subject to obstruction by the state.

We will work together with all citizens, organisations and groupings on projects — both national and international — which support, even in part, our beliefs.

As part of the movement of the European Greens we advocate just distribution structures which will guarantee a LASTING DEVELOP-MENT to the peoples of the Third World and help to prevent a collapse of the global ecosystem. We promote cross-border partnership in the joint ecological reform of environmental disaster areas.

With our belief in the fundamental change in our country we appeal to all interested citizens, irrespective of beliefs, religion or nationality. Out of concern for the catastrophic developments in our environment, responsibility for our children and the generations still unborn, join together at local regional level to form grassroots groups of the GREEN PARTY of the GDR. Elect speakers, draft proposals for the manifesto and the grassroots organisation. Elaborate a realistic assessment of the current situation in order to plan ALTERNATIVE STRATEGIES for your district, towns, regions and the whole GDR, formulate creative and prac-ticable proposals for the ecological transformation of society. Start with demonstrations!

The first plenary assembly which will decide on the manifesto, struc-ture and composition of the GREEN PARTY in the GDR will take place in early 1990 in one of the areas most seriously affected by environmen-tal destruction in the GDR.

FOR A GREEN REVOLUTION — THE GREEN PARTY!

Berlin, 5 November 1989

Document 9 Programme of the Party of Democratic Socialism

Our values
The values our party is committed to are:

1. *Individuality.* This includes the free development of thought and feeling, the abilities and talents of everybody, the implementation of
   individual aspirations and endeavours, rich social relations with other
   people, and independence in judgement and action of each
   individual.
2. *Solidarity.* We want to develop and shape solidarity among the working people, the generations, the sexes, the people, nations and
   nationalities.
3. *Justice.* Everybody, each social and national group, each democratic
   political force shall have the same chances and the same rights to
   represent their interests in society.
4. *Meaningful work and leisure time.* This presupposes efficient working
   conditions, gradual reduction and flexibility of working time in the
   interest of the employees and a work content which promotes the
   personality of the worker. There must be more possibilities to make
   creative use of leisure time according to one's wishes and so find the
   rest, relaxation, and stimulation necessary for the well-being and
   development of mankind.
5. *Freedom, democracy, and human rights.* Respect for the dignity and
   freedom of each individual is indispensable to life in a democratic
   society. For us, the human rights in their unity and universality are
   the decisive yardstick for all actions in society.
6. *Preservation of the natural foundations of life.* The existence of each
   individual depends on this. For this reason, economy and ecology
   must be connected with each other in a new way in the overall social
   reproduction process as well as on an international scale. Needs and
   life-style must be oriented to a healthy and attractive environment so
   as to preserve it for future generations.
7. *National and international peace.* A political life marked by non-violence,
   tolerance, mutual respect of all social groups, of sexes, generations,
   and nationalities, by dialogue and creative debates, love and peace,
   humanism, anti-Fascism, international friendship and by respect for
   other cultures is indispensable to the safeguarding of peace in our
   society and in all nations.

Our aims
We pursue a left-wing, socialist policy and stand for

— freedom for everybody to develop;
— a modern state under the rule of law, where individual and political
  as well as social, cultural, and collective human rights are put into
  practice;
— a market economy with a high degree of social and ecological

security, equal chances and personal freedom for all members of society;
— real social equality for men and women and a new way of their living together;
— a society which provides warmth, protection and assistance for children, senior citizens, handicapped, and all people with special needs;
— unbureaucratic structures and self-determined development for communities;
— broad possibilities for the political, professional and cultural development of young people;
— a society with a culture where the individual can develop, where science, education, culture and sports develop freely and are accessible to all people;
— peace, general and complete disarmament, cosmopolitan attitudes, friendship and solidarity with all nations, for a just international economic order and for the respect of the right to self-determination for all peoples.

To realise these aims we strive for a democratic socialism together with other left-wing and democratic forces.

Democratic socialism means to fight for a peaceful, humane society marked by solidarity, where everybody can freely develop alongside everybody else and all enjoy equal participation in economic, political, intellectual and cultural life.

Democratic socialism is not yet a completed system nor is it a social system which will soon exist on German soil. It is a road, a permanent task and challenge.

Berlin, 25 February 1990

The international aspects of German unity

Document 10 A New Era of Democracy, Peace and Unity — Charter of Paris for a new Europe

We, the Heads of State or Government of the States participating in the Conference on Security and Co-operation in Europe, have assembled in Paris at a time of profound change and historic expectations. The era of confrontation and division of Europe has ended. We declare that henceforth our relations will be founded on respect and co-operation.

Europe is liberating itself from the legacy of the past. The courage of men and women, the strength of the will of the peoples and the power of the ideas of the Helsinki Final Act have opened a new era of democracy, peace and unity in Europe.

Ours is a time for fulfilling the hopes and expectations our peoples have cherished for decades: steadfast commitment to democracy based on human rights and fundamental freedoms; prosperity through economic liberty and social justice; and equal security for all our countries.

The Ten Principles of the Final Act will guide us towards this ambitious future, just as they have lighted our way towards better relations for the past fifteen years. Full implementation of all CSCE commitments must form the basis for the initiatives we are now taking to enable our nations to live in accordance with their aspirations.

Human Rights, Democracy and Rule of Law

We undertake to build, consolidate and strengthen democracy as the only system of government of our nations. In this endeavour, we will abide by the following:

Human rights and fundamental freedoms are the birthright of all human beings, are inalienable and are guaranteed by law. Their protection and promotion is the first responsibility of government. Respect for them is an essential safeguard against an over-mighty State. Their observance and full exercise are the foundation of freedom, justice and peace.

Democratic government is based on the will of the people, expressed regularly through free and fair elections. Democracy has as its foundation respect for the human person and the rule of law. Democracy is the best safeguard of freedom of expression, tolerance of all groups of society, and equality of opportunity for each person.

Democracy, with its representative and pluralist character, entails accountability to the electorate, the obligation of public authorities to comply with the law and justice administered impartially. No one will be above the law.

We affirm that, without discrimination,

every individual has the right to:
freedom of thought, conscience and religion or belief,
freedom of expression,
freedom of association and peaceful assembly,
freedom of movement;

no one will be:

subject to arbitrary arrest or detention,
subject to torture or other cruel, inhuman or degrading treatment or punishment;

everyone also has the right:

to know and act upon his rights,
to participate in free and fair elections,
to fair and public trial if charged with an offence,
to own property alone or in association and to exercise individual enterprise,
to enjoy his economic, social and cultural rights.

We affirm that the ethnic, cultural, linguistic and religious identity of national minorities will be protected and that persons belonging to national minorities have the right freely to express, preserve and develop that identity without any discrimination and in full equality before the law.

We will ensure that everyone will enjoy recourse to effective remedies, national or international, against any violation of his rights.

Full respect for these precepts is the bedrock on which we will seek to construct the new Europe.

Our State will co-operate and support each other with the aim of making democratic gains irreversible.

Economic Liberty and Responsibility

Economic liberty, social justice and environmental responsibility are indispensable for prosperity.

The free will of the individual, exercised in democracy and protected by the rule of law, forms the necessary basis for successful economic and social development. We will promote economic activity which respects and upholds human dignity.

Freedom and political pluralism are necessary elements in our common objective of developing market economies towards sustainable economic growth, prosperity, social justice, expanding employment and efficient use of economic resources. The success of the transition to market economy by countries making efforts to this effect is important and in the interest of us all. It will enable us to share a higher level of prosperity which is our common objective. We will co-operate to this end.

Preservation of the environment is a shared responsibility of all our nations. While supporting national and regional efforts in this field, we must also look to the pressing need for joint action on a wider scale.

Friendly Relations among Participating States

Now that a new era is dawning in Europe, we are determined to expand and strengthen friendly relations and co-operation among the States of Europe, the United States of America and Canada, and to promote friendship among our peoples.

To uphold and promote democracy, peace and unity in Europe, we solemnly pledge our full commitment to the Ten Principles of the Helsinki Final Act. We affirm the continuing validity of the Ten Principles and our determination to put them into practice. All the Principles apply equally and unreservedly, each of them being interpreted taking into account the others. They form the basis for our relations.

In accordance with our obligations under the Charter of the United Nations and commitments under the Helsinki Final Act, we renew our pledge to refrain from the threat or use of force against the territorial integrity or political independence of any State, or from acting in any other manner inconsistent with the principles or purposes of those documents. We recall that non-compliance with obligations under the Charter of the United Nations constitutes a violation of international law.

We reaffirm our commitment to settle disputes by peaceful means. We decide to develop mechanisms for the prevention and resolution of conflicts among the participating States.

With the ending of the division of Europe, we will strive for a new quality in our security relations while fully respecting each other's freedom of choice in that respect. Security is indivisible and the security of every participating State is inseparably linked to that of all the others. We therefore pledge to co-operate in strengthening confidence and security among us and in promoting arms control and disarmament.

We welcome the Joint Declaration of Twenty-Two States on the improvement of their relations.

Our relations will rest on our common adherence to democratic values and to human rights and fundamental freedoms. We are convinced that in order to strengthen peace and security among our States, the advancement of democracy, and respect for and effective exercise of human rights, are indispensable. We reaffirm the equal rights of peoples and their right to self-determination in conformity with the Charter of the United Nations and with the relevant norms of international law, including those relating to territorial integrity of States.

We are determined to enhance political consultation and to widen co-operation to solve economic, social, environmental, cultural and humanitarian problems. This common resolve and our growing inter-dependence will help to overcome the mistrust of decades, to increase stability and to build a united Europe.

We want Europe to be a source of peace, open to dialogue and to co-operation with other countries, welcoming exchanges and involved in the search for common responses to the challenges of the future.

Security

Friendly relations among us will benefit from the consolidation of democracy and improved security.

We welcome the signature of the Treaty on Conventional Armed Forces in Europe by twenty-two participating States, which will lead to lower levels of armed forces. We endorse the adoption of a substantial new set of Confidence- and Security-building Measures which will lead to increased transparency and confidence among all participating States. These are important steps towards enhanced stability and security in Europe.

The unprecedented reduction in armed forces resulting from the Treaty on Conventional Armed Forces in Europe, together with new approaches to security and co-operation within the CSCE process, will lead to a new perception of security in Europe and a new dimension in our relations. In this context we fully recognize the freedom of States to choose their own security arrangements.

Unity

Europe whole and free is calling for a new beginning. We invite our peoples to join in this great endeavour.

We note with great satisfaction the Treaty on the Final Settlement with respect to Germany signed in Moscow on 12 September 1990 and sincerely welcome the fact that the German people have united to become one State in accordance with the principles of the Final Act of the Conference on Security and Co-operation in Europe and in full accord with their neighbours. The establishment of the national unity of Germany is an important contribution to a just and lasting order of peace for a united, democratic Europe aware of its responsibility for stability, peace and co-operation.

The participation of both North American and European States is a fundamental characteristic of the CSCE; it underlies its past achievements and is essential to the future of the CSCE process. An abiding adherence to shared values and our common heritage are the ties which bind us together. With all the rich diversity of our nations, we are united in our commitment to expand our co-operation in all fields. The challenges confronting us can only be met by common action, co-operation and solidarity.

The CSCE and the World

The destiny of our nations is linked to that of all other nations. We support fully the United Nations and the enhancement of its role in promoting international peace, security and justice. We reaffirm our commitment to the principles and purposes of the United Nations as enshrined in the Charter and condemn all violations of these principles. We recognize with satisfaction the growing role of the United Nations in world affairs and its increasing effectiveness, fostered by the improvement in relations among our States.

Aware of the dire needs of a great part of the world, we commit ourselves to solidarity with all other countries. Therefore, we issue a call from Paris today to all the nations of the world. We stand ready to join with any and all States in common efforts to protect and advance the community of fundamental human values.

Paris, 1990

Document 11 Overcoming the Division — a ten-point programme

A ten-point programme to overcome the division of Germany and Europe was presented by Chancellor Kohl on 28 November 1989 to the German Bundestag. His programme met with the approval of the vast majority of the representatives of most parties. Following are excerpts from the programme.

First: immediate measures need to be taken. These result from the events of the past few weeks, particularly from the movement of refugees and the new dimensions of inter-German traffic.

The Federal Government is prepared to provide immediate concrete aid where it is needed. We will assist in the humanitarian sector and provide medical assistance as far as is required.

We are also aware that the welcoming money, which is given once a year to every visitor from the GDR, can provide no long-term solution for the financing of journeys. The GDR must equip its nationals with the necessary currency. We are, however, prepared to contribute to a currency fund for the transition period. The prerequisites for this are, that the minimum sum of exchange imposed when travelling to the GDR must be relinquished, that entry into the GDR must be made easier and that the GDR itself makes a considerable contribution to this fund.

Our aim is to establish the most unhindered form of tourist traffic possible in both directions.

Second: The Federal Government will, as before, continue its co-operation with the GDR in all areas where it is of direct benefit to people on both sides. This is particularly true of economic, scientific and technological co-operation and of co-operation in cultural fields. It is of particular importance to intensify co-operation in the field of environmental protection.

Here we will be able to shortly take decisions concerning new projects.

Additionally, we also want to help to ensure that the telephone network in the GDR is extended as quickly as possible.

We are continuing negotiations pertaining to the extension of the railway network Hanover–Berlin. In addition, dialogue is necessary concerning fundamental questions of rail traffic within a Europe with open borders, and concerning the linking of the GDR network, with particular reference to modern high-speed trains.

Third: I have offered to **extensively extend our aid and co-operation,** should fundamental change of the political and economic system in the GDR be firmly agreed upon and put irrevocably in action. Irrevocably means that the leadership comes to an understanding with opposition groups concerning constitutional change and a new electoral law.

We support the demands for free, equal and secret elections in the GDR which incorporates independent and non-socialist parties. The power monopoly of the SED must be lifted.

The introduction of constitutional state conditions means, above all, the abolition of laws concerning political crimes.

Economic aid can only be effective if fundamental reforms within the economic system take place. Former experience with all COMECON states proves this. The bureaucratic planned economy must be dismantled.

We do not want to stabilise conditions which have become indefensible. Economic improvement can only occur if the GDR opens its doors to Western investment, if conditions of free enterprise are created and if private enterprise becomes possible. There are already examples of this in Hungary and Poland, examples which can be used by the GDR for orientation. Under these conditions, joint ventures would soon be possible. There is already a large degree of willingness to undertake such ventures both at home and abroad.

These are not official preconditions but factual prerequisites needed before our aid can take effect. Additionally there can be no doubt that the people in the GDR want an economic order which can also provide them with economic freedom and wealth.

Fourth: Prime Minister Modrow spoke in his governmental declaration of a 'contractual community'. We are prepared to accept these thoughts. The proximity and the special nature of the relationships between our two states in Germany demand an increasingly close-knit network of agreement in all sectors and at all levels.

This co-operation will also increasingly demand common institutions. Commissions which already exist can be given new tasks and further commissions can be called into being. Here I am particularly thinking of the economic, transport, environmental, scientific and technical, health and cultural sectors. It goes without saying that Berlin will be fully included in these co-operative efforts.

I call upon all social groups and institutions to actively participate in the development of such a contractual community.

Fifth: We are also prepared to take a further decisive step, namely, to develop **confederative structures** between the two states in Germany with the goal of creating a federation, a federal state order in Germany. A legitimate democratic government within the GDR is an unrelinquishable prerequisite.

We can envisage that after free elections the following institutions be formed:

— a common governmental committee for permanent consultation and political harmonisation,
— common technical committees,
— a common parliamentary gremium.

If in the future, a democratically legitimised, that is a freely elected government becomes our partner, totally new perspectives are available.

New forms of institutional co-operation could be created and further developed in stages. Such a coming together is in the interest of the continuation of German history. State organisations within Germany are always confederations of federations. At this time, we can once again make use of this historical precedence.

Nobody knows **how** a reunified Germany will look. I am however sure **that unity will come,** if it is wanted by the German nation.

Sixth: The development of inner-German relations remains bedded in the pan-European process and in East–West relations. **The future structure of Germany must fit into the future architecture of Europe as a whole.** The West has to provide pace-making aid here with its concept for a permanent and just European order of peace.

— The unlimited respect of the integrity and safety of each state. Each state has the right to choose its own political and social system.
— The unlimited respect of the principles and standards of international law, particularly, respect for the peoples' right of self-determination.
— The realisation of human rights.
— Respect for, and the upholding of the historically based cultures of the people of Europe.

With all these points we want to link on to the historically based European traditions and help to overcome the divisions in Europe.

Seventh: The powers of attraction and the aura of the **European Community** are and remain a constant feature in the pan-European development. We want to strengthen this future.

The European Community is now required to approach the reform-oriented states in Central, Eastern, and Southern Europe with openness and flexibility. This was ascertained unanimously by the Heads of State and Government of the EEC member states during their recent meeting in Paris.

This of course includes the GDR.

The Federal Government therefore approves the quick conclusion of a trade and co-operation agreement with the GDR. This would expand and secure the GDR's entry within the Common Market, including the perspectives of 1992.

We can envisage for the future specific forms of association which would lead the economies of the reform-oriented countries of Central and South-Eastern Europe to the EC, and thereby dismantle the economic and social gradients on our continent.

We understand the process leading to the recovery of the German unity to be of European concern. It must, therefore, be considered together with European integration. In keeping with this, the European Community must remain open to a democratic GDR and to other democratic countries from Central and South-Eastern Europe. The EC must not end on the Elba, but must remain open to the East.

Only in this way is it possible that the foundation of the EC truly includes a comprehensive European unity. Only in this way can it maintain, assert and develop an identity characteristic of all Europeans. This identity is not only based on the cultural diversity of Europe, but also, and especially, on the fundamental values of freedom, democracy, human rights and self-determination. If the countries of Central and South-Eastern Europe fulfil the necessary prerequisites, we would also greet their entrance into the European Council, especially into the convention for the Protection of Human Rights and Fundamental Freedoms.

Eight: The CSCE process is and remains a crucial part of the total European architecture and must be further advanced. In order to do this, the following CSCE forums must be taken advantage of:

— The Human Rights Conference in Copenhagen, in 1990, and in Moscow, in 1991.
— The Conference on Economic Cooperation in Bonn, in 1990.
— The Cultural Inheritance Symposium in Cracow, in 1991 and
— last but not least, the next CSCE meeting in Helsinki.

There we should think about new institutional forms for pan-European cooperation. We envisage a common Institution for the Coordination of East–West Economic Cooperation, as well as, the creation of a pan-European Environmental Council.

Ninth: Surmounting the separation of Europe and the division of Germany demands far-reaching and speedy steps pertaining to **disarmament and arms control.** Disarmament and arms control must keep step with political developments and therefore, might have to be accelerated . . . . We are trying — via bilateral discussions with the countries of the Warsaw Pact, including the GDR — to support this process.

Tenth: With this sweeping policy, we are working towards **the attainment of freedom within Europe, whereby the German people can, via free self-determination, restore their unity.** Reunification, the reattainment of German state unity, remains the political goal of the Federal Government. We are grateful that we once again found support pertaining to this point from our allies in the announcement made at the NATO Summit in Brussels, in May of this year.

The joining of the German question with pan-European developments and East–West relations, as I have explained in the previous ten points, enables an organic development which is of concern to all members and guarantees a peaceful co-existence in Europe.

We can only peacefully overcome the division of Europe and Germany together and in an atmosphere of mutual trust. We need discretion, understanding and sound judgement on all sides in order for the current developments to steadily and peacefully continue.

This process could not be hampered by reforms, but rather by the non-acceptance thereof. Freedom does not cause instability, but rather the oppression thereof. Every successful reform step means more stability and increased freedom and security for all of Europe.

Chancellor Helmut Kohl, German *Bundestag*, 28 November 1989

Document 12 Resolution on the German-Polish frontier[1]

The Bundestag adopted the following resolution on 21 June 1990, the day before the Two plus Four talks between the Foreign Ministers of the Four Powers (United States, United Kingdom, France, Soviet Union) and the two German Foreign Ministers in Berlin. An identical declaration was made by the East German Volkskammer on the same day.

The German Bundestag,

— conscious of its responsibility in the light of German and European history,
— firmly resolved to help achieve in free self-determination the unity and freedom of Germany so that Germany will serve the peace and freedom of the world as an equal partner in a united Europe based on the rule of law and respect for human rights,
— anxious to make a contribution through German unity to the development of a peaceful order in Europe in which frontiers no longer divide, which enables all European nations to live together in mutual trust and engage in comprehensive cooperation for the common benefit, and which ensures lasting peace, freedom and stability,
— conscious of the terrible suffering inflicted on the Polish people through crimes perpetrated by Germans and in the name of Germany,
— conscious of the great injustice done to millions of Germans who have been expelled from their native regions,
— desiring that a united Germany and the Republic of Poland, mindful of the tragic and painful chapters of history, systematically continue the policy of understanding and reconciliation between Germans and Poles, shape their relations with a view to the future and thus set an example of good-neighbourliness,
— convinced that special importance attaches to the young generation's commitment to reconciliation of the two nations,
— expecting the freely elected People's Chamber of the GDR to issue simultaneously an identical declaration,

expresses its will that the course of the frontier between the united Germany and the Republic of Poland be definitively confirmed, by a treaty under international law, as follows:

The course of the frontier between the united Germany and the Republic of Poland shall be as specified in the 'Agreement between the German Democratic Republic and The Polish Republic concerning the Demarcation of the Established and Existing German-Polish State Frontier' of 6 July 1950 as well as the accords implementing and supplementing the aforementioned agreement (Treaty of 22 May 1989 between the German Democratic Republic and the Polish People's Republic on the Delimitation of the Sea Areas in the Oder Bay. Instrument of 27 January 1951 confirming the Demarcation of the State Frontier between Germany and Poland) and by the 'Treaty between the Federal Republic of Germany and the Polish People's Republic concerning the Basis for Normalizing their Mutual Relations' of 7 December 1970.

The two sides reaffirm the inviolability of the frontier existing between them now and in the future and undertake to respect each other's sovereignty and territorial integrity without restriction.

The two sides declare that they have no territorial claims whatsoever against each other and that they will not assert such claims in the future.

The Government of the Federal Republic of Germany is formally called upon to communicate this resolution to the Republic of Poland as the expression of its will.

Note

1 The resolution was moved by all parliamentary groups (CDU/CSU, FDP, SPD, the Greens). 505 of the 519 members voted. The resolution was adopted with 487 votes for, 15 against and 3 abstentions. The East German Volkskammer, freely elected on 18 March 1990, adopted an identical resolution on 21 June 1990.

Document 13 Statement by Chancellor Kohl to the press concerning policy on Germany and his visit to the Soviet Union, Bonn, 17 July 1990 (excerpts)

1. Policy on Germany

For two weeks now the Germans in the Federal Republic of Germany and the GDR have been inseparably reunited with one another, without divisive borders. The entry into force of monetary, economic and social union was an important step on the road towards unity[1] and has been recognised as such all over the world.

The conversion to a different currency in the GDR went smoothly, indeed better than expected by many pessimists, thanks not least to the excellent preparatory efforts of all the authorities involved. A large number of laws have gone into effect in the GDR aimed at creating the legal prerequisites for establishing a social market economy system.

Everyone knows that the complete restructuring of the GDR will involve considerable difficulty in some cases, particularly in the initial phase. It will require hard work before we will have created wealth and social security for all Germans. No one will have to suffer undue hardship in the transitional phase. And we have every chance of achieving our goal in a relatively short time.

2. Results of the talks with President Gorbachev

I returned last night from my second trip this year to the Soviet Union. In connection with my first visit in February I was able to report to you that we Germans had been given the 'green light' by the Soviet leadership for our unification process and that we would be able to decide ourselves on the form, time frame and conditions involved.

Today I bring the good news for all Germans that an agreement has now been reached on all external aspects between ourselves and the Soviet Union. We want forward-looking treaties, comprehensive cooperation, mutual confidence and, not least, broad contacts between our peoples, in particular young people. In this context we want to help shape a durable and peaceful future for Europe as a whole . . . . President Gorbachev and I are agreed that this will be the basis of a comprehensive treaty of cooperation between united Germany and the Soviet Union which will be concluded as soon as possible after unification. The treaty will be concluded on the firm basis and the mutual and clear understanding that German-Soviet cooperation and our firm anchorage in the West constitute an indispensable contribution to stability in Central Europe and beyond.

On the basis of this — as President Gorbachev himself put it — common philosophy, we have resolved the practical problems that lie ahead of us on the road to Germany unity. I will summarise the major points:

First, the unification of Germany will involve the Federal Republic of Germany, the GDR and all of Berlin.

Second, with the establishment of the unity of Germany, Four-Power rights and responsibilities with regard to Germany as a whole and Berlin will be terminated. United Germany will acquire its full and unrestricted sovereignty at the time of unification.

Third, united Germany can decide freely and independently in exercise of its full and unrestricted sovereignty whether it wants to belong to an alliance and, if so, what alliance. This is in keeping with the CSCE Final Act.

I indicated that it was the view of the Government of the Federal Republic of Germany that a united Germany would like to be a member of the Atlantic Alliance and I know that this corresponds to the wishes of the GDR. Prime Minister de Maizière made this clear yesterday and we confirm this in our discussion this morning.

Fourth, united Germany will conclude with the Soviet Union a treaty on troop withdrawals from the GDR which, as the Soviet leadership indicated, are to be concluded in three to four years.

When I say 'three to four years' I mean Soviet forces will have left German territory by 1994 at the latest. In other words, the last Soviet troops will be gone 50 years after the day on which they first entered German territory during the Second World War.

In addition, a transitional agreement on the effects of introducing the deutschmark in the GDR is to be concluded for this period.

Fifth, as long as Soviet troops continue to be stationed on the territory of the present-day GDR, NATO structures will not be expanded to include this area. At the time of unification articles five and six of the NATO treaty will apply to the entire territory of united Germany.[2]

Sixth, non-integrated units of the Federal Armed Forces, i.e. territorial defence units, can be stationed in Berlin and on the territory of the present-day GDR immediately after the unification of Germany.

Seventh, we feel that troops of the Three Western Powers should remain in Berlin for the duration of Soviet military presence on the territory of the present-day GDR. The Government of the Federal Republic of Germany will request this of the Three Western Powers. A legal basis for the presence of the Western forces will have to be created by means of a treaty between the government of united Germany and the Three Powers. The number and equipment of these forces should not be stronger than at present.

Eighth, after the withdrawal of Soviet troops from the territory of the present-day GDR and Berlin it will also be possible for NATO-integrated troops to be stationed in this part of Germany, although without delivery systems for nuclear weapons. No foreign troops and nuclear weapons are to be deployed there.

Ninth, the government of the Federal Republic of Germany is prepared to commit itself in the on-going Vienna talks to reducing the strength of the armed forces of a united Germany to a level of 370,000 within three to four years. Reductions are to commence when the first Vienna treaty goes into effect. Based on the previous strength of the

Federal Armed Forces and the National People's Army, the armed forces of a future united Germany will be reduced by 45 per cent.

Tenth, united Germany will refrain from the manufacture, possession and use of ABC weapons and will remain a party to the Nuclear Non-Proliferation Treaty.[3]

I assume the the Three Western Powers as well as the Government of the GDR, with whom I have already spoken today in the person of Prime Minister de Maizière, will support this agreement.

Another aspect of my talks with President Gorbachev as well as of the talks held by Finance Minister Waigel with the Soviet counterparts was forward-looking and comprehensive economic and financial cooperation.

On the basis of the Three Western summits in Dublin, London and Houston, I was able to make it clear to President Gorbachev and the Soviet leadership that the West is pinning its hopes on the success of *perestroika* and wants to support it as much as possible. I would like to stress that this is the common interest and objective of our Western friends and partners . . . .

Notes

1 The last remaining intra-German border controls were discontinued upon the entry into force of the State Treaty of 18 May 1990.

2 Article V of the North Atlantic Treaty of 4 April 1949 reads: 'The Parties agree that an armed attack against one or more of them in Europe or North America shall be considered an attack against them all and consequently they agree that, if such an armed attack occurs, each of them, in exercise of the right of individual or collective self-defence recognised by article 51 of the Charter of the United Nations, will assist the Party or Parties so attacked by taking forthwith, individually and in concert with the other Parties, such action as it deems necessary, including the use of armed force, to restore and maintain the Security of the North Atlantic area. Any such armed attack and all measures taken as a result thereof shall immediately be reported to the Security Council. Such measures shall be terminated when the Security Council has taken the measures necessary to restore and maintain international peace and security.'

   Article 6 specifies the territory to which, for the purpose of article V, armed attack applies.

3 Treaty of 1 July 1968 on the Non-Proliferation of Nuclear Weapons. The Federal Republic of Germany signed this treaty as early as 28 November 1969.

Document 14 Treaty of 12 September 1990 on the Final Settlement with Respect to Germany

The Federal Republic of Germany, the German Democratic Republic, the French Republic, the Union of Soviet Socialist Republics, the United Kingdom of Great Britain and Northern Ireland and the United States of America,

Conscious of the fact that their peoples have been living together in peace since 1945;

Mindful of the recent historic changes in Europe which make it possible to overcome the division of the continent;

Having regard to the rights and responsibilities of the Four Powers relating to Berlin and to Germany as a whole, and the corresponding wartime and post-war agreements and decisions of the Four Powers;

Resolved in accordance with their obligations under the Charter of the United Nations to develop friendly relations among nations based on respect for the principle of equal rights and self-determination of peoples, and to take other appropriate measures to strengthen universal peace;

Recalling the principles of the Final Act of the Conference, on Security and Cooperation in Europe, signed in Helsinki;

Recognizing that those principles have laid firm foundations for the establishment of a just and lasting peaceful order in Europe:

Determined to take account of everyone's security interests

Convinced of the need finally to overcome antagonism and to develop cooperation in Europe:

Confirming their readiness to reinforce security, in particular by adopting effective arms control, disarmament and confidence-building measures; their willingness not to regard each other as adversaries but to work for a relationship of trust and cooperation and accordingly their readiness to consider positively setting up appropriate institutional arrangements within the framework of the Conference on Security and Cooperation in Europe;

Welcoming the fact that the German people, freely exercising their right of self-determination, have expressed their will to bring about the unity of Germany as a state so that they will be able to serve the peace of the world as an equal and sovereign partner in a united Europe;

Convinced that the unification of Germany as a state with definitive borders is a significant contribution to peace and stability in Europe;

Intending to conclude the final settlement with respect to Germany;

Recognizing that thereby, and with the unification of Germany as a democratic and peaceful state, the rights and responsibilities of the Four Powers relating to Berlin and to Germany as a whole lose their function;

Represented by their Ministers for Foreign Affairs who, in accordance with the Ottawa Declaration of 13 February 1990, met in Bonn on 5 May 1990, in Berlin on 22 June 1990, in Paris on 17 July 1990 with the participation of the Minister for Foreign Affairs of the Republic of Poland, and in Moscow on 12 September 1990;

Have agreed as follows;

ARTICLE 1

(1) The united Germany shall comprise the territory of the Federal Republic of Germany, the German Democratic Republic and the whole of Berlin. Its external borders shall be the borders of the Federal Republic of Germany and the German Democratic Republic and shall be definitive from the date on which the present Treaty comes into force. The confirmation of the definitive nature of the borders of the united Germany is an essential element of the peaceful order in Europe.

(2) The united Germany and the Republic of Poland shall confirm the existing border between them in a treaty that is binding under international law.

(3) The united Germany has no territorial claims whatsoever against other states and shall not assert any in the future.

(4) The Governments of the Federal Republic of Germany and the German Democratic Republic shall ensure that the constitution of the united Germany does not contain any provision incompatible with these principles. This applies accordingly to the provisions laid down in the preamble, the second sentence of Article 23, and Article 146 of the Basic Law for the Federal Republic of Germany.[1]

(5) The Governments of the French Republic, the Union of Soviet Socialist Republics, the United Kingdom of Great Britain and Northern Ireland and the United States of America take formal note of the corresponding commitments and declarations by the Governments of the Federal Republic of Germany and the German Democratic Republic and declare that their implementation will confirm the definitive nature of the united Germany's borders.

ARTICLE 2

The Governments of the Federal Republic of Germany and the German Democratic Republic reaffirm their declarations that only peace will emanate from German soil. According to the constitution of the united Germany, acts tending to and undertaken with the intent to disturb the peaceful relations between nations, especially to prepare for aggressive war, are unconstitutional and a punishable offence.[2] The Governments of the Federal Republic of Germany and the German Democratic Republic declare that the united Germany will never employ any of its weapons except in accordance with its constitution and the Charter of the United Nations.

ARTICLE 3

(1) The Governments of the Federal Republic of Germany and the German Democratic Republic reaffirm their renunciation of the manufacture and possession of and control over nuclear, biological and chemical weapons. They declare that the united Germany, too, will abide by these commitments. In particular, rights and obligations arising from the Treaty on the Non-Proliferation of Nuclear Weapons of 1 July 1968 will continue to apply to the united Germany.

(2) The Government of the Federal Republic of Germany, acting in full agreement with the Government of the German Democratic Republic, made the following statement on 30 August 1990 in Vienna at the Negotiations on Conventional Armed Forces in Europe:

'The Government of the Federal Republic of Germany undertakes to reduce the personnel strength of the armed forces of the united Germany to 370,000 (ground, air and naval forces) within three to four years. This reduction will commence on the entry into force of the first CFE agreement. Within the scope of this overall ceiling no more than 345,000 will belong to the ground and air forces which, pursuant to the agreed mandate, alone are the subject of the Negotiations on Conventional Armed Forces in Europe. The Federal Government regards its commitment to reduce ground and air forces as a significant German contribution to the reduction of conventional armed forces in Europe. It assumes that in follow-on negotiations the other participants in the negotiations, too, will render their contribution to enhancing security and stability in Europe, including measures to limit personnel strengths'.

The Government of the German Democratic Republic has expressly associated itself with this statement.

(3) The Governments of the French Republic, the Union of Soviet Socialist Republics, the United Kingdom of Great Britain and Northern Ireland and the United States of America take note of these statements by the Governments of the Federal Republic of Germany and the German Democratic Republic.

ARTICLE 4

(1) The Governments of the Federal Republic of Germany, the German Democratic Republic and the Union of Soviet Socialist Republics state that the united Germany and the Union of Soviet Socialist Republics will settle by treaty the conditions for and the duration of the presence of Soviet armed forces on the territory of the present German Democratic Republic and of Berlin, as well as the conduct of the withdrawal of these armed forces which will be completed by the end of 1994, in connection with the implementation of the undertaking of the Federal Republic of Germany and the German Democratic Republic referred to in paragraph 2 of Article 3 of the present Treaty.

(2) The Governments of the French Republic, the United Kingdom of Great Britain and Northern Ireland and the United States of America take note of this statement.

ARTICLE 5

(1) Until the completion of the withdrawal of the Soviet armed forces from the territory of the present German Democratic Republic and of Berlin in accordance with Article 4 of the present Treaty, only German territorial defence units which are not integrated into the alliance structures to which German armed forces in the rest of German territory are assigned will be stationed in that territory as armed forces of the united Germany. During that period and subject to the provisions of paragraph 2 of this Article, armed forces of other states will not be stationed in that territory or carry out any other military activity there.

(2) For the duration of the presence of Soviet armed forces in the territory of the present German Democratic Republic and of Berlin, armed forces of the French Republic, the United Kingdom of Great Britain and Northern Ireland and the United States of America will, upon German request, remain stationed in Berlin by agreement to this effect between the Government of the united Germany and the Governments of the states concerned. The number of troops and the amount of equipment of all non-German armed forces stationed in Berlin will not be greater than at the time of signature of the present Treaty. New categories of weapons will not be introduced there by non-German armed forces. The Government of the united Germany will conclude with the Governments of those states which have armed forces stationed in Berlin treaties with conditions which are fair taking account of the relations existing with the states concerned.

(3) Following the completion of the withdrawal of the Soviet armed forces from the territory of the present German Democratic Republic and of Berlin, units of German armed forces assigned to military alliance structures in the same way as those in the rest of German territory may also be stationed in that part of Germany, but without nuclear weapon carriers. This does not apply to conventional weapon systems which may have other capabilities in addition to conventional ones but which

in that part of Germany are equipped for a conventional role and designated only for such. Foreign armed forces and nuclear weapons or their carriers will not be stationed in that part of Germany or deployed there.

ARTICLE 6

The right of the united Germany to belong to alliances, with all the rights and responsibilities arising therefrom, shall not be affected by the present Treaty.

ARTICLE 7

(1) The French Republic, the Union of Soviet Socialist Republics, the United Kingdom of Great Britain and Northern Ireland and the United States of America hereby terminate their rights and responsibilities relating to Berlin and to Germany as a whole. As a result, the corresponding, related quadripartite agreements, decisions and practices are terminated and all related Four Power institutions are dissolved.

(2) The united Germany shall have accordingly full sovereignty over its internal and external affairs.

ARTICLE 8

(1) The present Treaty is subject to ratification or acceptance as soon as possible. On the German side it will be ratified by the united Germany. The Treaty will therefore apply to the united Germany.

(2) The instruments of ratification or acceptance shall be deposited with the Government of the united Germany. That Government shall inform the Governments of the other Contracting Parties of the deposit of each instrument of ratification or acceptance.

ARTICLE 9

The present Treaty shall enter into force for the united Germany, the French Republic, the Union of Soviet Socialist Republics, the United Kingdom of Great Britain and Northern Ireland and the United States of America on the date of deposit of the last instrument of ratification or acceptance by these states.

ARTICLE 10

The original of the present Treaty, of which the English, French, German and Russian texts are equally authentic, shall be deposited with the Government of the Federal Republic of Germany, which shall transmit certified true copies to the Governments of the other Contracting Parties.

Done at Moscow on 12 September 1990.

For the Federal Republic of Germany
Hans-Dietrich Genscher

For the German Democratic Republic
Lothar de Maizière

For the French Republic
Roland Dumas

For the United Kingdom of Great Britain
and Northern Ireland
Douglas Hurd

For the United States of America
James Baker

For the Union of Soviet Socialist Republics
Eduard Shevardnadze

AGREED MINUTE

to the Treaty on the Final Settlement with respect to Germany of 12 September 1990.

Any questions with respect to the application of the word 'deployed' as used in the last sentence of paragraph 3 of Article 5 will be decided by the Government of the united Germany in a reasonable and responsible way taking into account the security interests of each Contracting Party as set forth in the preamble.

Notes

1 This requirement was fulfilled by the provisions of article 4 amending the Basic Law.
2 Article 26 of the Basic Law reads: 'Acts tending to and undertaken with the intent to disturb the peaceful relations between nations,especially to prepare for aggressive war, shall be unconstitutional. They shall be made a punishable offence.'

Congratulatory letter from Mikhail Gorbachev, President of the Soviet Union, to Federal President Richard von Weizsäcker, 3 October 1990

I convey my congratulations to you and the whole German nation. The unification of Germany, which has taken place in agreement with your neighbours, with other states and peoples, is a great occasion for the Germans, but not for them alone. Unification has taken place on the boundary between two epochs. It has become a symbol and, I hope, it will also become a factor which will help to consolidate peace in general. Unification would not have been possible without the radical democratic reforms in our countries, if the right lessons from the tragedy of the most terrible war had not been drawn in real life.

On this significant day I wish to pay tribute to all those, both in my country and yours, who have overcome their bitterness, remembered the losses and commemorated the fallen, and at the same time have not yielded to prejudice and fear and have worked resolutely to build the future and made possible such a peaceful and honourable solution to the 'German question'.

We have high hopes of the new relationship with Germany. Our long history of mutual influence and attraction, the position of our countries in Europe and in the world, and their huge and mutually complementary potential, make wide-ranging cooperation possible and natural. This purpose will, I hope, be served by the treaty on good neighbourliness, partnership and cooperation which is soon to be concluded and is a suitable basis for the development of our relations.

I wish the great German nation happiness, prosperity and eternal peace within the framework of good neighbourly relations and friendship among the nations of Europe.

The treaties of German unification

Document 15 Treaty of 18 May 1990 between the Federal Republic of Germany and the German Democratic Republic establishing a Monetary, Economic and Social Union

THE HIGH CONTRACTING PARTIES,

Owing to the fact that a peaceful and democratic revolution took place in the German Democratic Republic in the autumn of 1989,

Resolved to achieve in freedom as soon as possible the unity of Germany within a European peace order,

Intending to introduce the social market economy in the German Democratic Republic as the basis for further economic and social development, with social compensation and social safeguards and responsibility towards the environment, and thereby constantly to improve the living and working condition of its population,

Proceeding from the mutual desire to take an initial significant step through the establishment of a monetary, economic and social union towards national unity in accordance with Article 23 of the Basic Law of the Federal Republic of Germany as a contribution to European unification, taking into account that the external aspects of establishing unity are the subject of negotiations with the Governments of the French Republic, the Union of Soviet Socialist Republics, the United Kingdom of Great Britain and Northern Ireland and the United States of America,

Recognizing that the establishment of national unity is accompanied by the development of federal structures in the German Democratic Republic,

Realizing that the provisions of this Treaty are intended to safeguard the application of European Community law following the establishment of national unity,

Have agreed to conclude a Treaty establishing a Monetary, Economic and Social Union, containing the following provisions.

CHAPTER I
BASIC PRINCIPLES

ARTICLE 1
Subject of the Treaty

(1) The Contracting Parties shall establish a Monetary, Economic and Social Union.
(2) Starting on 1 July 1990 the Contracting Parties shall constitute a Monetary union comprising a unified currency area and with the Deutsche Mark as the common currency. The Deutsche Bundesbank shall be the central bank in this currency area. The liabilities and claims expressed in Mark of the German Democratic Republic shall be converted into Deutsche Mark in accordance with this Treaty.
(3) The basis of the Economic Union shall be the social market economy as the common economic system of the two Contracting Parties. It shall be determined particularly by private ownership, competition, free pricing and, as a basic principle, complete freedom of movement of labour, capital, goods and services; this shall not preclude the legal admission of special forms of ownership providing for the participation of public authorities or other legal entities in trade and commerce as long as private legal entities are not subject to discrimination. It shall take into account the requirements of environmental protection.
(4) The Social Union together with the Monetary and Economic Union shall form one entity. It shall be characterized in particular by a system of labour law that corresponds to the social market economy and a comprehensive system of social security based on merit and social justice.

ARTICLE 2
Principles

(1) The Contracting Parties are committed to a free, democratic, federal and social basic order governed by the rule of law. To ensure the rights laid down in or following from this Treaty, they shall especially guarantee freedom of contract, freedom to exercise a trade, freedom of establishment and occupation, and freedom of movement of Germans in the entire currency area, freedom to form associations to safeguard and enhance working and economic conditions and, in accordance with Annex IX, ownership of land and means of production by private investors.
(2) Contrary provisions of the Constitution of the German Democratic Republic relating to its former socialist social and political system shall no longer be applied.

ARTICLE 3
Legal Basis

The establishment of a Monetary Union and the currency conversion shall be governed by the agreed provisions listed in Annex I. Pending the establishment of Monetary Union, the legislation of the Federal Republic of Germany concerning currency, credit, money and coinage as well as economic and social union referred to in Annex II shall be implemented in the German Democratic Republic; thereafter, it shall apply, as amended, in the entire currency area according to Annex II, unless this Treaty provides otherwise. The Deutsche Bundesbank, the Federal Banking Supervisory Office and the Federal Insurance Supervisory Office shall exercise the authority accorded to them under this Treaty and said legislation in the entire area of application of this Treaty.

ARTICLE 4
Legal Adjustments

(1) Legal adjustments in the German Democratic Republic necessitated by the establishment of the Monetary, Economic and Social Union shall be governed by the principles laid down in Article 2 (1) and the guidelines agreed in the Protocol; legislation remaining in force shall be interpreted and applied in accordance with said principles and guidelines. The German Democratic Republic shall repeal or amend the legislation referred to in Annex III and adopt the new legislation referred to in Annex IV prior to the establishment of Monetary union, provided that no other time limit is fixed in the Treaty or in the Annexes.
(2) The proposed amendments to legislation in the Federal Republic of Germany are listed in Annex V. The proposed legislative adjustments in the German Democratic Republic are listed in Annex VI.
(3) In the transmission of personal date, the principles contained in Annex VII shall apply.

ARTICLE 5
Administrative Assistance

The authorities of the Contracting Parties shall, subject to the provisions of domestic law, assist each other in the implementation of this Treaty. Article 32 of the Treaty shall remain unaffected.

ARTICLE 6
Recourse to the Courts

(1) Should any person's rights guaranteed by or following from this Treaty be violated by public authority he shall have recourse to the courts. In so far as no other jurisdiction has been established, recourse shall be to the ordinary courts.
(2) The German Democratic Republic shall guarantee recourse to the courts, including recourse for provisional court protection. In the absence of special courts for public-law disputes, special arbitration courts shall be set up at ordinary courts. Jurisdiction for such disputes shall be concentrated at specific regional and district courts.
(3) Pending the establishment of a special labour jurisdiction, legal disputes between employers and employees shall be settled by neutral arbitration bodies to be composed of an equal number of employers and employees and a neutral chairman. Their decisions shall be appealable.
(4) The German Democratic Republic shall permit free arbitration in the field of private law.

ARTICLE 7
Arbitral Tribunal

(1) Disputes concerning the interpretation or application of this Treaty, including the Protocol and the Annexes, shall be settled by the Governments of the two Contracting Parties through negotiation.
(2) If a dispute cannot thus be settled, either Contracting Party may submit the dispute to an arbitral tribunal. Such submission shall be admissible irrespective of whether a court has jurisdiction in accordance with Article 6 of this Treaty.
(3) The arbitral tribunal shall be composed of a chairman and four members. Within a period of one month following the entry into force of this Treaty, the Government of each Contracting Party shall appoint two regular and two deputy members. Within the same period, the chairman and the deputy chairman shall be appointed in agreement between the Governments of the two Contracting Parties. If the periods specified in the second and third sentences have not been observed, the necessary appointments shall be made by the President of the Court of Justice of the European Communities.
(4) The period of office shall be two years.
(5) The chairman and members of the arbitral tribunal shall exercise their office independently and free from instructions. Before commencing their activities, the chairman and members of the arbitral tribunal shall undertake to carry out their duties independently and conscientiously and to observe confidentiality.
(6) The provisions governing the convening and the procedure of the arbitral tribunal are laid down in Annex VIII.

ARTICLE 8
Intergovernmental Committee

The Contracting Parties shall appoint an Intergovernmental Commit-tee. The Committee shall discuss — and where necessary reach agree-ment on — questions relating to the implementation of the Treaty. The tasks of the Committee shall include the settlement of disputes under Article 7 (1) of the Treaty.

ARTICLE 9
Amendments to the Treaty

Should amendments or additions to this Treaty appear necessary in order to achieve any of its aims, such amendments or additions shall be agreed between the Contracting Parties.

CHAPTER II
PROVISIONS CONCERNING MONETARY UNION

ARTICLE 10
Prerequisites and Principles

(1) Through the establishment of a Monetary Union between the Contracting Parties, the Deutsche Mark shall be the means of payment, unit of account and means of deposit in the entire currency area. To this end, the monetary responsibility of the Deutsche Bundesbank as the sole issuing bank for this currency shall be extended to the entire currency area. The issuance of coin shall be the exclusive right of the Federal Republic of Germany.

(2) Enjoyment of the advantages of Monetary Union presupposes a stable monetary value for the economy of the German Democratic Republic, while currency stability must be maintained in the Federal Republic of Germany. The Contracting Parties shall therefore choose conversion modalities which do not cause any inflationary tendencies in the entire area of the Monetary Union and which at the same time increase the competitiveness of enterprises in the German Democratic Republic.

(3) The Deutsche Bundesbank, by deploying its instruments on its own responsibility and, pursuant to Section 12 of the Bundesbank Act, independent of instructions from the Governments of the Contrac-ting Parties, shall regulate the circulation of money and credit supply in the entire currency area with the aim of safeguarding the currency.

(4) Monetary control presupposes that the German Democratic republic establishes a free-market credit system. This shall include a system of commercial banks operating according to privatesector principles, with competing private, cooperative and publiclaw banks, as well as

a free money and a free capital market and non-regulated interest-rate fixing on financial markets.

(5) To achieve the aims described in paragraphs 1 to 4 above, the Contracting Parties shall, in accordance with the provisions laid down in Annex I, agree on the following principles for Monetary Union:

— With effect from 1 July 1990 the Deutsche Mark shall be introduced as currency in the German Democratic Republic. The banknotes issued by the Deutsche Bundesbank and denominated in Deutsche Mark, and the federal coins issued by the Federal Republic of Germany and denominated in Deutsche Mark or Pfennig, shall be sole legal tender from 1 July 1990.
— Wages, salaries, grants, pensions, rents and leases as well as other recurring payments shall be converted at a rate of one to one.
— All other claims and liabilities denominated in Mark of the German Democratic Republic shall be converted to Deutsche Mark at the rate of two to one.
— The conversion of bank notes and coin denominated in Mark of the German Democratic Republic shall only be possible for persons or agencies domiciled in the German Democratic Republic via accounts with financial institutions in the German Democratic Republic into which the cash amounts to be converted may be paid.
— Deposits with financial institutions held by individuals domiciled in the German Democratic Republic shall be converted upon application at a rate of one to one up to certain limits, there being a differentiation according to the age of the beneficiaries. Special regulations shall apply to deposits of persons domiciled outside the German Democratic Republic.
— Action shall be taken against abuse.

(6) Following an inventory of publicly owned assets and their earning power and following their primary use for the structural adaptation of the economy and for the recapitalization of the budget, the German Democratic Republic shall ensure where possible that a vested right to a share in publicly owned assets can be granted to savers at a later date for the amount reduced following conversion at a rate of two to one.

(7) The Deutsche Bundesbank shall exercise the powers accorded it by this Treaty and by the Deutsche Bundesbank Act in the entire currency area. It shall establish for this purpose a provisional office in Berlin with up to fifteen branches in the German Democratic Republic, which shall be located in the premises of the State Bank of the German Democratic Republic.

CHAPTER III
PROVISIONS CONCERNING ECONOMIC UNION

ARTICLE 11
Economic Policy Foundations

(1) The German Democratic Republic shall ensure that its economic and financial policy measures are in harmony with the social market system. Such measures shall be introduced in such a way that, within the framework of the market economy system, they are at the same time conducive to price stability, a high level of employment and foreign trade equilibrium, and thus steady and adequate economic growth.

(2) The German Democratic Republic shall create the basic conditions for the development of market forces and private initiative in order to promote structural change, the creation of modern jobs, a broad basis of small and medium-sized companies and liberal professions, as well as environmental protection. The corporate legal structure shall be based on the principles of the social market economy described in Article 1 of this Treaty, enterprises being free to decide on products, quantities, production processes, investment, employment, prices and utilization of profits.

(3) The German Democratic Republic, taking into consideration the foreign trade relations that have evolved with the member countries of the Council for Mutual Economic Assistance, shall progressively bring its policy into line with the law and the economic policy goals of the European Communities.

(4) In decisions which affect the economic policy principles referred to in paragraphs 1 and 2 above, the Government of the German Democratic Republic shall reach agreement with the Government of the Federal Republic of Germany within the framework of the Intergovernmental Committee appointed in accordance with Article 8 of this Treaty.

ARTICLE 12
Intra-German Trade

(1) The Berlin Agreement of 20 September 1951 concluded between the Contracting Parties shall be amended in view of monetary and economic union. The clearing system established by that Agreement shall be ended and the swing shall be finally balanced. Outstanding obligations shall be settled in Deutsche Mark.

(2) The Contracting Parties shall guarantee that goods which do not originate in the Federal Republic of Germany or the German Democratic Republic are transported across the intra-German border in accordance with a customs monitoring procedure.

(3) The Contracting Parties shall endeavour to create as soon as possible the preconditions for complete abolition of controls at the intra-German border.

ARTICLE 13
Foreign Trade and Payments

(1) In its foreign trade, the German Democratic Republic shall take into account the principles of free world trade, as expressed in particular in the General Agreement on Tariffs and Trade. The Federal Republic of Germany shall make its experience fully available for the further integration of the economy of the German Democratic Republic into the world economy.

(2) The existing foreign trade relations of the German Democratic Republic, in particular its contractual obligations towards the countries of the Council for Mutual Economic Assistance, shall be respected. They shall be further developed and extended in accordance with free-market principles, taking account of the facts established by Monetary and Economic Union and the interests of all involved. Where necessary, the German Democratic Republic shall adjust existing contractual obligations in the light of those facts, in agreement with its partners.

(3) The Contracting Parties shall cooperate closely in advancing their foreign trade interests, with due regard for the jurisdiction of the European Communities.

ARTICLE 14
Structural Adjustment of Enterprises

In order to promote the necessary structural adjustment of enterprises in the German Democratic Republic, the Government of the German Democratic Republic shall, for a transitional period and subject to its budgetary means, take measures to facilitate a swift structural adjustment of enterprises to the new market conditions. The Governments of the Contracting Parties shall agree on the specific nature of these measures. The objective shall be to strengthen the competitiveness of enterprises on the basis of the social market economy and to build up, through the development of private initiative, a diversified, modern economic structure in the German Democratic Republic, with as many small and medium-sized enterprises as possible, and thereby to create the basis for increased growth and secure jobs.

ARTICLE 15
Agriculture and Food Industry

(1) Because of the crucial importance of the European Community rules for the agriculture and food industry, the German Democratic Republic shall introduce a price support and external protection scheme in line with the EC market regime so that agricultural producer prices in the German Democratic Republic become adjusted to those in the Federal Republic of Germany. The German

Democratic Republic shall not introduce levies or refunds vis-à-vis the European Community, subject to reciprocity.

(2) For categories of goods in respect of which it is not possible to introduce a full price support system immediately upon the entry into force of this Treaty, transitional arrangements may be applied. Pending the legal integration of the agriculture and food industry of the German Democratic Republic into the EC agricultural market, specific quantitative restriction mechanisms shall be allowed for sensitive agricultural products in trade between the Contracting Parties.

(3) Without prejudice to the measures to be taken under Article 14 of this Treaty, the German Democratic Republic shall, within the limits of its budgetary means and for a transitional period, take suitable measures to promote the structural adaptation in the agricultural and food industry which is necessary to improve the competitiveness of enterprises, to achieve environmentally acceptable and quality-based production, and to avoid surpluses.

(4) The Governments of the Contracting Parties shall agree on the specific nature of the measures referred to in paragraph 2 and 3 above.

ARTICLE 16
Protection of the Environment

(1) The protection of human beings, animals and plants, soil, water, air, the climate and landscapes as well as cultural and other material property against harmful environmental influences is a major objective of both Contracting Parties. They shall pursue this objective on the basis of prevention, the polluter pays principle, and cooperation. Their aim is the rapid establishment of a German environmental union.

(2) The German Democratic Republic shall introduce regulation to ensure that, on the entry into force of this Treaty, the safety and environmental requirements applicable in the Federal Republic of Germany are the precondition for the granting of authorizations under environmental law for new plant and installations on its territory. For existing plant and installations the German Democratic Republic shall introduce regulations to bring them up to standard as quickly as possible.

(3) The German Democratic Republic shall, along with the development of the federal structure at Land level and with the establishment of an administrative jurisdiction, adopt the environmental law of the Federal Republic of Germany.

(4) In further shaping a common environmental law, the environmental requirements of the Federal Republic of Germany and the German Democratic Republic shall be harmonized and developed at a high level as quickly as possible.

(5) The German Democratic Republic shall harmonize the provisions

governing promotion of environmental protection measures with those of the Federal Republic of Germany.

CHAPTER IV
PROVISIONS CONCERNING THE SOCIAL UNION

ARTICLE 17
Principles of Labour Law

In the German Democratic Republic freedom of association, autonomy in collective bargaining, legislation relating to industrial action, corporate legal structure, codetermination at board level and protection against dismissal shall apply in line with the law of the Federal Republic of Germany; further details are contained in the Protocol on Guidelines and in Annexes II and III.

ARTICLE 18
Principles of Social Insurance

(1) The German Democratic Republic shall introduce a structured system of social insurance, to be governed by the following principles:

1. Pension, sickness, accident and unemployment insurance shall each be administered by self-governing bodies under public law subject to legal supervision by the state.
2. Pension, sickness, accident and unemployment insurance including employment promotion shall be financed primarily by contributions. Contributions to pension, sickness and unemployment insurance shall, as a rule, be paid half by the employee and half by the employer in line with the contribution rates applicable in the Federal Republic of Germany, and accident insurance contributions shall be borne by the employer.
3. Wage replacement benefits shall be based on the level of insured earnings.

(2) Initially, pension, sickness and accident insurance shall be administered by a single institution; income and expenditure shall be accounted for separately according to the type of insurance. Separate pension, sickness and accident insurance institutions shall be established, if possible by 1 January 1991. The aim shall be to create an organizational structure for social insurance which corresponds to that of the Federal Republic of Germany.

(3) For a transitional period the present comprehensive compulsory social insurance cover in the German Democratic Republic may be retained. Exemption from compulsory social insurance cover shall be granted to self-employed persons and professionals who can prove that they have adequate alternative insurance. In this connection, the

creation of professional pension schemes outside the pension insurance system shall be made possible.

(4) Wage-earners whose earnings in the last wage accounting period before 1 July 1990 were subject to a special tax rate under Section 10 of the Ordinance of 22 December 1952 on the Taxation of Earned Income (Law Gazette No. 182, p. 1413) shall receive until 31 December 1990 a supplement to their pension insurance contribution amounting to

— DM 30 for monthly wages up to DM 600,
— DM 20 for monthly wages of more than DM 600 up to DM 700,
— DM 10 for monthly wages of more than DM 700 up to DM 800.

Earnings from several employments shall be counted together. The supplement shall be paid to the wage-earner by the employer. Upon application the employer shall be reimbursed for these payments from the budget.

(5) The ceilings for compulsory insurance cover and for contribution assessment shall be fixed according to the principles of social insurance law applying in the Federal Republic of Germany.

ARTICLE 19
Unemployment Insurance and Employment Promotion

The German Democratic Republic shall introduce a system of unemployment insurance including employment promotion which shall be in line with the provisions of the Employment Promotion Act of the Federal Republic of Germany. Special importance shall be attached to an active labour market policy, such as vocational training and retraining. Consideration shall be given to the interests of women and disabled persons. In the transitional phase, special conditions in the German Democratic Republic shall be taken into account. The Governments of both Contracting Parties shall cooperate closely in the development of unemployment insurance including employment promotion.

ARTICLE 20
Pension Insurance

(1) The German Democratic Republic shall introduce all necessary measures to adapt its pension law to the pension insurance law of the Federal Republic of Germany, which is based on the principle of wage and contribution-related benefits. Over a transitional period of five years account shall be taken of the principle of bona fide rights protection in respect of persons approaching pensionable age.

(2) The pension insurance fund shall use its resources exclusively to meet its obligations with regard to rehabilitation, invalidity, old age, and death. The existing supplementary and special pensions

schemes shall be discontinued as of 1 July 1990. Accrued claims and entitlements shall be transferred to the pension insurance fund, and benefits on the basis of special arrangements shall be reviewed with a view to abolishing unjustified benefits and reducing excessive benefits. The additional expenditure incurred by the pension insurance fund because of such transfers shall be reimbursed from the budget.

(3) Upon conversion to Deutsche Mark current pensions from the pension insurance fund shall be fixed at a net replacement rate which, for a pensioner who has completed 45 insurance/working years and whose earnings were at all times in line with average earnings, shall be 70 per cent of average net earnings in the German Democratic Republic. For a greater or smaller number of insurance/working years, the percentage shall be correspondingly higher or lower. The basis for calculating the upgrading rate for individual pensions shall be the pension of an average wageearner in the German Democratic Republic, graduated according to year of entry, who has paid full contributions to the voluntary supplementary insurance scheme of the German Democratic Republic, over and above his compulsory social insurance contributions. If there is no upgrading on this basis a pension shall be paid in Deutsche Mark which corresponds to the amount of the former pension in Mark of the German Democratic Republic. Survivor's pensions shall be calculated on the basis of the pension which the deceased would have received after conversion.

(4) Pensions from the pension insurance fund shall be adjusted in line with the development of net wages and salaries in the German Democratic Republic.

(5) The voluntary supplementary pension insurance scheme in the German Democratic Republic shall be discontinued.

(6) The German Democratic Republic shall make a government contribution to its pension insurance fund to offset its expenditure.

(7) Persons who have transferred their habitual residence from the territory of either Contracting Party to that of the other Party after 18 May 1990 shall receive from the pension insurance institution hitherto responsible a pension calculated according to the regulations applicable to that institution for the period completed there.

ARTICLE 21
Health Insurance

(1) The German Democratic Republic shall introduce all necessary measures to adapt its health insurance law to that of the Federal Republic of Germany.

(2) Benefits which have hitherto been financed from the health insurance fund according to the legislation of the German Democratic Republic but which according to the legislation of the Federal Republic of Germany are not benefits covered by the health

insurance fund shall, for the time being, be financed from the budget of the German Democratic Republic.

(3) The German Democratic Republic shall introduce continued payment of wages in the event of sickness which is in line with legislation governing continued payment of wages in the Federal Republic of Germany.

(4) Pensioners shall be covered by health insurance. The contribution rate of the relevant health insurance fund shall be applicable. The health insurance contributions of pensioners shall be paid in a lump sum by the pension insurance fund to the health insurance fund. The amount to be paid shall be determined according to overall pension payments before deduction of the proportion of the health insurance contribution payable to pensioners. This shall not affect the net replacement rate envisaged after conversion of pensions.

(5) Investment in in-patient and out-patient facilities of the health service of the German Democratic Republic shall be financed from budget funds and not from contribution revenue.

ARTICLE 22
Public Health

(1) Medical care and health protection are of particular concern to the Contracting Parties.

(2) While provisionally continuing the present system, which is necessary to maintain public medical services, the German Democratic Republic shall gradually move towards the range of services offered in the Federal Republic of Germany with private providers, particularly by admitting registered doctors, dentists and pharmacists as well as independent providers of medicaments and remedial aids, and by admitting private providers of independent, non-profit-making hospitals.

(3) The German Democratic Republic shall create the necessary legal framework for the development of the necessary contractual relations — particularly as regards remuneration — between health insurance institutions and providers of services.

ARTICLE 23
Accident Insurance Pensions

(1) The German Democratic Republic shall introduce all necessary measures to adapt its accident insurance law to that of the Federal Republic of Germany.

(2) Upon conversion to Deutsche Mark, current accident insurance pensions shall be recalculated and paid on the basis of average gross earnings in the German Democratic Republic.

(3) Accident pensions to be determined after the conversion to Deutsche Mark shall be based on the average gross monthly earnings in the

twelve months prior to the accident.
(4) The provisions of Article 20 (4) and (7) shall apply mutatis mutandis.

ARTICLE 24
Social Assistance

The German Democratic Republic shall introduce a system of social assistance which shall correspond to the Social Assistance Act of the Federal Republic of Germany.

ARTICLE 25
Initial Financing

If, during a transitional period, contributions to the unemployment insurance fund of the German Democratic Republic and both the contributions and the government subsidy to the pension insurance fund of the German Democratic Republic do not fully cover expenditure on benefits, the Federal Republic of Germany shall provide temporary initial financing for the German Democratic Republic within the framework of the budgetary aid granted under Article 28 of this Treaty.

CHAPTER V
PROVISIONS CONCERNING THE BUDGET AND FINANCE

SECTION 1
The Budget

ARTICLE 26
Principles underlying the Fiscal Policy of the German Democratic Republic

(1) Public budgets in the German Democratic Republic shall be drawn up by the relevant national, regional or local authorities on their own responsibility, due account being taken of the requirements of general economic equilibrium. The aim shall be to establish a system of budgeting adapted to the market economy. Budgets shall be balanced as regards revenue and expenditure. All revenue and expenditure shall be included in the appropriate budget.
(2) Budgets shall be adapted to the budget structures of the Federal Republic of Germany. The following in particular shall be removed from the budget, starting with the partial budget for 1990 as of the establishment of monetary union:

— the social sector, in so far as it is wholly or mainly financed from charges or contributions in the Federal Republic of Germany,

- state undertakings by conversion into legally and economically independent enterprises,
- transport undertaking by making them legally independent,
- the Deutsche Reichsbahn and the Deutsche Post, which will be operated as special funds.

Government borrowing for housing shall be allocated to individual projects on the basis of their existing physical assets.

(3) National, regional and local authorities in the German Democratic Republic shall make every effort to limit deficits in drawing up and executing budgets. As regards expenditure this shall include:

- abolition of budget subsidies, particularly in the short term for industrial goods, agricultural products and food, autonomous price supports being permissible for the latter in line with the regulations of the European Communities, and progressively in the sectors of transport, energy for private households and housing, making allowance for the general development of income,
- sustained reduction of personnel expenditure in the public service,
- review of all items of expenditure, including the legal provisions on which they are based, to determine whether they are necessary and can be financed,
- structural improvements in the education system and preparatory division according to a federal structure (including the research sector).

As regards revenue, the limitation of deficits shall require, in addition to the measures under Section 2 of this Chapter, the harmonization or introduction of contributions and fees for public services corresponding to the system in the Federal Republic of Germany.

(4) An inventory shall be made of publicly owned assets. Publicly owned assets shall be used primarily for the structural adaption of the economy and for the recapitalization of the budget in the German Democratic Republic.

ARTICLE 27
Borrowing and Debts

(1) Borrowing authorizations in the budgets of the local, regional and national authorities of the German Democratic Republic shall be limited to 10 billion Deutsche Mark for 1990 and 14 billion Deutsche Mark for 1991 and allocated to the different levels of government in agreement with the Minister of Finance of the Federal Republic of Germany. A borrowing limit of 7 billion Deutsche Mark for 1990 and 10 billion Deutsche Mark for 1991 shall be established for the advance financing of proceeds expected to accrue from the realization of assets currently held in trust. In the event of a fundamental change

in conditions, the Minister of Finance of the Federal Republic of Germany may permit these credit ceilings to be exceeded.
(2) The raising of loans and the granting of equalization claims shall be conducted in agreement between the Minister of Finance of the German Democratic Republic and the Minister of Finance of the Federal Republic of Germany. The same shall apply to the assumption of sureties, warranties or other guarantees and for the total authorizations for future commitments to be appropriated in the budget.
(3) After accession, debt accrued in the budget of the German Democratic Republic shall be transferred to the assets held in trust in so far as it can be redeemed by proceeds expected to accrue from the realization of the assets held in trust. The remaining debt shall be assumed in equal parts by the Federal Government and the Länder newly constituted on the territory of the German Democratic Republic. Loans raised by Länder and local authorities shall remain their responsibility.

ARTICLE 28
Financial Allocations granted by the Federal Republic of Germany

(1) The Federal Republic of Germany shall grant the German Democratic Republic financial allocations amounting to 22 billion Deutsche Mark for the second half of 1990 and 35 billion Deutsche Mark for 1991 for the specific purposes of balancing its budget. Furthermore, initial financing shall be made available from the federal budget, in accordance with Article 25, amounting to 750 million Deutsche Mark for the second half of 1990 for pension insurance as well as 2 billion Deutsche Mark for the second half of 1990 and 3 billion Deutsche Mark for 1991 for unemployment insurance. Payments shall be made as required.
(2) The Contracting Parties agree that the transit sum payable under Article 18 of the Agreement of 17 December 1971 on the Transit of Civilian Persons and Goods between the Federal Republic of Germany and Berlin (West) shall lapse upon the entry into force of this Treaty. The German Democratic Republic shall cancel with effect for the two Contracting Parties the regulations on fees laid down in that Agreement and in the Agreement of 31 October 1979 on the Exemption of Road Vehicles from Taxes and Fees. In amendment of the Agreement of 5 December 1989, the Contracting Parties agree that from 1 July 1990 no more payments shall be made into the hard-currency fund (for citizens of the German Democratic Republic travelling to the Federal Republic of Germany). A supplementary agreement shall be concluded between the Finance Ministers of the Contracting Parties on the use of any amounts remaining in the fund upon the establishment of Monetary Union.

ARTICLE 29
Transitional Regulations in the Public Service

Government of the German Democratic Republic shall guarantee, with due regard for the first sentence of Article 2 (1), that in collective bargaining agreements or other settlements in the public administration sector the general economic and financial conditions in the German Democratic Republic and the exigencies of budget consolidation are taken into account, with any new service regulations being of a transitional nature only. The Federal Representation of Staff Act shall be applied mutatis mutandis.

SECTION 2
Finance

ARTICLE 30
Customs and Special Excise Taxes

(1) In accordance with the principle set out in Article 11 (3) of this Treaty, the German Democratic Republic shall adopt step by step the customs law of the European Communities, including the Common Customs Tariff, and the special excise taxes stipulated in Annex IV to this Treaty.
(2) The Contracting Parties are agreed that their customs territory shall comprise the area of application of this Treaty.
(3) Equalization at the border between the fiscal territories for excise taxes of both Contracting Parties, except those on tobacco, shall be discontinued. Fiscal jurisdiction shall remain unaffected. Separate agreements shall be made to offset shifts in excise revenue.
(4) The movement of untaxed excisable goods between the fiscal territories shall be permitted as stipulated in the regulations on movements of untaxed goods within one fiscal territory.
(5) Tax relief for export goods shall be granted only upon proof of export to territories other than two fiscal territories.

ARTICLE 31
Taxes on Income, Property, Net Worth and Transactions

(1) The German Democratic Republic shall regulate taxes on income, property, net worth and transactions in accordance with Annex IV to this Treaty.
(2) For the purposes of turnover tax there shall be no tax frontier between the Contracting Parties; in consequence, there shall be no equalization of turnover tax burdens at the frontier. Fiscal jurisdiction shall remain unaffected. The right of input tax deduction shall extend to the tax on turnovers which are subject to the turnover tax of the other Contracting Party. Compensation for the reduced yield

resulting from this shall be settled by special agreement.

(3) Where there is unlimited net worth tax liability in the territory of one Contracting Party, that Party shall have the exclusive right to tax; where there is unlimited net worth tax liability in the territories of both Contracting Parties, this shall apply to the Party with which the taxpayer has the closer personal and economic ties (centre of vital interests) or in whose territory he has effective management as a legal person. Property located in the territory of the other Contracting Party shall be assessed according to the regulations for domestic property applying in that territory.

(4) Where there is unlimited inheritance tax or gift tax liability in the territory of one Contracting Party, that Party shall have the exclusive right to tax transfers on which tax is payable after 31 December 1990. Where there is unlimited tax liability in the territory of both Contracting Parties, this shall apply to the Party with which the testator or donor had the closer personal and economic ties when the tax liability was incurred (centre of vital interests), or in whose territory he had effective management as a legal person. The second sentence of paragraph 3 above shall be applied mutatis mutandis to evaluation.

(5) Paragraph 4 shall apply accordingly to transfer of property by reason of death on which taxes are incurred after 30 June 1990 and before 1 January 1991. Transfers of property by reason of death from citizens of the Contracting Parties who had established residence in the territory of the other Party after 8 November 1989 or who for the first time had their customary abode there and who still had their residence or customary abode there at the time of death cannot be subjected to any higher inheritance tax than would be imposed where there is unlimited tax liability in the territory of the first-mentioned Contracting Party.

(6) Disclosure and notification obligations resulting from the inheritance tax and gift tax legislation of the Contracting Parties shall in each case apply also with regard to the revenue authorities of the other Party.

ARTICLE 32
Exchange of Information

(1) The Contracting Parties shall exchange such information as is necessary for the execution of their taxation and monopoly legislation. The Ministers of Finance of the Contracting Parties, together with the authorities empowered by them, shall be responsible for the exchange of information. Any information received by a Contracting Party shall be treated as secret in the same manner as information obtained under the domestic laws of that party and shall be disclosed only to those persons or authorities (including courts and administrative bodies) involved in the assessment or collection of, the enforcement or prosecution in respect of, or the determination of

appeals in relation to the taxes and monopolies falling within this Section. Such persons or authorities shall use the information for these purposes only. They may disclose the information in public court proceedings or in judicial decisions.

(2) The provisions of paragraph 1 shall not commit either Contracting Party

— to carry out administrative measures at variance with the laws and administrative practice of that or of the other Contracting Party;

— to supply information which is not obtainable under the laws or in the normal course of the administration of that or of the other Contracting Party;

— to supply information which would disclose any trade, business, industrial, commercial or professional secret or trade process, or information the disclosure of which would be contrary to public policy.

ARTICLE 33
Consultation Procedure

(1) The Contracting Parties shall endeavour to avoid double taxation in respect of taxes on income, property, net worth and transactions by reaching agreement on the appropriate delimitation of the tax base. They shall also strive to eliminate by mutual agreement any difficulties or doubts which result from the interpretation or application of their law on the taxes and monopolies that fall within this Section.

(2) To reach agreement as mentioned in paragraph 1 above, the Minister of Finance of the Federal Republic of Germany and the Minister of Finance of the German Democratic Republic may communicate directly with each other.

ARTICLE 34
Structure of the Revenue Administration

(1) The German Democratic Republic shall create the legal basis for a three-tier revenue administration in line with the Revenue Administration Act of the Federal Republic of Germany, incorporating the amendments arising from this Treaty, and shall establish the administrations accordingly.

(2) Before the establishment of monetary, economic and social union, the first priority shall be to set up efficient tax and customs administrations.

CHAPTER VI
FINAL PROVISIONS

ARTICLE 35
International Treaties

This Treaty shall not affect the international treaties which the Federal Republic of Germany and the German Democratic Republic have concluded with third countries.

ARTICLE 36
Review of the Treaty

The provisions of this Treaty shall be reviewed in the light of any fundamental changes in the situation.

ARTICLE 37
Berlin Clause

Consistent with the Quadripartite Agreement of 3 September 1971 this Treaty will, in accordance with established procedures, be extended to Berlin (West).

ARTICLE 38
Entry into Force

This Treaty, including the Protocol and Annexes I–IX, shall enter into force on the date on which the Governments of the Contracting Parties have informed each other that the necessary constitutional and other national requirements for such entry into force have been fulfilled.

Done at Bonn on 18 May 1990 in duplicate in the German language.

For the
Federal Republic of Germany
Dr Theo Waigel

For the
German Democratic Republic
Dr Walter Romberg

PROTOCOL ON GUIDELINES
To supplement the Treaty establishing a Monetary, Economic and Social Union, the High Contracting Parties have agreed on the following guidelines which shall be binding in accordance with the first sentence of Article 4 (1) of the Treaty.

A. GENERAL GUIDELINES

I. GENERAL PROVISIONS

1. The law of the German Democratic Republic will be modelled on the principles of a free, democratic federal and social order governed by the rule of law and be guided by the legal regime of the European Communities.
2. Regulations which commit individual or state institutions, including the legislature and the judiciary, to a socialist system of law, a socialist body politic, the aims and targets of centralized economic control and planning, a socialist sense of justice, socialist convictions, the convictions of individual groups or parties, socialist morality, or comparable notions, will no longer be applied. The rights and obligations of parties to legal relations shall be bounded by public morals, the principle of good faith, and the necessity of protecting the economically weaker party from undue disadvantage.
3. Authorizations should be required only for compelling reasons of the common weal. Their preconditions should be clearly defined.

II. ECONOMIC UNION

1. Economic activity should primarily occur in the private sector and on the basis of competition.
2. Freedom of contract will be guaranteed. Intervention in the freedom of economic activity must be kept to a minimum.
3. Business decisions will be free from planning targets (e.g. regarding production, purchasing, deliveries, investment, employment, prices and utilization of profits).
4. Private enterprises and liberal professions will not be subjected to worse treatment than state and cooperative enterprises.
5. Prices will be freely set, except where they are established by the government for compelling reasons in cases where the economy as a whole is affected.
6. For economic activity, the freedom to acquire, dispose of and use land and other factors of production will be guaranteed.
7. Enterprises under direct or indirect state ownership will be managed according to the principles of economic efficiency. They will be organized competitively as quickly as possible and transferred to private ownership as far as possible. The aim is to open up opportunities for small and medium-sized enterprises in particular.

8. In respect of posts and telecommunications, the regulatory and organizational principles contained in the Structure of Posts and Telecommunications Act of the Federal Republic of Germany will be adopted step by step.

III. SOCIAL UNION

1. Everyone has the right to form or join organizations to safeguard and enhance working and economic conditions, to leave such organizations and to remain outside them. Furthermore, the right to be active within such organizations is guaranteed. All agreements which restrict these rights will be void. Trade unions and employers' associations will be protected as regards their establishment, existence, organizational autonomy and proper activity.
2. Trade unions and employers' associations able to conclude collective agreements must be freely formed, not include members from the other side, be organized on a supra-company level and independent, and accept existing legislation on collective bargaining as binding; they must also be able to conclude collective agreements by exerting pressure on their bargaining partner.
3. Wages and other working conditions will not be determined by the state but through free negotiation between trade unions, employers' associations and employers.
4. Legislation providing for special participation rights for the Free German Trade Unions' Federation, company-level union organizations and union management will no longer be applied.

B. GUIDELINES FOR INDIVIDUAL FIELDS OF LAW

I JUDICIAL SYSTEM

1. Regulations providing for the participation of collectives, social organs, trade unions, works, social prosecutors and defenders in the judicial system and their right to be informed about proceedings will no longer be applied; the right of trade unions to advice and legal representation in labour disputes will remain unaffected by this provision.
2. Regulations on cooperation between the courts and local representations of the people and other organs, the duty of judges to inform the latter, as well as criticism of the courts will no longer be applied.
3. Regulations concerning the involvement of public prosecutors in the judicial system will only be applicable in criminal cases and in family law, parent and child and guardianship cases.
4. Principles contained in the Criminal Code of the German Democratic Republic which relate to the socialist system of law and the socialist body politic, as well as regulations which serve to maintain a centrally planned economy, conflict with a future unification of the two

German states or are contrary to principles of a free democratic state, will not be applied to offences committed after the entry into force of this Treaty.

5. Provisions of the Criminal Code which relate to socialist property will not be applied to offences committed after the entry into force of this Treaty; regulations concerning personal or private property will also be applied to other property and assets after the entry into force of this Treaty.

6. To the extent that the legislation referred to in Annex II provides for fines or penalties and cannot be incorporated in the system of sanctions of the German Democratic Republic, the German Democratic Republic will adapt it to its own law as far as possible in line with the legislation of the Federal Republic of Germany.

II. ECONOMIC LAW

1. For the purpose of establishing collateral for credits, rights equivalent to those in the Federal Republic of Germany, especially rights in rem, will be created in the German Democratic Republic.

2. Conditions for a free capital market will be created in the German Democratic Republic. They will include particularly the liberalization of interest rates and the admission of tradeable securities (stocks and bonds).

3. Conditions will be created so that administrative decisions and other rulings made by authorities referred to in the third sentence of Article 3 of the Treaty can be enforced against persons domiciled in the German Democratic Republic.

4. The existing insurance monopoly in the German Democratic Republic will be abolished, premium control removed from those insurance branches where tariffs are not part of the business statutes, and current legislation and rules on general conditions for insurance companies repealed.

5. Existing barriers in the payment transactions system of the German Democratic Republic will be removed and its structuring under private law promoted.

6. Foreign trade and payments will be free. Restrictions will be permissible only for compelling reasons in cases where the economy as a whole is affected, on the basis of intergovernmental agreements. The German Democratic Republic will abolish its external trade monopoly.

7. In order to achieve a comparable basis, the German Democratic Republic will adjust its statistics to those of the Federal Republic of Germany and, in cooperation with the Federal Statistical Office or the Deutsche Bundesbank, make information available in accordance with federal statistical standards for the following areas: labour market, prices, production, turnover, foreign trade and payments and retail trade.

III. BUILDING LAW

In order to establish a reliable basis for construction planning and investment, the German Democratic Republic will create as soon as possible a legal framework consistent with the Building Code and the Regional Planning Act of the Federal Republic of Germany.

IV. LABOUR AND SOCIAL LAW

1. Employers in the German Democratic Republic may agree with employees from the Federal Republic of Germany who are temporarily employed in the German Democratic Republic that the labour legislation of the Federal Republic of Germany be applied.
2. Persons in temporary employment may be exempt from compulsory social insurance if they have other cover.
3. The regulations of the German Democratic Republic governing occupational safety and health will be adapted within an appropriate transitional period to the industrial safety laws of the Federal Republic of Germany.
4. In changing its legal minimum period of notice for employment contracts, the German Democratic Republic will not exceed the statutory minimum periods of notice applicable in the Federal Republic of Germany in respect of wage-earners and salaried employees.
5. The German Democratic Republic will create a legal basis for summary dismissal for important reasons in conformity with Sections 626 and 628 of the Civil Code of the Federal Republic of Germany.

STATEMENTS FOR THE RECORD

At the signing of the Treaty between the Federal Republic of Germany and the German Democratic Republic establishing a Monetary, Economic and Social Union, the following statements were made with reference to the Treaty:

1. The two Contracting Parties state the following with regard to the second sentence of Article 2 (1) of the Treaty: Freedom of movement within the meaning of this provision also includes the entry into the currency area of individuals, including members of ethnic minorities, who are in possession of an identity card, a passport or document in lieu of a passport of the Federal Republic of Germany or the German Democratic Republic.
2. The German Democratic Republic states that it will grant nationals and enterprises of all member states of the European Communities equal treatment with individuals and enterprises of the Federal Republic of Germany on a reciprocal basis in so far as the jurisdiction of the European Communities might be affected and in so far as nothing to the contrary is explicitly agreed in this Treaty; the protocol

(to the EEC Treaty) on German internal trade remains unaffected by this provision.

3. The two Contracting Parties understand the three-month FIBOR within the meaning of the third sentence of Article 8 of Section 4 (1) of Annex I to be the respective interest rate which is determined in Frankfurt/Main every three months on the second business day prior to the beginning of an interest period, according to Section 2 (3) of the Conditions for the Bond of the Federal Republic of Germany of 1990 (Securities Code No. 113–478) without the discount envisaged in it.

4. In connection with Section 1 (3) of Annex IV the German Democratic Republic states: To ensure competition for public contracts appropriate directives will be established without delay and applied by public authorities with effect from 1 January 1991 at the latest.

Bonn, 18 May 1990

For the   For the
Federal Republic of Germany   German Democratic Republic
Dr Theo Waigel   Dr Walter Romberg

(505 of the 519 Members of the Bundestag took part in the vote. 444 voted for, 60 against, and there was one abstention.)

Document 16 Statement by Lothar de Maizière, Prime Minister of the German Democratic Republic, on the occasion of the signing of the treaty, Bonn, 18 May 1990

This is an important day for us; it marks the beginning of the realization of Germany's unity. Monetary, economic and social union makes the unification process irreversible. What we are doing here today constitutes a decisive step towards our goal of achieving German unity in freedom within a peaceful European order.

The State Treaty is a treaty between the two Governments in Germany. Its content shows that both Governments are determined not to tailor the unification process from above. The coalescence of the divided Germany begins rather with the people and their living conditions. In our discussions and negotiations over the past few weeks we were guided by the interests of the people in the two German states.

The spirit in which this treaty was formulated is consonant with the aspirations and desires of the people in the GDR for freedom, prosperity and social justice. This was not a case of foreign states negotiating, but of compatriots and friends refusing to be estranged any longer . . . .

This Treaty is a compromise. Yet is in not the result of haggling, but a good and balanced piece of work. It is a sound blueprint for the introduction of an ecologically-oriented social market economy.

At this juncture I should like to turn first of all to the citizens of the GDR.

The introduction of the Deutschmark, of dynamic pensions and unemployment insurance, and the aid for the GDR's national budget, are a generous political gesture on the part of the Federal Republic of Germany. No one should forget what the Ostmark would really be worth today on a free market. And no one should be under any illusion as to the seriousness of the crisis in the GDR's economy. We could not and cannot carry on as before.

Not every rosy dream which some people have associated with the State Treaty could be fulfilled. But no one will be worse off than before. On the contrary: what country has ever been afforded as good a starting position as we have with this Treaty?

We in the GDR must now make the best of it. Adopting a realistic view of the situation, we must set to work with a new pioneering spirit, with commitment, faith and confidence in our own strength. In doing so, we will never lose sight of social justice. Our social commitment will hardly be surpassed by anyone.

To the citizens of the Federal Republic of Germany I should like to say the following:

My Government is responsible first and foremost for the Germans in the GDR and for their interests. This is in line with the mandate given us by the electorate in our newly-won democracy.

At the same time, however, we and the Federal Government are jointly responsible for an undivided future. Our aim in the GDR, too, is to ensure the stability of the Deutschmark and to safeguard an overall economic balance in the Federal Republic and in the GDR, in other words in the new joint economic area. I promise that we will do everything in our power to ensure that the funds from the Federal Republic of Germany are invested wisely.

We consider your aim to be help for self-help. In the long term, we want to receive no free gifts. We wish to safeguard our future through our own efforts.

Document 17 Treaty of 31 August 1990 between the Federal Republic of Germany and the German Democratic Republic on the establishment of German unity (Unification Treaty)

On 31 August 1990 Wolfgang Schäuble, Federal Minister of the Interior, and GDR State Secretary Günther Krause signed the Unification Treaty in East Berlin. The Treaty entered into force upon the GDR's accession to the Federal Republic on 3 October 1990. This date was chosen by the GDR *Volkskammer* on 23 August 1990.

The Federal Republic of Germany and the German Democratic Republic,

Resolved to achieve in free self-determination the unity of Germany in peace and freedom as an equal partner in the community of nations,

Mindful of the desire of the people in both parts of Germany to live together in peace and freedom in a democratic and social federal state governed by the rule of law,

In grateful respect to those who peacefully helped freedom prevail and who have unswervingly adhered to the task of establishing German unity and are achieving it,

Aware of the continuity of German history and bearing in mind the special responsibility arising from our past for a democratic development in Germany committed to respect for human rights and to peace,

Seeking through German unity to contribute to the unification of Europe and to the building of a peaceful European order in which borders no longer divide and which ensures that all European nations can live together in a spirit of mutual trust,

Aware that the inviolability of frontiers and of the territorial integrity and sovereignty of all states in Europe within their frontiers constitutes a fundamental condition for peace,

Have agreed to conclude a Treaty on the Establishment of German Unity, containing the following provisions:

CHAPTER I
EFFECT OF ACCESSION

ARTICLE 1
LÄNDER

(1) Upon the accession of the German Democratic Republic to the Federal Republic of Germany in accordance with Article 23 of the Basic Law taking effect on 3 October 1990 the Länder of Brandenburg, Mecklenburg-Western Pomerania, Saxony, Saxony-Anhalt and Thuringia shall become Länder of the Federal Republic of Germany.[1] The establishment of these Länder and their boundaries shall be governed by

the provisions of the Constitutional Act of 22 July 1990 on the Establishment of Länder in the German Democratic Republic (Länder Establishment Act) (Law Gazette I, No. 51, p. 955) in accordance with Annex II.

(2) The 23 boroughs of Berlin shall form Land Berlin.

ARTICLE 2
CAPITAL CITY, DAY OF GERMAN UNITY

(1) The capital of Germany shall be Berlin. The seat of the parliament and government shall be decided after the establishment of German unity.

(2) 3 October shall be a public holiday known as the Day of German Unity.

CHAPTER II
BASIC LAW

ARTICLE 3
ENTRY INTO FORCE OF THE BASIC LAW

Upon the accession taking effect, the Basic law of the Federal Republic of Germany, as published in the Federal Law Gazette Part III, No. 100–1, and last amended by the Act of 21 December 1983 (Federal Law Gazette I, p. 1481), shall enter into force in the Länder of Brandenburg, Mecklenburg-Western Pomerania, Saxony, Saxony-Anhalt and Thuringia and in the part of Land Berlin where it has not been valid to date,[2] subject to the amendments arising from Article 4, unless otherwise provided in the Treaty.

ARTICLE 4
AMENDMENTS TO THE BASIC LAW RESULTING FROM ACCESSION

The Basic Law of the Federal Republic of Germany shall be amended as follows:

1. The Preamble shall read as follows:
   'Conscious of their responsibility before God and men,
   Animated by the resolve to serve world peace as an equal partner in a united Europe, the German people have adopted, by virtue of their constituent power, this Basic Law.
   The Germans in the Länder of Baden-Württemberg, Bavaria, Berlin, Brandenburg, Bremen, Hamburg, Hesse, Lower Saxony, Mecklenburg-Western Pomerania, North-Rhine/Westphalia, Rhineland-Palatinate, Saarland, Saxony, Saxony-Anhalt, Schleswig-Holstein and Thuringia have achieved the unity and freedom of Germany in free self-

determination. This Basic Law is thus valid for the entire German People.'
2. Article 23 shall be repealed.
3. Article 51 (2) shall read as follows:
'(2) Each Land shall have at least three votes; Länder with more than two million inhabitants shall have four, Länder with more than six million inhabitants five, and Länder with more than seven million inhabitants six votes.'[3]
4. The existing text of Article 135a[4] shall become paragraph 1. The following paragraph shall be inserted after paragraph1:
'(2) Paragraph 1 above shall be applied mutatis mutandis to liabilities of the German Democratic Republic or its legal entities as well as to liabilities of the Federation or other corporate bodies and institutions under public law which are connected with the transfer of properties of the German Democratic Republic to the Federation, Länder and communes (Gemeinden), and to liabilities arising from measures taken by the German Democratic Republic or its legal entities.'
5. The following new Article 143 shall be inserted in the Basic Law:

'Article 143
(1) Law in the territory specified in Article 3 of the Unification Treaty may deviate from provisions of this Basic Law for a period not extending beyond 31 December 1992 in so far as and as long as no complete adjustment to the order of the Basic Law can be achieved as a consequence of the different conditions. Deviations must not violate Article 19 (2)[5] and must be compatible with the principles set out in Article 79 (3).[6]
(2) Deviations from sections II, VIII, VIIIa, IX, X and XI are permissible for a period not extending beyond 31 December 1995.
(3) Notwithstanding paragraphs 1 and 2 above, Article 41 of the Unification Treaty and the rules for its implementation shall remain valid in so far as they provide for the irreversibility of interferences with property in the territory specified in Article 3 of the said Treaty.'
6. Article 146 shall read as follows:
'Article 146
This Basic Law, which is valid for the entire German people following the achievement of the unity and freedom of Germany, shall cease to be in force on the day on which a constitution adopted by a free decision of the German people comes into force.'

ARTICLE 5
FUTURE AMENDMENTS TO THE CONSTITUTION

The Governments of the two Contracting Parties recommend to the legislative bodies of the united Germany[7] that within two years they should deal with the questions regarding amendments or additions to the Basic Law as raised in connection with German unification, in particular

— with regard to the relationship between the Federation and the
Länder in accordance with the Joint Resolution of the Minister
Presidents of 5 July 1990,[8]
— with regard to the possibility of restructuring the Berlin/Brandenburg
area in derogation of the provisions of Article 29 of the Basic Law[9]
by way of an agreement between the Länder concerned,
— with considerations on introducing state objectives into the Basic
Law, and
— with the question of applying Article 146 of the Basic Law and of
holding a referendum in this context.

ARTICLE 6
EXCEPTION

For the time being, Article 131 of the Basic Law shall not be applied
in the territory specified in Article 3 of this Treaty.[10]

ARTICLE 7
FINANCIAL SYSTEM

(1) The financial system of the Federal Republic of Germany shall be
extended to the territory specified in Article 3 unless otherwise provided
in this Treaty.
(2) Article 106 of the Basic Law shall apply to the apportionment of tax
revenue among Federation as well as the Länder and communes
(associations of communes) in the territory specified in Article 3 of this
Treaty with the proviso that

1. paragraph 3, fourth sentence, and paragraph 4 shall not apply up to
31 December 1994;[11]
2. up to 31 December 1996 the share of income tax revenue received by
the communes in accordance with Article 106 (5) of the Basic Law
shall be passed on from the Länder to the communes not on the basis
of the amount of income tax paid by their inhabitants, but according
to the number of inhabitants in the communes;
3. up to December 1994, in derogation of Article 106 (7) of the Basic
Law, an annual share of at least 20 per cent of the Land share of total
revenue from joint taxes and of the total revenue from Land taxes as
well as 40 per cent of the Land share from the German Unity Fund[12]
according to paragraph 5, item 1, shall accrue to the communes
(associations of communes).

(3) Article 107[13] of the Basic Law shall be valid in the territory
specified in Article 3 of this Treaty with the proviso that up to 31
December 1994 the provisions of paragraph 1, fourth sentence, shall not
be applied between the Länder which have until now constituted the
Federal Republic of Germany and the Länder in the territory specified

in Article 3 of this Treaty and that there shall be no all-German financial equalization between the Länder (Article 107 (2) of the Basic Law).

The Land share of turnover tax throughout Germany shall be divided up into an eastern component and a western component in such a way that the average share of turnover tax per inhabitant in the Länder of Brandenburg, Mecklenburg-Western Pomerania, Saxony, Saxony-Anhalt and Thuringia amounts

in 1991 to 55 per cent
in 1992 to 60 per cent
in 1993 to 65 per cent
in 1994 to 70 per cent

of the average share of turnover tax per inhabitant in the Länder of Baden-Württemberg, Bavaria, Bremen, Hesse, Hamburg, Lower Saxony, North-Rhine/Westphalia, Rhineland-Palatinate, Saarland and Schleswig-Holstein. The share of Land Berlin shall be calculated in advance on the basis of the number of inhabitants. The provisions contained in this paragraph shall be reviewed for 1993 in the light of the conditions obtaining at the time.

(4) The territory specified in Article 3 of this Treaty shall be incorporated in the provisions of Article 91 a, 91 b and 104 a (3) and (4) of the Basic Law,[13a] including the pertinent implementing provisions, in accordance with this Treaty with effect from 1 January 1991.

(5) Following the establishment of German unity the annual allocations from the German Unity Fund shall be distributed as follows:

1. 85 per cent as special assistance to the Länder of Brandenburg, Mecklenburg-Western Pomerania, Saxony, Saxony-Anhalt and Thuringia as well as to Land Berlin to cover their general financial requirements and divided up among these Länder in proportion to their number of inhabitants, excluding the inhabitants of Berlin (West), and
2. 15 per cent to meet public requirements at a central level in the territory of the aforementioned Länder.

(6) In the event of a fundamental change in conditions, the Federation and the Länder shall jointly examine the possibilities of granting further assistance in order to ensure adequate financial equalization for the Länder in the territory specified in Article 3 of this Treaty.

CHAPTER III
HARMONIZATION OF LAW

ARTICLE 8
EXTENSION OF FEDERAL LAW

Upon the accession taking effect, federal law shall enter into force in the territory specified in Article 3 of this Treaty unless its area of application is restricted to certain Länder or parts of Länder of the Federal Republic of Germany and unless otherwise provided in this Treaty, notably Annex I.

ARTICLE 9
CONTINUED VALIDITY OF LAW OF THE GERMAN DEMOCRATIC REPUBLIC

(1) Law of the German Democratic Republic valid at the time of the signing of this Treaty which is Land Law according to the distribution of competence under the Basic Law shall remain in force in so far as it is compatible with the Basic Law, notwithstanding Article 143, with the federal law put into force in the territory specified in Article 3 of this Treaty and with the directly applicable law of the European Communities, and unless otherwise provided in this Treaty. Law of the German Democratic Republic which is federal law according to the distribution of competence under the Basic Law and which refers to matters not regulated uniformly at the federal level shall continue to be valid as Land Law under the conditions set out in the first sentence pending a settlement by the federal legislator.

(2) The law of the German Democratic Republic referred to in Annex II shall remain in force with the provisos set out there in so far as it is compatible with the Basic Law, taking this Treaty into consideration, and with the directly applicable law of the European Communities.

(3) Law of the German Democratic Republic enacted after the signing of this Treaty shall remain in force to the extent agreed between the Contracting Parties. Paragraph 2 above shall remain unaffected.

(4) Where law remaining in force according to paragraphs 2 and 3 above refers to matters within the exclusive legislative power of the Federation, it shall remain in force as federal law. Where it refers to matters within concurrent legislative powers or outlining legislation, it shall continue to apply as federal law if and to the extent that it relates to fields which are regulated by federal law in the remaining area of application of the Basic Law.

(5) The church tax legislation enacted by the German Democratic Republic in accordance with Annex II shall continue to apply as Land Law in the Länder named in Article 1 (1) of this Treaty.

ARTICLE 10
LAW OF THE EUROPEAN COMMUNITIES

(1) Upon the accession taking effect, the Treaties on the European Communities together with their amendments and supplements as well as the international agreements, treaties and resolutions which have come into force in connection with those Treaties shall apply in the territory specified in Article 3 of this Treaty.

(2) Upon the accession taking effect, the legislative acts enacted on the basis of the Treaties on the European Communities shall apply in the territory specified in Article 3 of this Treaty unless the competent institutions of the European Communities enact exemptions. These exemptions are intended to take account of administrative requirements and help avoid economic difficulties.

(3) Legislative acts of the European Communities whose implementation or execution comes under the responsibility of the Länder shall be implemented or executed by the latter through provisions under Land Law.

CHAPTER IV
INTERNATIONAL TREATIES AND AGREEMENTS

ARTICLE 11
TREATIES OF THE FEDERAL REPUBLIC OF GERMANY

The Contracting Parties proceed on the understanding that international treaties and agreements to which the Federal Republic of Germany is a contracting party, including treaties establishing membership of international organizations or institutions, shall retain their validity and that the rights and obligations arising therefrom, with the exception of the treaties named in Annex I, shall also relate to the territory specified in Article 3 of this Treaty. Where adjustments become necessary in individual cases, the all-German Government shall consult with the respective contracting parties.

ARTICLE 12
TREATIES OF THE GERMAN DEMOCRATIC REPUBLIC

(1) The Contracting Parties are agreed that, in connection with the establishment of German unity, international treaties of the German Democratic Republic shall be discussed with the contracting parties concerned with a view to regulating or confirming their continued application, adjustment or expiry, taking into account protection of confidence, the interests of the states concerned, the treaty obligations of the Federal Republic of Germany as well as the principles of a free, democratic basic order governed by the rule of law, and respecting the competence of the European Communities.

(2) The united Germany shall determine its position with regard to the adoption of international treaties of the German Democratic Republic following consultations with the respective contracting parties and with the European Communities where the latter's competence is affected.

(3) Should the united Germany intend to accede to international organizations or other multilateral treaties of which the German Democratic Republic but not the Federal Republic of Germany is a member, agreement shall be reached with the respective contracting

parties and with the European Communities where the latter's competence is affected.

CHAPTER V
PUBLIC ADMINISTRATION AND THE ADMINISTRATION OF JUSTICE

ARTICLE 13
FUTURE STATUS OF INSTITUTIONS

(1) Administrative bodies and other institutions serving the purposes of public administration or the administration of justice in the territory specified in Article 3 of this Treaty shall pass under the authority of the government of the Land in which they are located. Institutions whose sphere of activities transcends the boundaries of a Land shall come under the joint responsibility of the Länder concerned. Where institutions consist of several branches each of which is in a position to carry out its activities independently, the branches shall come under the responsibility of the government of the respective Land in which they are located. The Land government shall be responsible for the transfer of winding-up. Section 22 of the Länder Establishment Act of 22 July 1990 shall remain unaffected.

(2) To the extent that before the accession took effect the institutions or branches mentioned in paragraph 1, first sentence, performed tasks that are incumbent upon the Federation according to the distribution of competence under the Basic Law, they shall be subject to the competent supreme federal authorities. The latter shall be responsible for the transfer of winding-up.

(3) Institutions under paragraph 1 and 2 above shall also include such

1. cultural, educational, scientific and sports institutions,
2. radio and television establishments as come under the responsibility of public administrative bodies.

ARTICLE 14
JOINT INSTITUTIONS OF THE LÄNDER

(1) Institutions or branches of institutions which, before the accession took effect, performed tasks that are incumbent upon the Länder according to the distribution of competence under the Basic Law shall continue to operate as joint institutions of the Länder pending a final settlement by the Länder named in Article 1 (1) of this Treaty. This shall apply only to the extent that it is necessary for them to remain in place under this transitional arrangement so as to allow the Länder to carry out their responsibilities.

(2) The joint institutions of the Länder shall be under the authority of the Land plenipotentiaries pending the election of minister presidents in

the Länder. Subsequently they shall be under the authority of the minister presidents. The latter may charge the responsible Land minister with their supervision.

ARTICLE 15
TRANSITIONAL ARRANGEMENTS FOR LAND ADMINISTRATION

(1) The Land spokesmen in the Länder named in Article 1 (1) of this Treaty and the government plenipotentiaries in the districts shall continue to discharge their present responsibilities on behalf of the Federal Government and subject to its instructions, from the date when the accession takes effect until the election of minister presidents. The Land spokesmen shall, as Land plenipotentiaries, be in charge of the administration of their respective Länder and have the right to give instructions to district administrative authorities and, in the case of delegated responsibilities, also to communes and rural districts. Where Land commissioners were appointed in the Länder named in Article 1 (1) of this Treaty before the accession took effect, they shall be vested with the responsibilities and powers of the Land spokesman as set out in the first and second sentences.

(2) The other Länder and the Federation shall render administrative assistance in setting up Land administrative authorities.

(3) At the request of the minister presidents of the Länder named in Article 1 (1) of this Treaty the other Länder and the Federation shall render administrative assistance in the execution of certain technical responsibilities for a period not extending beyond 30 June 1991. The minister president shall grant any agencies and individuals from the Länder and the Federation a right to give instructions to the extent that they render administrative assistance in the execution of technical responsibilities.

(4) The Federation shall make available the necessary budget resources to the extent that it renders administrative assistance in the execution of technical responsibilities. The resources employed shall be deducted from the share of the respective Land in the German Unity Fund allocations or from its share of import turnover tax.

ARTICLE 16
TRANSITIONAL PROVISION PENDING THE CONSTITUTION OF A SINGLE LAND GOVERNMENT FOR BERLIN

Until the constitution of a single Land government for Berlin its responsibilities shall be discharged by the Berlin Senat[14] jointly with the Magistrat.[14a]

ARTICLE 17
REHABILITATION

The Contracting Parties reaffirm their intention to create without delay a legal foundation permitting the rehabilitation of all persons who have been victims of a politically motivated punitive measure or any court decision contrary to the rule of law or constitutional principles. The rehabilitation of these victims of the iniquitous SED regime shall be accompanied by appropriate arrangements for compensation.

ARTICLE 18
CONTINUED VALIDITY OF COURT DECISIONS

(1) Decisions handed down by the courts of the German Democratic Republic before the accession took effect shall retain their validity and may be executed in conformity with the law put into force according to Article 8 of this Treaty or remaining in force according to Article 9. This law shall be taken as the yardstick when checking the compatibility of decisions and their execution with the principles of the rule of law. Article 17 of this Treaty shall remain unaffected.

(2) Subject to Annex I, persons sentenced by criminal courts of the German Democratic Republic are granted by this Treaty a right of their own to seek the quashing of final decisions through the courts.

ARTICLE 19
CONTINUED VALIDITY OF DECISIONS TAKEN BY PUBLIC
ADMINISTRATIVE BODIES

Administrative acts of the German Democratic Republic performed before the accession took effect shall remain valid. They may be revoked if they are incompatible with the principles of the rule of law or with the provisions of this Treaty. In all other respects the rules on the validity of administrative acts shall remain unaffected.

ARTICLE 20
LEGAL STATUS OF PERSONS IN THE PUBLIC SERVICE

(1) The agreed transitional arrangements set out in Annex I shall apply to
the legal status of persons in the public service at the time of accession.

(2) The exercise of public responsibilities (state authority as defined in Article 33 (4) of the Basic Law) shall be entrusted as soon as possible to professional civil servants. Public service law shall be introduced in accordance with the agreed arrangements set out in Annex I. Article 92 of the Basic Law shall remain unaffected.

(3) Military personnel law shall be introduced in accordance with the agreed arrangements set out in Annex I.

CHAPTER VI
PUBLIC ASSETS AND DEBTS

ARTICLE 21
ADMINISTRATIVE ASSETS

(1) The assets of the German Democratic Republic which are used directly for specific administrative purposes (administrative assets) shall become federal assets unless their designated purpose as of 1 October 1989 was primarily to meet administrative responsibilities which, under the Basic Law, are to be exercised by Länder, communes (associations of communes) or other agencies of public administration. Where administrative assets were primarily used for the purposes of the former Ministry of State Security/ Office of National Security,[15] they shall accrue to the Trust Agency[16] unless they have already been given over to new social or public purposes since the above-mentioned date.

(2) Where administrative assets are not federal assets under paragraph 1 above, they shall accrue, upon the accession taking effect, to the agency of public administration which, under the Basic Law, is responsible for the relevant administrative purpose.

(3) Assets which have been made available free of charge by another corporate body under public law to the central government or to the Länder and communes (associations of communes) shall be returned free of charge to this corporate body or its legal successor; former Reich assets shall become federal assets.

(4) Where administrative assets become federal assets under paragraphs 1 to 3 above or by virtue of a federal law, they shall be used for public purposes in the territory specified in Article 3 of this Treaty. This shall also apply to the use of proceeds from the sale of assets.

ARTICLE 22
FINANCIAL ASSETS

(1) Public assets of legal entities in the territory specified in Article 3 of this Treaty, including landed property and assets in agriculture and forestry, which do not directly serve specific administrative purposes (financial assets), with the exception of social insurance assets, shall, unless they have been handed over to the Trust Agency or will be handed over by law according to Section 1 (1), second and third sentences, of the Trusteeship Act, to communes, towns and cities or rural districts, come under federal trusteeship upon the accession taking effect. Where financial assets were primarily used for the purposes of the former Ministry of State Security/ National Security Office, they shall accrue to the Trust Agency unless they have already been given over to

new social or public purposes since 1 October 1989. Financial assets shall be divided by federal law between the Federation and the Länder named in Article 1 of this Treaty in such a way that the Federation and the Länder named in Article 1 each receive one half of the total value of the assets. The communes (associations of communes) shall receive an appropriate share of the Länder portion. Assets accruing to the Federation under this provision shall be used for public purposes in the territory specified in Article 3 of this Treaty. The Länder share should in principle be distributed to the respective Länder in such a way that the relationship between the total values of the assets apportioned to the respective Länder corresponds to the relationship between the population sizes of these Länder on the date the accession takes effect, excluding the inhabitants of Berlin (West). Article 21 (3) of this Treaty shall be applied mutatis mutandis.

(2) Pending legislative arrangements the financial assets shall be administered by the authorities currently responsible unless the Federal Minister of Finance orders the assumption of administrative responsibilities by authorities responsible for the administration of assets at the federal level.

(3) On demand the federal, regional or local authorities referred to in paragraphs 1 and 2 above shall provide each other with information about, and grant each other access to, land registers, files and other materials containing information on assets whose assignment in law and in fact is unresolved or the subject of dispute between the said authorities.

(4) Paragraph 1 above shall not apply to publicly owned property used for residential purposes and coming under the legal responsibility of publicly owned housing enterprises. This shall also apply to publicly owned property which is already the subject of concrete plans for residential use. Upon the accession taking effect, these assets shall become the property of the local authorities, which shall also assume their respective shares of the debts. Taking into consideration social concerns, the local authorities shall step by step place their housing stock on the basis obtaining in a market economy. Privatization shall be speeded up in this context, among other things to encourage individual home ownership. As regards the publicly owned housing stock of state institutions, in so far as it does not come under Article 21 of this Treaty, paragraph 1 above shall remain unaffected.

ARTICLE 23
DEBT ARRANGEMENTS

(1) Upon the accession taking effect, the total debts of the central budget of the German Democratic Republic which have accumulated up to this date shall be taken over by a federal Special Fund without legal capacity, which shall meet the obligations arising from debt servicing. The Special Fund shall be empowered to raise loans:

1. to pay off debts of the Special Fund,
2. to cover due interest and loan procurement costs,
3. to purchase debt titles of the Special Fund for the purposes of market cultivation.

(2) The Federal Minister of Finance shall administer the Special Fund. The Special Fund may, in his name, conduct legal transactions, sue and be sued. The general legal domicile of the Special Fund shall be at the seat of the Federal Government. The Federation shall act as guarantor for the liabilities of the Special Fund.

(3) From the day the accession takes effect until 31 December 1993 the Federation and the Trust Agency shall each repay one half of the interest payments made by the Special Fund.
Repayment shall be made by the first of the month following the month in which the Special Fund has made the payments referred to in the first sentence.

(4) With effect from 1 January 1994 the Federation and the Länder named in Article 1 of this Treaty as well as the Trust Agency shall take over the total debts which have accumulated in the Special Fund up to 31 December 1993 in accordance with Article 27 (3) of the Treaty of 18 May 1990 between the Federal Republic of Germany and the German Democratic Republic Establishing a Monetary, Economic and Social Union. The distribution of the debts shall be settled in detail by a separate law in accordance with Article 34 of the Act of 25 July 1990 concerning the Treaty of 18 May 1990 (*Federal Law Gazette 1990* 11, p. 518). The portions of the total amount for the Länder named in Article 1 of this Treaty to be taken over by each of the Länder named in Article 1 shall be calculated in relation to their number of inhabitants on the date the accession takes effect, excluding the inhabitants of Berlin (West).

(5) The Special Fund shall be abolished at the end of 1993.

(6) Upon the accession taking effect, the Federal Republic of Germany shall take over the sureties, guarantees and warranties assumed by the German Democratic Republic and debited to its state budget prior to unification. The Länder named in Article 1 (1) of this Treaty and Land Berlin for that part in which the Basic Law has not been in force to date shall assume jointly and severally a counter-surety to the amount of 50 per cent of the total debt transferred in the form of sureties, guarantees and warranties to the Federal Republic of Germany. The losses shall be divided among the Länder in proportion to their number of inhabitants on the date the accession takes effect, excluding the inhabitants of Berlin (West).

(7) The German Democratic Republic's share of the Staatsbank Berlin may be transferred to the Länder named in Article 1 of this Treaty. The rights arising from the German Democratic Republic's share of the Staatsbank Berlin shall accrue to the Federation pending the transfer of the share according to the first sentence or a transfer according to the third sentence. The Contracting Parties shall, notwithstanding an examination from the viewpoint of antitrust legislation, provide for the

possibility of transferring the Staatsbank Berlin wholly or partially to a credit institution under public law in the Federal Republic of Germany or to other legal entities. In the event that not all assets and liabilities are covered by a transfer, the remaining part of the Staatsbank Berlin shall be wound up. The Federation shall assume the liabilities resulting from the German Democratic Republic acting as guarantor for the Staatsbank Berlin. This shall not apply to liabilities arising after the transfer of the share according to the first sentence or a transfer according to the third sentence. The fifth sentence shall apply mutatis mutandis to new liabilities created by the Staatsbank Berlin during winding-up. If claims are made on the Federation in its capacity as guarantor, the burden shall be incorporated upon the accession taking effect into the total debt of the central budget of the German Democratic Republic and be taken over by the Special Fund under paragraph 1 above, which has no legal capacity.

ARTICLE 24
SETTLEMENT OF CLAIMS AND LIABILITIES VIS-À-VIS FOREIGN COUNTRIES AND THE FEDERAL REPUBLIC OF GERMANY

(1) In so far as they arise from the monopoly on foreign trade and foreign currency or from the performance of other state tasks of the German Democratic Republic vis-à-vis foreign countries and the Federal Republic of Germany up to 1 July 1990, the settlement of the claims and liabilities remaining when the accession takes effect shall take place under instructions from, and under the supervision of, the Federal Minister of Finance. Debt rescheduling agreements contracted by the Government of the Federal Republic of Germany after the accession takes effect shall also incorporate the claims mentioned in the first sentence. The claims concerned shall be held in trust by the Federal Minister of Finance or transferred to the Federation to the extent that the claims are adjusted.

(2) The Special Fund as defined in Article 23 (1) of this Treaty shall, up to 30 November 1993, assume payment of the necessary administrative expenditure, the interest costs arising from the difference between interest payments and interest revenue and the other losses incurred by the institutions charged with the settlement of claims and liabilities during the settlement period in so far as the institutions are unable to balance them out of their own resources. After 30 November 1993 the Federation and the Trust Agency shall each assume one half of the expenditure and costs referred to in the first sentence and of the loss compensation. Further details shall be determined by federal law.

(3) Claims and liabilities arising from membership of the German Democratic Republic or its institutions in the Council for Mutual Economic Assistance may be the subject of separate arrangements by the Federal Republic of Germany. These arrangements may also refer to claims and liabilities which will arise or have arisen after 30 June 1990.

ARTICLE 25
ASSETS HELD IN TRUST

The Privatization and Reorganization of Publicly Owned Assets Act (Trusteeship Act) of 17 June 1990 (Law Gazette 1, No. 33, p. 300) shall continue to apply after the accession takes effect with the following proviso:

(1) The Trust Agency shall continue to be charged, in accordance with the provisions of the Trusteeship Act, with restructuring and privatizing the former publicly owned enterprises to bring them into line with the requirements of a competitive economy. It shall become a direct institution of the Federation vested with legal capacity and subject to public law. Technical and legal supervision shall be the responsibility of the Federal Minister of Finance, who shall exercise technical supervision in agreement with the Federal Minister of Economics and the respective federal minister. Stakes held by the Trust Agency shall be indirect stakes of the Federation. Amendments to the Charter shall require the agreement of the Federal Government.

(2) The number of members of the Administrative Board of the Trust Agency shall be raised from 16 to 20, and for the first Administrative Board to 23. Instead of the two representatives elected from the members of the Volkskammer, the Länder named in Article 1 of this Treaty shall each receive one seat on the Administrative Board of the Trust Agency. Notwithstanding Section 4 (2) of the Trusteeship Act, the chairman and the remaining members of the Administrative Board shall be appointed by the Federal Government.

(3) The Contracting Parties reaffirm that the publicly owned assets shall be used exclusively for the purpose of activities in the territory specified in Article 3 of this Treaty, regardless of budgetary responsibilities. Revenue of the Trust Agency shall accordingly be used in line with Article 26 (4) and Article 27 (3) of the Treaty of 18 May 1990. As part of the structural adjustment of the agricultural sector, revenue of the Trust Agency may also be used in individual cases for debt relief to agricultural enterprises. First of all, their own assets shall be used. Debts attributed to branches of enterprises which are to be hived off shall be disregarded. Assistance with debt relief may also be granted with the proviso that enterprises pay back the funds granted in whole or in part, depending on their economic capabilities.

(4) The power to raise loans granted to the Trust Agency by Article 27 (1) of the Treaty of 18 May 1990 shall be increased from a maximum total of 17 billion Deutsche Mark to a maximum total of 25 billion Deutsche Mark. The aforementioned loans should, as a rule, be repaid by 31 December 1995. The Federal Minister of Finance may permit an extension of the loan periods and, in the event of a fundamental change in conditions, give permission for the loan ceilings to be exceeded.

(5) The Trust Agency shall be empowered, in agreement with the Federal Minister of Finance, to assume sureties, guarantees and other warranties.

(6) In accordance with Article 10 (6) of the Treaty of 18 May 1990

possibilities shall be provided for savers at a later date to be granted a vested right to a share in publicly owned assets for the amount reduced following conversion at a rate of two to one.

(7) The interest and capital payments on loans raised before 30 June 1990 shall be suspended until the adoption of the opening balance in Deutsche Mark. The interest payments due shall be repaid to the Deutsche Kreditbank AG and the other banks by the Trust Agency.

ARTICLE 26
SPECIAL FUND OF THE DEUTSCHE REICHSBAHN

(1) Upon the accession taking effect, the property and all other property rights of the German Democratic Republic and the Reich property in Berlin (West) belonging to the special fund of the Deutsche Reichsbahn within the meaning of Article 26 (2) of the Treaty of 18 May 1990 shall become the property of the Federal Republic of Germany as the special fund of the Deutsche Reichsbahn. This further includes all property rights acquired since 8 May 1945 with resources from the special fund of the Deutsche Reichsbahn as well as those which were attached to its operation or that of its predecessor administrations, regardless of which legal entity they were acquired for, unless they were subsequently given over to another purpose with the consent of the Deutsche Reichsbahn. Property rights claimed by the Deutsche Reichsbahn up to 31 January 1991 pursuant to Section 1 (4) of the Decree of 11 July 1990 on the Registration of Claims with Regard to Property Rights (Law Gazette 1, No. 44, p. 718) shall not be regarded as property given over to another purpose with the consent of the Deutsche Reichsbahn.

(2) Associated liabilities and claims shall be transferred simultaneously with the property rights to the special fund of the Deutsche Reichsbahn.

(3) The Chairman of the Board of the Deutsche Bundesbahn and the Chairman of the Board of the Deutsche Reichsbahn shall be responsible for coordinating the two special funds. In carrying out this responsibility they shall work towards the objective of technically and organizationally merging the two railways.

ARTICLE 27
SPECIAL FUND OF THE DEUTSCHE POST

(1) The property and all other property rights belonging to the special fund of the Deutsche Post shall become the property of the Federal Republic of Germany. They shall be combined with the special fund of the Deutsche Bundespost. Associated liabilities and claims shall be transferred simultaneously with the property rights to the special fund of the Deutsche Bundespost. Property serving sovereign and political purposes, together with associated liabilities and claims, shall not become part of the special fund of the Deutsche Bundespost.

The special fund of the Deutsche Post shall also include all property rights which, as of 8 May 1945, belonged to the special fund of the Deutsche Reichspost or, after 8 May 1945, were either acquired with resources from the former special fund of the Deutsche Reichspost or attached to the operation of the Deutsche Post, regardless of which legal entity they were acquired for, unless they were subsequently given over to another purpose with the consent of the Deutsche Post. Property rights claimed by the Deutsche Post up to 31 January 1991 pursuant to Section 1 (4) of the Decree of 11 July 1990 on the Registration of Claims with Regard to Property Rights shall not be regarded as property given over to another purpose with the consent of the Deutsche Post.

(2) After consulting the enterprises of the Deutsche Bundespost the Federal Minister of Posts and Telecommunications shall finally determine the division of the special fund of the Deutsche Post among the partial special funds of the three enterprises. After consulting the three enterprises of the Deutsche Bundespost, the Federal Minister of Posts and Telecommunications shall, within a transitional period of three years, determine which items of property serve sovereign and political purposes. He shall take them over without compensation.

ARTICLE 28
ECONOMIC ASSISTANCE

(1) Upon the accession taking effect, the territory specified in Article 3 of this Treaty shall be incorporated into the arrangements of the Federation existing in the territory of the Federal Republic for economic assistance, taking into consideration the competence of the European Communities. The specific requirements of structural adjustment shall be taken into account during a transitional period. This will make a major contribution to the speediest possible development of a balanced economic structure with particular regard for small and medium-sized businesses.

(2) The relevant ministries shall prepare concrete programmes to speed up economic growth and structural adjustment in the territory specified in Article 3 of this Treaty. The programmes shall cover the following fields:

— measures of regional economic assistance accompanied by a special programme for the benefit of the territory specified in Article 3 of this Treaty; preferential arrangements shall be ensured for this territory;
— measures to improve the general economic conditions in the communes, with particular emphasis being given to infrastructure geared to the needs of the economy;
— measures to foster the rapid development of small and medium-sized businesses;
— measures to promote the modernization and restructuring of the economy, relying on restructuring schemes drawn up by industry of its own accord (e.g. rehabilitation programmes, including ones for

exports to COMECON countries);
— debt relief for enterprises following the examination of each case individually.

ARTICLE 29
FOREIGN TRADE RELATIONS

(1) The established foreign trade relations of the German Democratic Republic, in particular the existing contractual obligations vis-à-vis the countries of the Council for Mutual Economic Assistance, shall enjoy protection of confidence. They shall be developed further and expanded, taking into consideration the interests of all parties concerned and having regard for the principles of a market economy as well as the competence of the European Communities. The all-German Government shall ensure that appropriate organizational arrangements are made for these foreign trade relations within the framework of departmental responsibility.

(2) The Federal Government, or the all-German Government, shall hold consultations with the competent institutions of the European Communities on which exemptions are required for a transitional period in the field of foreign trade, having regard to paragraph 1 above.

CHAPTER VII
LABOUR, SOCIAL WELFARE, FAMILY, WOMEN, PUBLIC HEALTH AND ENVIRONMENTAL PROTECTION

ARTICLE 30
LABOUR AND SOCIAL WELFARE

(1) It shall be the task of the all-German legislator

1. to recodify in a uniform manner and as soon as possible the law on employment contracts and the provisions on working hours under public law, including the admissibility of work on Sundays and public holidays, and the specific industrial safety regulations for women;
2. to bring public law on industrial safety into line with present-day requirements in accordance with the law of the European Communities and the concurrent part of the industrial safety law of the German Democratic Republic.

(2) Employed persons in the territory specified in Article 3 of this Treaty shall be entitled, upon reaching the age of 57, to receive early retirement payments for a period of three years, but not beyond the earliest possible date on which they become entitled to receive a retirement pension under the statutory pension scheme. The early retirement payment shall amount to 65 per cent of the last average net earnings; for employed persons whose entitlement arises on or before 1 April 1991

early retirement payments shall be raised by an increment of five percentage points for the first 312 days. The early retirement payments shall be made by the Federal Institute for Employment along similar lines to unemployment pay, notably the provisions of Section 105c of the Employment Promotion Act. The Federal Institute for Employment may reject an application if it is established that there is a clear lack of manpower in the region to carry out the occupational duties so far discharged by the applicant. The early retirement payments shall be refunded by the Federation in so far as they reach beyond the period of entitlement to unemployment pay. The provisions on early retirement payments shall be applied to new claims up to 31 December 1991. The period of validity may be prolonged by one year.

In the period from this Treaty taking effect up to 31 December 1990, women shall be entitled, on reaching the age of 55, to receive early retirement payments for a period not exceeding five years.

(3) The social welfare supplement to pension, accident and unemployment payments introduced in the territory specified in Article 3 of this Treaty in conjunction with the Treaty of 18 May 1990 shall be limited to new cases up to 31 December 1991. The payments shall be made for a period not extending beyond 30 June 1995.

(4) The transfer of tasks incumbent upon the social insurance scheme to separate agencies shall take place in such a way as to ensure that payments are made and financed and sufficient staff is available to perform the said tasks. The distribution of assets and liabilities among the separate agencies shall be definitively settled by law.

(5) The details regarding the introduction of Part VI of the Social Code (pension insurance) and the provisions of Part III of the Reich Insurance Code (accident insurance) shall be settled in a federal Act.

For persons whose pension under the statutory pension scheme begins in the period from 1 January 1992 to 30 June 1995

1. a pension shall be payable which is in principle at least as high as the amount they would have received on 30 June 1990 in the territory specified in Article 3 of this Treaty according to the pension law valid until that time, without regard for payments from supplementary or special pension schemes,
2. a pension shall also be paid where, on 30 June 1990, a pension entitlement would have existed in the territory specified in Article 3 of this Treaty under the pension law valid until that time.

In all other respects, the introduction should have the goal of ensuring that as wages and salaries in the territory specified in Article 3 of this Treaty are brought into line with those in the other Länder, so are pensions.

(6) In developing further the ordinance on occupational diseases it shall be examined to what extent the arrangements which have applied until now in the territory specified in Article 3 of this Treaty can be taken into account.

ARTICLE 31
FAMILY AND WOMEN

(1) It shall be the task of the all-German legislator to develop further the legislation on equal rights for men and women.

(2) In view of different legal and institutional starting positions with regard to the employment of mothers and fathers, it shall be the task of the all-German legislator to shape the legal situation in such a way as to allow a reconciliation of family and occupational life.

(3) In order to ensure that day care centres for children continue to operate in the territory specified in Article 3 of this Treaty, the Federation shall contribute to the costs of these centres for a transitional period up to 30 June 1991.

(4) It shall be the task of the all-German legislator to introduce regulations no later than 31 December 1992 which ensure better protection of unborn life and provide a better solution in conformity with the Constitution of conflict situations faced by pregnant women — notably through legally guaranteed entitlements for women, first and foremost to advice and public support — than is the case in either part of Germany at present. In order to achieve these objectives, a network of advice centres run by various agencies and offering blanket coverage shall be set up without delay with financial assistance from the Federation in the territory specified in Article 3 of this Treaty. The advice centres shall be provided with sufficient staff and funds to allow them to cope with the task of advising pregnant women and offering them necessary assistance, including beyond the time of confinement. In the event that no regulations are introduced within the period stated in the first sentence, the substantive law shall continue to apply in the territory specified in Article 3 of this Treaty.

ARTICLE 32
VOLUNTARY ORGANIZATIONS

Voluntary welfare and youth welfare organizations play an indispensable part through their institutions and services in fashioning the socially oriented state described in the Basic Law. The establishment and expansion of voluntary welfare and youth welfare organizations shall be promoted in the territory specified in Article 3 of this Treaty in line with the distribution of competence under the Basic Law.

ARTICLE 33
PUBLIC HEALTH

(1) It shall be the task of the legislators to create the conditions for effecting a rapid and lasting improvement in in-patient care in the territory specified in Article 3 of this Treaty and for bringing it into line with the situation in the remainder of the federal territory.

(2) In order to avoid deficits arising form expenditure on prescribed drugs by the health insurance scheme in the territory specified in Article 3 of this Treaty, the all-German legislator shall introduce temporary regulations providing for a reduction in producers' prices within the meaning of the Ordinance on the Price of Drugs corresponding to the gap between the income subject to insurance contributions in the territory specified in Article 3 of this Treaty and that in the present federal territory.

ARTICLE 34
PROTECTION OF THE ENVIRONMENT

(1) On the basis of the German environmental union established under Article 16 of the Treaty of 18 May 1990 in conjunction with the Skeleton Environment Act of the German Democratic Republic of 29 June 1990 (Law Gazette 1, No. 42, p. 649), it shall be the task of the legislators to protect the natural basis of man's existence, with due regard for prevention, the polluter-pays principle, and cooperation, and to promote uniform ecological conditions of a high standard at least equivalent to that reached in the Federal Republic of Germany.

(2) With a view to attaining the objective defined in paragraph 1 above, ecological rehabilitation and development programmes shall be drawn up for the territory specified in Article 3 of this Treaty, in line with the distribution of competence under the Basic Law. Measures to ward off dangers to public health shall be accorded priority.

CHAPTER VIII
CULTURE, EDUCATION AND SCIENCE, SPORT

ARTICLE 35
CULTURE

(1) In the years of division, culture and the arts — despite different paths of development taken by the two states in Germany — formed one of the foundations for the continuing unity of the German nation. They have an indispensable contribution to make in their own right as the Germans cement their unity in a single state on the road to European unification. The position and prestige of a united Germany in the world depend not only on its political weight and its economic strength, but also on its role in the cultural domain. The overriding objective of external cultural policy shall be cultural exchange based on partnership and cooperation.

(2) The cultural substance in the territory specified in Article 3 of this Treaty shall not suffer any damage.

(3) Measures shall be taken to provide for the performance of cultural tasks, including their financing, with the protection and promotion of culture and the arts being the responsibility of the new Länder and local

authorities in line with the distribution of competence under the Basic Law.

(4) The cultural institutions which have been under central management to date shall come under the responsibility of the Länder or local authorities in whose territory they are located. In exceptional cases, the possibility of the Federation making a contribution to financing shall not be ruled out, particularly in Land Berlin.

(5) The parts of the former Prussian state collections which were separated as a result of post-war events (including State Museums, State Libraries, Secret State Archives, IberoAmerican Institute, State Musicology Institute) shall be joined together again in Berlin. The Prussian Cultural Heritage Foundation shall assume responsibility for the time being. Future arrangements shall likewise involve an agency that is responsible for the former Prussian state collections in their entirety and is based in Berlin.

(6) The Cultural Fund shall be continued up to 31 December 1994 on a transitional basis in the territory specified in Article 3 of this Treaty to promote culture, the arts and artists. The possibility of the Federation making a contribution to financing in line with the distribution of competence under the Basic Law shall not be ruled out. Discussions on a successor institution shall be held in the framework of the talks on the accession of the Länder named in Article 1 (1) of this Treaty to the Cultural Foundation of the Länder.

(7) In order to offset the effects of the division of Germany the Federation may help to finance, on a transitional basis, individual cultural programmes and institutions in the territory specified in Article 3 of this Treaty to enhance the cultural infrastructure.

ARTICLE 36
BROADCASTING

(1) The Rundfunk der DDR and the Deutscher Fernsehfunk shall be continued as an autonomous joint institution having legal capacity by the Länder named in Article 1 of this Treaty and by Land Berlin in respect of that part where the Basic Law has not been valid to date for a period not extending beyond 31 December 1991 in so far as they perform tasks coming under the responsibility of the Länder. The institution shall have the task of providing the population in the territory specified in Article 3 of this Treaty with a radio and television service in accordance with the general principles governing broadcasting establishments coming under public law. The studio equipment which has belonged to the Deutsche Post to date shall be made over to the institution together with the immovable property serving production and administrative purposes for radio and television. Article 21 of this Treaty shall be applied mutatis mutandis.

(2) The executive bodies of the institution shall be

1. the Broadcasting Commissioner,

2. the Advisory Council on Broadcasting.

(3) The Broadcasting Commissioner shall be elected by the Volkskammer on the proposal of the Prime Minister of the German Democratic Republic. Should the Volkskammer fail to elect a Broadcasting Commissioner, he shall be elected by the Land spokesmen of the Länder named in Article 1 (1) of this Treaty and by the First Mayor of Berlin by a majority vote. The Broadcasting Commissioner shall be in charge of the institution and represent it in and out of court. He shall be responsible for fulfilling the mission of the institution within the limits of the available resources and shall, without delay, draw up a budget for 1991 in which revenue and expenditure are balanced.

(4) The Advisory Council on Broadcasting shall comprise 18 acknowledged public figures as representatives of socially relevant groups. The parliaments of the Länder named in Article 1 (1) of this Treaty and the Berlin Municipal Assembly shall each elect three members. The Advisory Council on Broadcasting shall have a consultative voice on all questions of programming and a right to participation in major personnel, economic and budget decisions. The Advisory Council on Broadcasting may recall the Broadcasting Commissioner by a majority vote of two thirds of its members. It may elect a new Broadcasting Commissioner by a majority vote of two thirds of its members.

(5) The institution shall be financed mainly by revenue raised through licence fees paid by radio and television users resident in the territory specified in Article 3 of this Treaty. To that extent it shall be the recipient of radio and television licence fees. For the rest, it shall cover its expenditure by advertising revenue and other revenue.

(6) Within the period laid down in paragraph 1 above the institution shall be dissolved in accordance with the federal structure of broadcasting through a joint treaty between the Länder named in Article 1 of this Treaty or converted to agencies under public law of one or more Länder. Should a treaty under the first sentence fail to materialize by 31 December 1991, the institution shall be deemed to have been dissolved on that date. The assets and liabilities existing on that date shall be shared out among the Länder named in Article 1 of this Treaty. The amount of the shares to be transferred shall be calculated in proportion to the licence fee revenues as of 30 June 1991 in the territory specified in Article 3 of this Treaty. This shall not affect the obligation of the Länder to continue to provide a broadcasting service in the territory specified in Article 3 of this Treaty.

(7) Upon the entry into force of the treaty under paragraph 6 above, but no later than 31 December 1991, paragraph 1 to 6 above shall cease to have effect.

ARTICLE 37
EDUCATION

(1) School, vocational or higher education certificates or degrees obtained or officially recognized in the German Democratic Republic shall continue to be valid in the territory specified in Article 3 of this Treaty. Examinations passed or certificates obtained in the territory specified in Article 3 or in the other Länder of the Federal Republic of Germany, including Berlin (West), shall be considered equal and shall convey the same rights if they are of equal value. Their equivalence shall be established by the respective competent agency on application. Legal provisions of the Federation and the European Communities regarding the equivalence of examinations and certificates, and special provisions set out in this Treaty shall have priority. In all cases this shall not affect the right to use academic professional titles and degrees obtained or officially recognized or conferred.

(2) The usual recognition procedure operated by the Conference of Ministers of Education and Cultural Affairs shall apply to teaching diploma examinations. The said Conference shall make appropriate transitional arrangements.[17]

(3) Examination certificates issued under the trained occupation scheme and the skilled workers' training scheme as well as final examinations and apprentices' final examinations in recognized trained occupations shall be considered equal.

(4) The regulations necessary for the reorganization of the school system in the territory specified in Article 3 of this Treaty shall be adopted by the Länder named in Article 1. The necessary regulations for the recognition of examinations under educational law shall be agreed by the Conference of Ministers of Education and Cultural Affairs. In both cases they shall be based on the Hamburg Agreement and the other relevant agreements reached by the said Conference.

(5) Undergraduates who move to another institution of higher education before completing their studies shall have their study and examination record up to that point recognized according to the principles laid down in Section 7 of the General Regulations on Degree Examination Procedures (ABD) or within the terms of the rules governing admission to state examinations.

(6) The entitlements to study at an institution of higher education confirmed on leaving certificates issued by engineering and technical schools of the German Democratic Republic shall be valid in accordance with the resolution of 10 May 1990 of the Conference of Ministers of Education and Cultural Affairs and its Annex B. Further principles and procedures for the recognition of technical school and higher education certificates for the purpose of school and college studies based on them shall be developed within the framework of the Conference of Ministers of Education and Cultural Affairs.

ARTICLE 38
SCIENCE AND RESEARCH

(1) In the united Germany science and research shall continue to constitute important foundations of the state and society. The need to renew science and research in the territory specified in Article 3 of this Treaty while preserving efficient institutions shall be taken into account by an expert report on publicly maintained institutions prepared by the Science Council and to be completed by 31 December 1991, with individual results to be implemented step by step before that date.

The following provisions are intended to make possible the preparation of this report and ensure the incorporation of science and research in the territory specified in Article 3 of this Treaty into the joint research structure of the Federal Republic of Germany.

(2) Upon the accession taking effect, the Academy of Sciences of the German Democratic Republic shall be separated as a learned society from the research institutes and other institutions. The decision as to how the learned society of the Academy of Sciences of the German Democratic Republic is to be continued shall be taken under Land law. For the time being the research institutes and other institutions shall continue to exist up to 31 December 1991 as institutions of the Länder in the territory specified in Article 3 of this Treaty in so far as they have not been previously dissolved or transformed. Transitional arrangements shall be made for the financing of these institutes and institutions up to 31 December 1991; the requisite funds shall be provided in 1991 by the Federation and the Länder named in Article 1 of this Treaty.

(3) The employment contracts of the staff employed at the research institutes and other institutions of the Academy of Sciences of the German Democratic Republic shall continue to exist up to 31 December 1991 as limited employment contracts with the Länder to which these institutes and institutions are transferred. The right to cancel these employment contracts with or without notice under the conditions listed in Annex 1 to this Treaty shall remain unaffected.

(4) Paragraphs 1 to 3 above shall apply mutatis mutandis to the Academy of Architecture and the Academy of Agricultural Sciences of the German Democratic Republic and to the scientific institutions subordinate to the Ministry of Food, Agriculture and Forestry.

(5) The Federal Government shall begin negotiations with the Länder with a view to adapting or renewing the Federation-Länder agreements under Article 91 b of the Basic Law in such a way that educational planning and the promotion of institutions and projects of scientific research of supraregional importance are extended to the territory specified in Article 3 of this Treaty.

(6) The Federal Government shall seek to ensure that the proven methods and programmes of research promotion in the Federal Republic of Germany are applied as soon as possible to the entire federal territory and that the scientists and scientific institutions in the territory specified in Article 3 of this Treaty are given access to current research promotion schemes. Furthermore, certain schemes for promoting research and

development which have expired in the territory of the Federal Republic of Germany shall be reopened for the territory specified in Article 3 of this Treaty; this shall not include fiscal measures.

(7) Upon the accession of the German Democratic Republic taking effect, the Research Council of the German Democratic Republic shall be dissolved.

ARTICLE 39
SPORT

(1) The sporting structures which are in a process of transformation in the territory specified on Article 3 of this Treaty shall be placed on a self-governing basis. The public authorities shall give moral and material support to sport in line with the distribution of competence under the Basic Law.

(2) To the extent that it has proved successful, top-level sport and its development shall continue to receive support in the territory specified in Article 3 of this Treaty. Support shall be given within the framework of the rules and principles existing in the Federal Republic of Germany and in line with the public-sector budgets in the territory specified in Article 3 of this Treaty. Within this framework, the Physical Training and Sport Research Institute (FKS) in Leipzig, the doping control laboratory recognized by the International Olympic Committee (IOC) in Kreischa (near Dresden) and the Sports Equipment Research and Development Centre (FES) in Berlin (East) shall — each in an appropriate legal form and to the extent necessary — be continued as institutions in the united Germany or attached to existing institutions.

(3) The Federation shall support sport for the disabled for a transitional period until 31 December 1992.

CHAPTER IX
TRANSITIONAL AND FINAL PROVISIONS

ARTICLE 40
TREATIES AND AGREEMENTS

(1) The obligations under the Treaty of 18 May 1990 between the Federal Republic of Germany and the German Democratic Republic establishing a Monetary, Economic and Social Union shall continue to be valid unless otherwise provided in this Treaty and unless they become irrelevant in the process of establishing German unity.

(2) Where rights and duties arising from other treaties and agreements between the Federal Republic of Germany or its Länder and the German Democratic Republic have not become irrelevant in the process of establishing German unity, they shall be assumed, adjusted or settled by the competent national entities.

ARTICLE 41
SETTLEMENT OF PROPERTY ISSUES

(1) The Joint Declaration of 15 June 1990 on the Settlement of Open Property Issues (Annex III) issued by the Government of the Federal Republic of Germany and the Government of the German Democratic Republic shall form an integral part of this Treaty.

(2) In accordance with separate legislative arrangements there shall be no return of property rights to real estate or buildings if the real estate or building concerned is required for urgent investment purposes to be specified in detail, particularly if it is to be used for the establishment of an industrial enterprise and the implementation of this investment decision deserves support from a general economic viewpoint above all if it creates or safeguards jobs. The investor shall submit a plan showing the major features of his project and shall undertake to carry out the plan on this basis. The legislation shall also contain arrangements for compensation to the former owner.

(3) The Federal Republic of Germany shall not otherwise enact any legislation contradicting the Joint Declaration referred to in paragraph 1 above.

ARTICLE 42
DELEGATION OF PARLIAMENTARY REPRESENTATIVES

(1) Before the accession of the German Democratic Republic takes effect, the Volkskammer shall, on the basis of its composition, elect 144 Members of Parliament to be delegated to the 11th German Bundestag together with a sufficient number of reserve members. Relevant proposals shall be made by the parties and groups represented in the Volkskammer.

(2) The persons elected shall become members of the 11th German Bundestag by virtue of a statement of acceptance delivered to the President of the Volkskammer, but not until the accession takes effect. The President of the Volkskammer shall without delay communicate the result of the election, together with the statement of acceptance, to the President of the German Bundestag.

(3) The eligibility for election to, and loss of membership of, the 11th German Bundestag shall otherwise be subject to the provisions of the Federal Election Act as promulgated on 1 September 1975 (Federal Law Gazette 1, p. 2325) and last amended by the Act of 29 August 1990 (Federal Law Gazette 11, p. 813).

In the event of cessation of membership, the member concerned shall be replaced by the next person on the reserve list. He must belong to the same party as, at the time of his election, the member whose membership has ceased. The reserve member to take his seat in the German Bundestag shall, before the accession takes effect, be determined by the President of the Volkskammer, and thereafter by the President of the German Bundestag.

ARTICLE 43
TRANSITIONAL RULE FOR THE BUNDESRAT PENDING THE
FORMATION OF LÄNDER GOVERNMENTS

From the formation of the Länder named in Article 1 (1) of this Treaty
until the election of minister presidents, the Land plenipotentiaries may
take part in the meetings of the Bundesrat in a consultative capacity.

ARTICLE 44
PRESERVATION OF RIGHTS

Rights arising from this Treaty in favour of the German Democratic
Republic or the Länder named in Article 1 of this Treaty may be asserted
by each of these Länder after the accession has taken effect.

ARTICLE 45
ENTRY INTO FORCE OF THE TREATY

(1) This Treaty, including the attached Protocol and Annexes I to III,
shall enter into force on the day on which the Governments of the
Federal Republic of Germany and the German Democratic Republic have
informed each other that the internal requirements for such entry into
force have been fulfilled.
(2) The Treaty shall remain valid as federal law after the accession has
taken effect.

Done at Berlin on 31 August 1990 in duplicate in the German
language.

For the Federal Republic of Germany
Wolfgang Schäuble

For the German Democratic Republic
Günther Krause

PROTOCOL

At the signing of the Treaty between the Federal Republic of Germany
and the German Democratic Republic on the Establishment of German
Unity the following explanations were made in respect of this Treaty:

I. RE ARTICLES AND ANNEXES OF THE TREATY

1. Re Article 1:

(1) The boundaries of Land Berlin shall be those defined by the

Establishment of a New Municipality of Berlin Act of 27 April 1920[18] (Prussian Law Gazette 1920, p. 123) with the proviso

— that the note in the protocol concerning Article 1 of the Agreement of 31 March 1988 between the Senat and the Government of the German Democratic Republic on the Inclusion of Further Enclaves and Other Small Territories in the Agreement of 20 December 1971 on the Settlement of Questions of Enclaves by the Exchange of Territories[19] shall be extended to all boroughs and shall continue to apply between the Länder of Berlin and Brandenburg;
— that all territories in which an election to the House of Representatives or to the Municipal Assembly of Berlin took place after 7 October 1949 are constituent parts of the boroughs of Berlin.

(2) The Länder of Berlin and Brandenburg shall review the course of the boundary arising from paragraph 1 above and produce a documentary record of it within one year.

2. Re Article 2 (1):

The Contracting Parties agree that decisions under the second sentence shall be the prerogative of the legislative bodies of the Federation after the election of the first all-German Bundestag and after the establishment of full rights of participation for the Länder named in Article 1 (1) of this Treaty.[20]

3. Re Article 2 (2):

The Contracting Parties agree that the character of 3 October 1990 as a public holiday does not rule out actions which have already been decided irreversibly when the Treaty enters into force.

4. Re Article 4, item 5:

Article 143 (1) and (2) has only temporary significance; it is therefore not binding on future legislation.

5. Re Article 9 (5):

The two Contracting Parties take note of the statement by Land Berlin that the church tax legislation valid in Berlin (West) shall, with effect from 1 January 1991, be extended to that part of Berlin in which it has not been valid to date.

6. Re Article 13:

Institutions or their branches which, up to the accession taking effect, have performed tasks that in future are no longer to be carried out by the public administration shall be wound up as follows:

(1) Where a substantive link exists with public tasks, the institutions or their branches shall be wound up by the body which is responsible for these public tasks (Federation, Land, Länder jointly).

(2) In all other cases the institutions or their branches shall be wound up by the Federation.

In cases of doubt the Land concerned or the Federation may have recourse to an agency established by the Federation and the Länder.

7. Re Article 13 (2):

Where Institutions are wholly or partially transferred to the Federation, suitable existing staff shall be taken on to an appropriate extent as necessary for the performance of tasks.

8. Re Article 15:

The administrative assistance of the Federation and the Länder for the organization of Land administration and the performance of certain technical tasks shall be coordinated in a clearing agency to be established by the Federation and the Länder.

9. Re Article 16:

The two Contracting Parties take note of the announcement by Land Berlin that the First Mayor will, on 3 October 1990, be appointed a member of the Bundesrat and that the members of the Magistrat, like other members of the Land Government of Berlin, will be entitled to deputize for the appointed members of the Bundesrat.[21]

10. Re Article 17:

This provision shall also apply to persons who, due to committal to a psychiatric institution contrary to the rule of law, became victims within the meaning of Article 17.

11. Re Article 20 (2):

The introduction of professional civil service law in accordance with the agreed arrangements set out in Annex 1 shall take place in line with the principles governing the staffing of permanently required posts of the Federal Republic of Germany.

12. Re Article 21 (1),first sentence:

The Länder shall be informed about the continued use of immovable property employed for military purposes. The Länder concerned shall be consulted before immovable property which has been used to date for military purposes and becomes federal property is given over to another use.

13. Re Article 22 (4):

Publicly owned land used for housing purposes by the housing cooperatives shall also be covered by paragraph 4 and shall ultimately be made over to the housing cooperatives, with its present purpose being maintained.

14. Re Article 35:

The Federal Republic of Germany and the German Democratic Republic declare in connection with Article 35 of the Treaty:

1. There shall be freedom of commitment to the distinctive Sorbian way of life and to Sorbian culture.[22]
2. The maintenance and further development of Sorbian culture and traditions shall be guaranteed.
3. The Sorbian people and their organizations shall be free to cultivate and preserve the Sorbian language in public life.
4. The distribution of competence between the Federation and the Länder as set out in the Basic Law shall remain unaffected.

15. Re Article 38:

Agreements concluded by the Academy of Sciences, the Academy of Architecture and the Academy of Agricultural Sciences of the German Democratic Republic with organizations in other states or with international agencies shall be reviewed in accordance with the principles laid down in Article 12 of the Treaty.

16. Re Article 40:

The Federal Government shall settle cases in which it has agreed to assume the costs of medical care for Germans from the territory specified in Article 3 of the Treaty.
(. . .)

II. STATEMENT FOR THE RECORD

The two Contracting Parties are agreed that the provisions of the Treaty are adopted without prejudice to the rights and responsibilities of the Four Powers in respect of Berlin and Germany as a whole still existing at the time of signing and to the still outstanding results of the talks[23] on the external aspects of the establishment of German unity.

Notes

1 On 23 August 1990 the East German Volkskammer voted in favour of the accession of the German Democratic Republic to the Federal

Republic of Germany with effect from 3 October 1990. 363 of the 400 members were present, 294 voted for, 62 against, and there were 7 abstentions.

2 I.e. East Berlin.

3 Old version: 'Each Land shall have at least three votes; Länder with more than 2 million inhabitants shall have four, Länder with more than 6 million inhabitants five votes.'

4 Article 135a of the Basic Law concerns the procedure for settling the liabilities of the German Reich and the former Land of Prussia as well as a number of cases of the immediate post-war era.

5 Article 19 (2) of the Basic Law: 'In no case may the essential content of a basic right be encroached upon.'

6 Article 79 (3) of the Basic Law: 'Amendments of the Basic Law affecting the division of the Federation into Länder, the participation of the Länder in legislation, or the basic principles laid down in articles 1 and 20, shall be inadmissible.' Article 1 concerns human dignity and the state's duty to protect it. Article 20 relates to the fundamental structure of the state and the right to resist anyone seeking to abolish the constitutional order.

7 The legislative bodies of the Federal Republic of Germany are the German Bundestag as the directly elected parliament and the Bundesrat (Federal Council) representing the Länder (federal states).

8 Decision of the Ministers President of the Länder amending the number of votes of each Land in the Bundesrat.

9 Article 29 of the Basic Law concerns the reorganization of the federal territory through the formation of new Länder.

10 Article 131 of the Basic Law concerns the legal position of persons who at the time of the capitulation in 1945 were employed in the public service.

11 Article 106 of the Basic Law concerns the apportionment of tax revenue. The provisions which under the Unification Treaty do not apply concern the proportions of the income tax, corporation tax and turnover tax falling to the Federation and the Länder.

12 On 16 May 1990 the Federal and the State governments set up a Fund of DM 115 billion to assist the GDR.

13 Article 107 of the Basic Law concerns financial equalization. It takes account of the differing financial resources of the federal states.

13a These provisions govern the Federation's involvement in fulfilling the responsibilities of the Länder as well as the distribution of expenditure as between the Federation and the Länder.

14 State and City Government of West Berlin.

14a City Government of East Berlin.

15 The East German Ministry for State Security. After the revolution it was renamed the Office of National Security. This ministry, popularly known as the 'Stasi', had more than 100,000 official and unofficial employees and was the regime's most dreaded instrument of repression.

16 Cf. Article 25 of the Unification Treaty. By means of the Privatization and Reorganisation of Publicly Owned Assets Act (Trusteeship

Act) of 17 June 1990 the East German Volkskammer charged the Trust Agency with converting the former state-owned enterprises into private companies.

17 The Standing Conference of Ministers of Education and Cultural Affairs is responsible for cooperation among the Länder on matters of culture and education. Under the constitution cultural affairs and education are the responsibility of the Länder.

18 This law adopted by the Prussian Land Parliament merged Berlin with Charlottenburg, Köpenick, Lichtenberg, Neukölln, Schöneberg, Spandau and Wilmersdorf, which until then were independent towns, together with 59 rural districts and 27 estates to form 'Greater Berlin'. The city covered a total area of 878 square kilometers and was divided up into 20 administrative districts.

19 The basic agreement on the exchange of territory which the Berlin Senat and the East German Government signed on 20 December 1971 with a view to improving travel and visitor traffic was followed by another territory exchange agreement of 31 March 1988. In 1971, 17.1 hectares of Eastern territory was exchanged for 15.6 hectares of Western territory to settle problems arising in connection with a number of small enclaves in Brandenburg (East Germany) west and south-west of Berlin but belonging to the city. A special road had been built connecting the enclave of Steinstücken to the city in order to give the people living there direct and uncontrolled access to their homes.

20 This provision concerns the establishment of the seat of parliament and government.

21 Unlike the situation in the five new Länder, whose interests in the Bundesrat until the election of their respective parliaments on 14 October 1990 and subsequently of their minister presidents were looked after by appointed representatives. Land Berlin was represented in the Bundesrat until the election of the Berlin Parliament, the House of Representatives (which took place on 2 December jointly with the election for the first all-German Bundestag) and the formation of the new Senat by members of the West Berlin Senat and the East Berlin Magistrat (city council) which remained in existence until that date.

22 The Sorbs are a group of about 100,000 people living in the former GDR whose Slavic language, culture and school system were specially protected by law.

23 The special rights and responsibilities of the Victorious Powers were suspended prior to the entry into force of the Two plus Four Settlement by means of a declaration by the Four Powers immediately before the day of German unity, until their final termination.

Document 18 Address by Federal President Richard von Weizsäcker of 3 October 1990 (excerpts)

I

The preamble to our constitution, which is now valid for all Germans, expresses the quintessence of what is uppermost in our minds today: We have achieved the unity and freedom of Germany in free self-determination. We are resolved to serve world peace in a united Europe. In pursuing this aim we are conscious of our responsibility to God and man.

Our hearts are filled with gratitude and joy, and at the same time we are aware of the magnitude and seriousness of our commitment. History in Europe and Germany now offers us a chance we have never had before. We are going through one of those rare phases in history when something really can be changed for the better. Let us not for one moment forget what this means to us.

Massive problems confront us at home and abroad. We do not ignore them. We take the reservations expressed by our neighbours seriously. We also realize how difficult it will be to fulfil the expectations placed in us by all sides. But we will be guided by confidence, not fear and doubt. Decisive for us is our firm determination to see our responsibilities clearly and to face up to them together. That determination gives us the strength to see our day-to-day problems in the perspective of our history and future in Europe.

For the first time we Germans are not a source of dispute in Europe. Our unity was not forced upon anyone but agreed peacefully. It is part of a historical process embracing the whole of Europe aimed at securing freedom for the nations and establishing a new peaceful order in our continent. We Germans wish to serve this aim. Our unity is directed to its achievement.

We now have a state which we ourselves no longer regard as provisional and whose identity and integrity are no longer disputed by our neighbours. On this day the united German nation finds its acknowledged place in Europe.

What this means is obvious for the significance of frontiers. No European country has as many neighbours as we. For centuries frontiers have been a source of violence and terrible bloodshed. Now all our neighbours and we ourselves live within secure borders. These borders are protected not only by the renunciation of force but by the clear awareness of their changed function. Those who were forced to leave their homeland suffered immeasurably. But there is no point in any new dispute over national boundaries. All the greater is our desire to remove their divisive character. We want all Germany's frontiers to be bridges to our neighbours.

II

The ideals of the French Revolution, together with the constitutional evolution in the United States and the United Kingdom, laid the foundations for Western democracy. A perception of freedom based on humanity and the rule of law emerged which has increasingly become the standard. It cannot be applied everywhere right away, but wherever the urge for political freedom, or a system marked by efficiency, social justice and respect for human rights breaks through — even into the heart of Peking — the values and rules of the Western democracies are everyone's yardstick.

We Germans participated in the democratic evolution at a very early stage but we applied its ideals and principles only half-heartedly. The rule of law in our country had grown from our own traditions. In the Prussian reforms[1] of the Napoleonic era local self-government became the source of democratic convictions. The people sought unity, right and freedom as personified by the St. Paul's Church parliament.[2] They definitely wanted to be united, and this aim was finally achieved in 1871,[3] but they had no say in the matter. Time and again the Germans went on a romantic search for a third road to their country's internal order and its place in Europe. But that was an illusion. The Weimar Republic, too, failed to establish a viable democracy.[4]

When the Federal Republic of Germany was founded[5] there was deep concern at first that its integration with the West might perpetuate the division of Germany. This time, however, the path did not lead to a dead end. Initially only one part of Germany was allowed to follow that path, but from today we can together make a new beginning. The unification of Germany is more than the mere enlargement of the Federal Republic. The day has come when, for the first time in history, Germany as a whole can take its permanent place among the Western democracies.

To us and to all our neighbours this is a process of fundamental importance. It will change the centre of Europe. We shall play a major part in the process, jointly with our Western partners with whom we are closely linked by virtue of our common values and objectives.

III

Amidst our European neighbours we were destined to remain divided for over forty years. For the one part of the country this proved to be a boon, for the other a burden, but it was, and remains, our common German fate. A fate which embraces the past and the responsibility for its consequences. The SED (Socialist Unity Party) in East Germany tried to decree the country's division. It thought it sufficient to proclaim the socialist society of the future in order to free itself from the burden of history.

But in the German Democratic Republic the people saw, and felt, it differently. They had to carry a far greater part of the burden of the war than their countrymen in the West and they have always felt that recalling the past with a sense of responsibility would give them the indispensable strength to free themselves for the future. Hardly had the imposed ideological parlance gone then they faced up squarely to history's outstanding questions. The world has noted with great respect how sincerely the free forces, and especially young people, in Eastern Germany considered it their responsibility to make up for the old regime's failure to bear its share of the responsibility for the past. The recent visit to Israel by the presidents of both freely elected parliaments to commemorate the holocaust, the most heinous of all crimes, left a deep impression in that country. It symbolizes the common identity of the Germans precisely as regards their historical responsibility. Nazi tyranny and the war it unleashed brought untold suffering and injustice on nearly the whole of Europe and our own country. We will always remember the victims, and we are grateful for the growing signs of reconciliation between people and nations.

IV

At no time in the post-war era did the Germans, particularly the Berliners, cease to hope that freedom would return and that the division of Europe would be overcome. And yet no one had the imagination to predict the course of events. So what is happening today is to us a gift. This time history was well disposed towards us Germans. But this is all the more reason for conscientious reflection.

After the Second World War the division of Germany epitomized the division of Europe. It was not the result of the joint will of the victors but rather of their disagreement. The growing East-West confrontation cemented that division. But we will not use that as an excuse. No one in our country will forget that there would have been no division if the war started by Hitler had not happened.

Against the background of the Cold War and under the protective shield of the nuclear stalemate, the social systems in East and West competed with one another for over forty years. That phase is now drawing to a close.

The Soviet leadership under President Gorbachev has realized that reforms leading to democracy and a market economy have become inevitable. But without freedom such reforms would be doomed to failure. As a result, courageous decisions were taken. The Soviet Union ceased dominating its allies and respected their right to decide their own political future. This led to the unprecedented peaceful revolutions in Central, Eastern and South Eastern Europe. It led to the acceptance of the German people's free decision in favour of national unity.

The success of the reform course pursued by the Soviet leadership is still in considerable jeopardy, but it has already gone down in history as a worthy endeavour. And many people, including we Germans, have reason to be grateful.

We are grateful to the civil rights movements and peoples in Hungary,

Poland and Czechoslovakia. The citizens of Warsaw, Budapest and Prague have set examples. They saw the path leading to freedom in the German Democratic Republic as part of a common historical process and gave it their encouragement.

Nor will we forget the help they gave to the refugees, which was a very direct contribution towards overcoming the wall and the barbed wire. In future the united Germany will seek an open, a close neighbourly relationship with them.

The defence of freedom and human rights is fundamental to the commitment of our Western allies and friends, above all the Americans, the French and the British. Their protection, their resolve and cooperation, have been of crucial assistance to us. Most important of all, they placed their confidence in us. For this we are deeply grateful.

How important our partners understanding was for German unification is apparent from the unequivocal and constructive position taken by the European Community. I take great pleasure in welcoming among us today the President of the European Commission, Jacques Delors, and his colleagues and wish to express our respect and thanks for their farsightedness.

Our thanks today go out in particular to those Germans in the German Democratic Republic who summoned the courage to rise up against oppression and despotism. For over ten years meetings and prayers for peace in the churches developed and spread the ideas which ultimately sparked the peaceful revolution. But the power of the state security services remained omnipresent. The use of force was imminent well into the autumn of 1989. It would have been quite understandable if the people had backed down and retreated. But it was no longer possible to suppress the hope lodged in their hearts.

'We are the people'. With these four simple and magnificent words a whole system was shattered. Those words expressed the desire of the people to take the country, the res publica, into their own hands. Thus the peaceful revolution in Germany became truly republican. The fact that it happened after almost 60 years of bitter oppression makes it all the more amazing and credible. Democrats had joined forces in the cause of freedom and solidarity, both forming one mission for us all.

But on this occasion we must also thank the people in the West. If they had not trusted us Germans we would not have been able to unite. That trust has grown with the development of the Federal Republic over a period of forty years. Our people have established themselves in a free and democratic system and in the European consciousness.

The Germans have become predictable, reliable and respected partners. This was a crucial factor which won our neighbours and the whole world's approval for the country's unification.

V

Now those four words have developed into many thousands. In an almost incredible effort, agreements and treaties have been completed which made it possible for us to set the seal today on both the internal and the external aspects of our unity. The subject-matter was often very complex and there was no lack of controversy. The pressure of time was constantly mounting. All concerned worked day and night — something we can do, of course, when it matters.

In future there will be more than one doubt to clear up, more than one dispute to settle. But all in all we can only admire what has been achieved.

I wish to thank the political leaders on both sides, their parliaments, and not least the many excellent staff of the public authorities for the work they have done. Their devotion to the cause was exemplary. Their accomplishment is reward in itself.

The form of unity has been determined. Now we must give it substance. Parliaments, governments and parties must help in this task, but only the sovereign nation, the minds and hearts of the people themselves, can translate it into practice. Everyone is aware how much still has to be done. It would be neither sincere nor helpful if at this hour we sought to conceal how much still separates us.

The external constraints of division were devised to estrange us. This they failed to do. Inhumane as the Wall and barbed wire were, they only served to strengthen the people's will to come together. We felt this above all in Berlin, that city which was and will remain of crucial significance to the nation. The sight of the Wall day by day never let us stop believing in, hoping for, the other side. Now the Wall has gone, and that's what matters.

But now that we have our freedom we must prove ourselves worthy of it. Today we have a clearer picture of the consequences of our different courses of development. The gap in our material standards is what strikes us most. Although the people in the German Democratic Republic had to cope with shortage day in, day out, made the best of their situation and worked hard — this we will not forget — the magnitude of their problems and the gulf between them and the West became fully clear only during recent months. If we are to close the gap soon we shall not only have to help but also, and above all, to respect one another.

To the Germans in the former German Democratic Republic unification is a transformation process which affects them directly in their daily lives, touches their very existence. This often confronts them with demands beyond their human capacity. A woman wrote to me that the people in East Germany were sincerely grateful for their freedom but had not realized how nerve-racking changes would be which required them to take leave of themselves, as it were. After all, — they yearned for nothing more than to rid themselves of their regime. But replacing nearly all elements of one's life with something new, something unknown, overnight is beyond human measure.

The people in the West were overjoyed when the Wall came down, but many fail to realize or consider it most unwelcome that unification has something to do with their personal lives. This must not remain so. We shall first have to learn to understand one another better. Not until we really appreciate that both sides have gained valuable experience and acquired important qualities which are worth keeping in unity will we be on the right road.

First, let us look at the West. There is one development here which deserves special emphasis. Over the years the people have developed an affection for their state which is free from ungenuine feelings and nationalistic pathos. True, in the forty-year history of the Federal Republic there have been many serious conflicts between the generations and between the different social and political groups. They were often bitter struggles but without a destructive tendency as during the Weimar Republic. The revolt by young people in the late sixties, notwithstanding all the offence it caused, ultimately helped strengthen the people's commitment to democracy.

As we learnt how to settle conflicts we developed a mutual confidence in the constitution. The internal uncertainty has gone. We are no longer constantly comparing ourselves with other nations. Conditions in other countries must not be altogether bad to make ours look good. Conversely, favourable conditions are not only to be found beyond our borders. We have become more self-assured in our judgement, in our awareness of life.

Some in the West are only now really discovering the merits of their own country. Some of the severest critics of conditions in the Federal Republic are worried today that our open-mindedness, our federalism, our integration with Europe, might suffer in the united Germany. I do not share their anxiety . . . .

Notes

1 Aimed at loosening the petrified structures of the Prussian state. The main elements were: Decree of October 1807 liberating the peasants, Public Administration Act (1808), Municipal Code (1808), agricultural reform attempts from 1811 to 1820, industrial reform (1810/11), customs laws (1818) and emancipation of the Jews.
2 The Frankfurt Parliament in the 1848 revolution.
3 Creation of the first German nation-state.
4 First German republic in 1918. 'Weimar Republic' refers to the old German cultural center Weimar, in Thuringia, where Goethe, Schiller, Herder and other famous people used to live and where the constituent national assembly was held in February 1919.
5 On 23 May 1949 in Bonn.

Document 19
Results of elections to the *Volkskammer*, *Landtag* and *Bundestag* in the *Länder* of the former GDR (%)

Party	*Volkskammer*	*Landtag*	*Bundestag*
Mecklenburg–West Pomerania			
CDU	36.3	38.3	41.2
SPD	23.4	27.0	26.6
Left List/PDS	22.8	15.7	14.2
Alliance 90	4.4	6.4	5.9
FDP	3.6	5.5	9.1
other*	9.5	7.1	2.9
Brandenburg			
CDU	33.6	29.4	36.3
SPD	29.9	38.2	32.9
LL/PDS	18.3	13.4	11.0
Alliance 90	5.4	7.2	6.6
FDP	4.7	6.6	9.7
other	8.1	3.1	3.4
Saxony-Anhalt			
CDU	44.5	39.0	38.6
SPD	23.7	26.0	24.7
LL/PDS	14.0	12.0	9.4
Alliance 90	4.0	5.3	5.3
FDP	7.7	13.5	19.7
other	6.1	4.2	2.3
Saxony			
CDU	43.4	53.8	49.5
SPD	15.1	19.4	18.2
LL/PDS	13.6	10.2	9.0
Alliance 90	4.7	5.6	5.9
FDP	5.7	5.3	12.4
other	17.5	6.0	4.9
Thuringia			
CDU	52.6	45.4	45.2
SPD	17.5	22.8	21.9
LL/PDS	11.4	9.7	8.3
Alliance 90	4.1	6.5	6.1
FDP	4.6	9.3	14.6
other	9.8	6,4	3.9

Source: *Frankfurter Rundschau* 4 December 1990; 'other' includes votes for the DSU

Results by region of the *Volkskammer* elections (18.3.90)

	CDU	DSU	DA	SPD	PDS	Liberals	Alliance 90
total	40.82	6.31	0.92	21.88	16.4	5.28	2.91
Berlin (East)	18.28	2.23	1.02	34.85	30.22	3.00	6.33
Cottbus	42.76	4.77	0.79	19.25	17.87	5.23	2.67
Dresden	44.97	13.81	1.08	9.68	14.76	5.55	3.65
Erfurt	56.25	2.46	1.91	18.73	9.94	4.54	1.82
Frankfurt/Oder	27.82	3.51	0.72	31.9	22.5	4.23	3.15
Gera	48.88	8.21	1.68	16.49	12.55	5.1	2.58
Halle	45.11	2.75	0.58	20.82	13.81	9.98	2.39
Karl-Marx-Stadt	44.95	14.79	0.98	15.64	11.29	5.98	2.07
Leipzig	39.64	10.09	0.69	21.53	14.49	5.39	3.33
Magdeburg	44.22	1.95	0.68	27.47	14.22	4.41	1.95
Neubrandenburg	36.03	2.05	0.52	21.19	25.81	3.03	1.59
Potsdam	31.23	2.94	0.75	34.36	16.55	4.92	3.82
Rostock	34.32	2.79	0.66	24.82	23.16	3.38	2.67
Schwerin	39.78	1.96	0.58	25.36	17.83	4.55	2.54
Suhl	50.58	8.91	0.96	16.09	12.55	4.15	1.88

Final results of the elections to the *Bundestag* on 2 December 1990 in the *Länder* of the West and the new *Länder* of the East (in %)

Party	Eastern voting area	Western voting area*
CDU	43.4	35.0
CSU	—	9.1
SPD	23.6	35.9
FDP	13.4	10.6
Greens	—	4.7
All.90/Greens	5.9	—
PDS	9.9	0.3

Source: *Frankfurter Rundschau*, 4 Dember 1990, p. 6 (* excluding West Berlin)

Document 20 The German *Länder*

Germany is divided into sixteen provinces. The total area is 357,050 km^2; the number of inhabitants is 78.5 million.

Baden-Württemburg
Area: 35,751 km^2
Population: 9.62 million
Capital: Stuttgart

Bavaria
Area: 70,554 km^2
Population: 11.2 million
Capital: Munich

Berlin
Area: 883 km^2
Population: 3.41 million
Capital: Berlin

Brandenburg
Area: 29,060 km^2
Population: 2.64 million
Capital: Potsdam

Bremen
Area: 4.4 km^2
Population: 0.67 million
Capital: Bremen

Hamburg
Area: 755 km^2
Population: 1.6 million
Capital: Hamburg

Hesse
Area: 21,114 km^2
Population: 1.96 million
Capital: Wiesbaden

Lower Saxony
Area: 47,348 km^2
Population: 7.28 million
Capital: Hanover

Mecklenburg-Western Pomeriana
Area: 23,835 km^2
Population: 1.96 million
Capital: Schwerin

North Rhine-Westphalia
Area: 34,068 km²
Population: 17.1 million
Capital: Düsseldorf

Rhineland-Palatinate
Area: 19,849 km²
Population: 3.7 million
Capital: Mainz

Saarland
Area: 2,570 km²
Population: 1.06 million
Capital: Saarbrücken

Saxony
Area: 18,338 km²
Population: 4.9 million
Capital: Dresden

Saxony-Anhalt
Area: 20,443 km²
Population: 2.96 million
Capital: Magdeburg

Schleswig-Holstein
Area: 15,730 km²
Population: 2.59 million
Capital: Kiel

Thuringia
Area: 16,251 km²
Population: 2.68 million
Capital: Erfurt

Index